ROUTLEDGE LIBRARY EDITIONS: EARLY WESTERN RESPONSES TO SOVIET RUSSIA

Volume 8

RUSSIA UNVEILED

RUSSIA UNVEILED

PANAÏT ISTRATI

Routledge
Taylor & Francis Group
LONDON AND NEW YORK

First published in French in 1929 under the title 'La Russie Nue'
First published in Great Britain in 1931 by George Allen & Unwin Ltd

This edition first published in 2018
by Routledge
2 Park Square, Milton Park, Abingdon, Oxon OX14 4RN

and by Routledge
711 Third Avenue, New York, NY 10017

Routledge is an imprint of the Taylor & Francis Group, an informa business

British Library Cataloguing in Publication Data
A catalogue record for this book is available from the British Library

ISBN: 978-1-138-04993-2 (Set)
ISBN: 978-1-315-11072-1 (Set) (ebk)
ISBN: 978-1-138-08459-9 (Volume 8) (hbk)
ISBN: 978-1-138-08467-4 (Volume 8) (pbk)
ISBN: 978-1-315-11172-8 (Volume 8) (ebk)

Publisher's Note
The publisher has gone to great lengths to ensure the quality of this reprint but points out that some imperfections in the original copies may be apparent.

RUSSIA UNVEILED

by

PANAÏT ISTRATI

Translated by

R. J. S. CURTIS, M.A.

LONDON
GEORGE ALLEN & UNWIN LTD
MUSEUM STREET

The French original, "La Russie Nue", was first published in Paris in 1929

FIRST PUBLISHED IN GREAT BRITAIN IN 1931

PRINTED IN GREAT BRITAIN BY
UNWIN BROTHERS LTD., WOKING

FOREWORD

PANAIT ISTRATI

No modern writer can have had a more astonishing, a more adventurous, career than the author of this book. His life-story is so extraordinary that its rightful place seems almost to be in the realm of fiction rather than of fact.

Born at Braila (Rumania) in 1884, he was the child of a Greek smuggler and a Rumanian peasant woman. His mother, who after her husband's death earned her living by smuggling Turkish tobacco into Rumania, was a person of great character and devoted to her son. But when he was only twelve years old Istrati's vagabond instincts were irrepressible, and he left her to begin his wanderings throughout the world.

For the next twenty years he roamed about the Levant and Asia Minor, following all kinds of trades. He was by turns a cabaret waiter, baker, sandwich-man, sign-painter, journalist, domestic servant, navvy, mechanic, and wharf-porter. Travelling sometimes as a stowaway, sometimes as an unpaying passenger on goods trains, he wandered about Egypt, Greece, Italy to Jaffa, Beyrout, Damascus, and Lebanon. He tells us of the miseries and hardships of these years of vagabondage, and it is only by his deft touch that we are enabled to realise the depths of his degradation.

During this period Istrati became acquainted with the great Russian authors, of whom he is now considered almost an equal. In 1913 he went back to Rumania, where he met the exiled Rakovsky, who was later to become Soviet Ambassador in London. Istrati fell under his influence and quickly became an enthusiastic convert to revolutionary ideas, a militant Socialist, and an agitator upon whom the Rumanian police did not look with favour. About this time he married and became a pig farmer, but on the eve of the war he was once more a homeless wanderer. His pigs died and his wife deserted him.

In 1917 he arrived in Switzerland; in 1918 he reached France. In 1921, at Nice, when he was nearly dying of hunger, he made an attempt to commit suicide by cutting his throat, but was only half successful. On his person a letter addressed to Romain Rolland was found, and this, duly forwarded, brought the great writer hurrying to the vagabond's bedside. This singular epistle appealed to Rolland's imagination, for though it was the farewell letter of a man determined to take his life, it was twice interrupted by humorous anecdotes of his adventurous past. Rolland later described how Istrati's words had affected him. "I read," he said, "and I was seized with the tumult of genius, a burning wind on the plain. It was the confession of a new Gorki of the Balkan countries."

After six months in hospital Istrati recovered, and was persuaded by Rolland, by this time his friend and admirer, to write down some reminiscences of his amazing career. In 1923, while he was still working as a photographer on the *plages* of Brittany and Normandy, his first book, *Kyra Kyralina*, was published and immediately brought him fame. This was followed shortly by other works, such as *Les récits d'Adrien Zograffi*, *Oncle Anghel*, *Présentation des Haïdoucs*, etc.

In 1929 Istrati wrote three books on Soviet Russia, *Après seize mois en U.R.S.S.*, *Soviets 1929*, and *La Russie nue*; this last appears here in an English translation. Before the war he was on intimate terms with many who are now prominent in the Soviet régime, and quite recently threw himself whole-heartedly into the greatest experiment of all time, serving enthusiastically in Soviet institutions. But when he returned to Paris, instead of extolling the virtues of the system, he gave the world an account of the sufferings which it had brought to one hundred and fifty million people, and described how they were being crucified for its theories of Socialism and Communism. No one is better qualified to reveal the inmost secrets of the Soviet régime than Panaït Istrati; few men have been in a position to write so intimately of the foremost of European problems and the greatest scourge in the memory of mankind. A man of exceptional mentality, he was thoroughly acquainted with Russia, both in Tsarist and Bolshevist times; he had learnt to speak the language fluently, and, being an extreme revolutionary himself, at once became an ardent supporter of the Bolshevist cause. He put his unbounded enthusiasm and great mental qualities at the service of what he at first believed to be an ideal system. Yet it was not long before his illusions were shattered. With his exceptional knowledge—for a foreigner—of Russia and her language, and his wonderful capacity for sifting evidence and seeking out the truth, he was soon able to see through the veil of masking propaganda and perceive that the Soviet system was, in practice, both oppressive and unworkable.

PREFACE

The author of this work undertakes to tell the truth, the whole truth—as far as is possible in two hundred and sixty-two pages—and nothing but the truth.

He does not ask his readers to accept his statements unconditionally, but, rather, to have recourse to the established facts. With this end in view he will continually refer to them, together with all the evidence upon which they are founded; and these facts, being exclusively of Soviet origin, are therefore free from any suspicion of being intentionally directed against the system of government born of the great Russian Revolution. In our opinion such facts, to be of any real value, must be deduced from a survey of the situation as a whole, and will depend on this for their characteristic interest. No importance must be attached to incidental happenings and events, temporary and exceptional conditions, or to unforeseen occurrences. These facts may be of general value in two definite ways. Where they occur frequently they may provide a picture of the daily life of the great masses; or, where they are of rare occurrence and inconceivable unless found under the conditions specially favourable to them, they may give a singularly striking insight into some particular situation and its ambient influences.

If an outside observer is to judge these basic facts with the discernment necessary, he must have lived in Soviet territory, not as a *persona grata* (though that is far from being a waste of time), but on a common footing with ordinary mortals; and lived long enough there to have learnt to distinguish the realities from beneath the masking veil of Red propaganda and to have made a deep and prolonged study of Russia, both old and new, together with all her reactionary and revolutionary movements. Finally, he must feel a deep love for the Russian peoples, and, at the outset, take his part in their struggle for freedom.

These conditions, at least, will be found to have been fulfilled by the author of this book.

CONTENTS

RUSSIA UNVEILED

CHAPTER I

AN INTRODUCTION TO SOVIET LIFE

Fénelon's land of enchantment—The Soviet legend—Before Lenin's death—The tourist in Soviet Russia—Appearances and realities—The new and old régime—The heritage of the past—Statistical methods—Socialism or Capitalism—The scope of this book—The dogma of infallibility—Self-criticism—Russia's sham élite.

"From afar we espied an island of sugar-candy and caramel, with streams of syrup flowing through the countryside. The inhabitants, who were great epicures, used to lick the surface of the roads, and having dipped their fingers in the rivers, would suck them. There were forests of liquorice as well, and lofty trees from which honey-wafers fell and were carried by the wind into the travellers' mouths, were they open ever so little."

"As so many sweet things seemed insipid to us we wished to pass over to some other country where dishes of a more elevated flavour could be found. We were informed that ten leagues away there was another island where there were mines of hams, sausages, and peppered stews. These are worked just as the gold-mines are in Peru. Streams of onion-sauce are to be found there, and the walls of the houses are made of pie-crust. When the sky is overcast rain falls in the form of deep-coloured wine, and on the finest days white wine always replaces the morning dew."

"Hardly had I got to bed than I heard a great noise; I was frightened and called for help. I was told that this was caused by the earth gaping open. I thought I was lost, but was reassured on being informed that at a certain hour every night it opened in this way, and, straining, belched forth boiling streams of frothy chocolate and iced liquors in every shape and form. I arose hastily to taste of the latter and found them delicious. Then I went back to bed and dreamed that the whole world was made of crystal, that men lived on perfumes when it so pleased them, that they fain must dance when they walked and sing when they talked; that they had wings and fins with which to soar into the air and pass through the seas."

Viewed in the light of modern conditions, this description might appear at first sight to have been taken from a book of travel written by one of those salaried or benevolent apologists who go about the world extolling the system of government established in Russia since the death of Lenin. It will not require much thought, however, to identify this passage from among the memories of childhood's days as coming from *Travels in the Isle of Pleasure*. But how feeble is Fénelon's imagination beside the inventive and deceptive powers of those who, for the benefit of a particularly credulous public, are now busy with fabrications concerning Soviet Russia, describing it as a veritable Paradise! The Russian Revolution, like all its predecessors, has been harried and vilified by those with whose interests it has necessarily wrought havoc. It has successfully resisted the bitter attacks made upon it. After the death of Lenin, the new leaders, suffering from some amazing form of mental aberration, exposed it to even a greater danger; they eulogised it systematically, approved it fanatically, almost slandered it with their extravagant praise; and the results of this policy have been more definitely harmful and lasting than any that preceded it.

The Soviet Republic will depend for its existence on the conscious solidarity of the working classes in all countries, and they cannot become conscious of that solidarity unless they have a full knowledge of the difficulties which hamper the progress of Socialism in Russia. The Soviet legend, invented, propagated, and kept alive at the instigation of the Government in Moscow, only succeeds in arousing a superficial and entirely verbal solidarity amongst the most backward elements in the working class, at the same time introducing deceptions which will result in an irreparable alienation of sympathy.

In Lenin's time the first non-Russian supporters of Bolshevism did not deceive the mass of workers in the West. They called on them to support the Revolution, recounting stories of the misery and suffering with which the peoples of Russia found themselves overwhelmed in their struggle for freedom. Far from keeping silent concerning the disorganisation in their country, the decay of its productive powers, and the devastating effect of famine throughout vast districts, they relied upon these revelations to stimulate increased support for the movement.

This period was certainly not free from illusions. Amid scenes of unspeakable horror the war was drawing to a close. Europe was being shaken by revolutionary movements, and scientific objectivity was not favoured by this tide of frenzy and passion. The time for impartial discussions had not yet come. Those courageous souls who were so daring as to attack the principles of present-day society (and they are quite right not to regret having done so) needed resolute support. Therefore, each partially successful effort to check disorder, each well-conceived attempt to work on original lines, each improvisation that turned out well—all were hailed as bearing promise of a happy future. But no Communist would have dreamed of claiming that all was for the best in the best of revolutions. No one denied that there were such things as cold and hunger in Russia, or attempted to conceal the immensity of the task in prospect, or the anæmic character of the remedial measures at the disposal of the authorities.

Then there were the "pilgrim tourists" who visited the Russia of that day and brought back with them artless tales of the conditions prevailing in that country. But these personal opinions, not very common, were not an expression of any existing system, and were dependent for their veracity upon their authors' word alone. It was not on this basis that the Soviet authorities and the qualified representatives of the International Communist movement founded their policy. The documents dealing with this period are still accessible and show how keen was the anxiety of the leaders to ascertain the real conditions and disclose them in the minutest detail so that, ultimately, they might become masters of the situation.

That was in Lenin's time.

After the disappearance of this unchallenged leader the whole situation underwent a change. It became an act of high treason against the Revolution to state the truth or to make known the actual facts, even when this was done in a spirit which conformed most strictly to Communist inclinations. Also, even the most scrupulously loyal and reforming criticism was considered an open attack upon the system. That is the reason why so many of Lenin's companions in arms have, one after another, been seen to take the road leading to prison, to exile, or to deportation.

Up to 1924 Lenin used to mount the tribune in Soviet or Communist assemblies and, when he deemed it necessary, did not hesitate to say for the whole world to hear that in such a case or in such a debate, "We were wrong." Far from benefiting the enemy, this clarity and candour enlightened the revolutionary conscience.

Since 1924 Lenin's successor has claimed that he has never been in error; that in six times three hundred and sixty-five days he has made no mistake. If the Communist and Soviet Press of all countries is closely examined, not the slightest allusion will be found even to the mildest faults committed by the Soviet authority incarnate in that unique and self-sufficing person, the Secretary of the Communist Party of the United Republics of Soviet Russia.

The population of the greater part of the two Continents does not yet know that amongst mere mortals an infallible personage resides at the Kremlin in Moscow. That is doubtless the reason why this omniscient individual has, with boundless foresight, thought good to organise a troop of sycophants who, under various designations, endeavour to sing his praises on every hand.

Is it true to say, as these sycophants declare, that all is for the best in the best of revolutions? There are at least two ways of discovering if this is so: either by going to Russia to gain first-hand information or by studying, perhaps at a distance, Soviet documents not intended for foreign propaganda. If they are to be efficacious, both these methods will require at least two indispensable qualities: first, above everything, a disposition friendly to the Russian Revolution, and, secondly, a previous knowledge of the subject. Real understanding of the problem will be impossible unless there is an instinctive or reasoned sympathy for an event so widespread and complex as the matter under review. It is also useless to claim that any proper estimation can be made without a knowledge of Russia and of the Revolution. Those who are ignorant of these subjects must first gain the requisite information before they start to discuss the question themselves.

A visit to Soviet Russia is not necessarily a revelation in itself; everything depends on the conditions under which the tour is carried out and on the intellectual and moral worth of the traveller himself. Anyone who tours the country guided and surrounded by specially appointed cicerones, following prearranged itineraries and visiting specially chosen places often prepared for his coming, and avails himself of modes of travel which are aristocratic and comfortable to a degree otherwise unknown in Russia at the present day, who, further, frequents the society of officials, functionaries, and privileged persons—this kind of traveller, I say, is not, on his return, entitled to criticise. Sleeping-cars, motor-cars, comfortably appointed hotels, have nothing in common with the life at the present time of 150 million people in the U.S.S.R. With regard to other aspects of the problem, they may be judged from within or from without. The difference existing between the outward aspect of things and their intimate purport is not peculiar to Russia. Admirers of ancient ruins in any country stand filled with wonder at their picturesqueness without a moment's thought for those unfortunates condemned to spend their lives in such surroundings. Friends of old Paris protest on archæological grounds against the proposed demolition of the sordid hovels on the Ile St. Louis, while they themselves live in their new, clean houses at Auteuil. The glorious tints and hues of the countryside which enrapture visitors do not, however, hinder men from living there in filth and squalor. Passers-by who gather round workmen engaged in some difficult street operation evince an interest of which the involuntary actors would doubtless like to deprive them.

In the U.S.S.R. conditions are the same as anywhere else, but with certain specific complications. It is rare that a foreigner arrives knowing Russian, and his relations are therefore limited to a few officials or officious people who can easily deceive him. If the traveller wishes to have personal contact with some trustworthy person either in his own language or with the aid of an interpreter, it then becomes necessary for the latter to exercise discretion in this responsible rôle and be assured as to the accuracy of his translation. He must also see to it that there is present no third person who might denounce the individual giving the information. Also, if the foreigner is successfully to carry out his inquiry, he must be on his guard against accepting the favours granted him out of politeness or in gratitude when visiting State institutions, as this would be contrary to the very spirit in which his journey was undertaken. Finally, it is all-important to know how to distinguish what, in Soviet Russia, is Soviet from what is Russian, not attributing to the new régime the characteristics of the old, and *vice versa*.

Here it is necessary to give several examples.

A so-called "delegate" of a Western workers' organisation (in reality a functionary nominated by other functionaries who are in their turn dependent upon higher officials at Moscow), hearing that a strike had been declared recently in a Moscow factory, announced that he wished to get to the bottom of the matter. He therefore went to the spot, accompanied by an interpreter and various other "delegates" of his own type, and then in the presence of the factory manager and the secretary of the Communist nucleus and of the factory committee, etc., questioned a workman. It appears that the latter answered that he had heard nothing, and thus found it possible to avoid contradicting the story of the strike without in any way compromising himself. Our inquiring friend declared himself perfectly satisfied. But if the workman had told the truth he would have been suspended after the visitor's departure, deprived of his livelihood, and sentenced, with his wife and children, to a life of terror and misery. This will be proved later on in this book by indisputable evidence. If he had taken it upon himself to pronounce an opinion unfavourable to those in power at that time, he would have paid for it by a term of imprisonment or by deportation to Siberia, after being condemned in secret without any trial or opportunity of offering a defence. The inquiry, conducted in this fashion, was therefore valueless; the workman should have been examined under conditions which would have ensured complete freedom of speech.

Another "delegate" in the same factory (one of those specially selected for visits of this kind) learned that tramway motors, manufactured there, were turned out at almost a pre-war figure. He made a note of this comparatively satisfactory result and passed on the information to the author of this book who, having friends in the concern in question, made inquiries and was given the precise details. The work of the factory was confined to assembling engine-parts imported from Germany before the Revolution. The net cost of motors manufactured entirely in Russia would have been three or four times that amount. Moreover, anyone able to read the reports of metallurgical trusts and articles in economic papers could ascertain the real costs of production.

Other "delegates" at the time of the tenth anniversary of the Revolution saw from their charabanc a long queue of people and were informed by their guide that these were all waiting to subscribe to a Government loan. In reality these poor wretches had been standing about for many weary hours, waiting to buy the primary necessities of life.

How many incompetent, unscrupulous investigators, over-eager with their defensive arguments in favour of the new régime, have attributed the main principles of the Tsarist and pre-revolutionary periods to Soviet creation? One of these, an artist as well as a fabricator of unreliable evidence, has placed his abilities as a draughtsman at the service of the "living Russia" and her works. He has made a sketch of the Kremlin, and is guilty of a stupendous anachronism by introducing it, as the frontispiece, into his book on modern Russia. Another has written in glowing terms of the *corps de ballet* and the chorus at the Grand Theatre where Bolshevism plays no part at all. A third almost swoons with emotion at the mere mention of the revolutionary songs (none of which date from the October Revolution), and of Soviet chants, which are not of Soviet origin, but consist of new words set to ancient melodies. This kind of writer also sings the praises of the Matisse and Cézanne pictures in the galleries of Western art, quite as if their choice and acquisition were not due to two Capitalists. There are some who so far forget themselves as to insult Lenin by paying him a special tribute on the grounds that he resisted the temptation of having a pair of boots made for himself out of the canvas from the Van Gogh pictures. The same writer praises the scenery in Georgia just as if it were a result of Soviet rule, and it is most probable that somebody else will attribute to Leninism the loftiness of the Elbruz and Kazbek peaks and the eternal snows of the Caucasian mountains.

The same sycophants, who ascribe quite unmerited values to the so-called Soviet régime, hasten to blame the old order for everything that tends to interfere with their public expression of satisfaction with regard to State affairs. The "heritage of the past" is the excuse for everything. But if there are some traces of past difficulties still to efface, there are others which probably no longer exist in this, the twelfth, year after the Revolution. If, on the other hand, so many evils remain which the new system cannot possibly root out in a quarter of a century, that is no reason to deny their existence, cloaking them with idyllic descriptions, or to confuse them with the faults and evils of the new régime itself.

In this connection it is quite sufficient to recall the tragic lot of the abandoned children, doomed to an unutterably dreadful physical and moral decadence, to a life of crime, begging, and plunder. The hirelings of the Soviet legend at first denied their existence, but the scourge was so evident, so alarming, that the Soviet leaders were obliged to denounce it openly in their Press.

The people's Health Commissary wrote in the "Izvestia" on September 4th 1925: "The dirty, half-naked children, covered with vermin, seen in the towns and at the stations, are a *living reproach* to our conscience." Vinokurov, one of the highest magistrates of the Soviet tribunal, calculated that there were *at least four hundred thousand* of these little vagabonds ("Izvestia", March 2nd 1926). This figure may certainly be regarded as an under-estimate of the true number, if the difficulties of taking a census are kept in mind. Alexandra Rakovsky, wife of the Soviet Ambassador in Paris, gave 600,000 as being the correct figure ("L'Œuvre", June 25th 1926). Those who had travelled and stayed in Russia at the expense of workmen and peasants, and who could not fail to notice the hundreds of thousands of abandoned children, were able to escape from their embarrassment as soon as the "heritage of the past" was pointed out to them as the obvious scapegoat. But someone was found to speak the truth, couched in very prudent language certainly, but whose word could not very easily be disputed. This was N. Krupskaya, Lenin's widow, who wrote in "Pravda" on December 2nd 1925:

"Most comrades, even within the Party, believe that the abandoned children are the legacy of the Great War and of economic chaos. In reality, 75 per cent. of the abandoned children who are swarming this year in the streets of Moscow are the product, not of past shortcomings and calamities, but of present conditions, due principally to the pitiable condition of the peasant classes and to unemployment. Certainly the matter is connected with the war, but only by the bond that ordinarily links past and present. I also wrote some time ago that the abandonment of children was a consequence of the war and of economic chaos, but now, after closely examining the question, I see that there must be an end to such talk, that the origins of the scourge must be said to be rooted not only in the past, but also in the present."

Thus one authoritative, but unfortunately *privileged*, voice was raised to denounce the falsity of the everlasting allusion to the "heritage of the past". If any ordinary Communist, who had not had the good fortune to marry Lenin, had timidly ventured to make an observation in the same sense, he would have paid for it by a term of imprisonment or by deportation to Siberia. Nevertheless, the calamitous condition of these deserted, unprotected children has undergone a definite improvement in the course of the last three years, thanks solely to the public criticism of which we have given several examples above. This improvement would not have been possible if the Soviet authorities had had only to reckon with their own hirelings.

We refer to this particular example of the effect of criticism as being undeniably important as well as specially striking; but a hundred others could be cited. Isolated incidents must on no account be seized upon in order to characterise a whole situation. Those who systematically attacked the Revolution followed this method when forging the anti-Soviet legend, to which attack the more or less legitimate heirs of Lenin thought good to retort with the Soviet legend. But the exact opposite of an ironical statement is not necessarily the truth. Each of these myths is perfectly good in its way, but far from offering mutual support they remain incompatible and leave the problem entirely unsolved. Although prompted by conflicting motives, they are both the issue of identically the same system which consists in generalising from exceptional facts, the only difference being that the rival parties do not choose the same examples.

The truth is not to be found in a happy combination composed partly of one and partly of the other doctrine. It stands by itself, clear and unmistakable, and though it may involve certain facts which are contained in the rival legends, yet it only does so by reducing them to their right proportions and by restoring to them their true meaning. In his *Social History of the French Revolution*, Jaurès said that Taine, the historian of the Revolution, had searched the archives with almost no other purpose than that of finding how many windows were broken by the mobs during the revolutionary period. Public opinion on both sides of the Atlantic has for several years been struck by these tales of the number of window-panes broken in the course of the Russian Revolution. Clumsy enthusiasts are now trying to refute them by publishing the number of windows replaced. But although the Bolsheviks can flatter themselves that they have puttied up a few windows, yet this has not enabled them to announce that the final struggle and social transformation are now at hand.

People who never miss an opportunity of slandering the Soviet Revolution have long ago been discredited, and even when true their statements are no longer accepted. Though they now quote authentic extracts from Russian Communist publications in support of their declarations, no further trust is placed in them. In this way the organised attacks of the first few years of the Revolution have disqualified the sober and justified criticism of more recent times, and even afford a kind of protection to the present Bolshevist leaders. Having heard and read so many anathemas, the public pays no further attention to the vital truths.

The out-and-out apologists, working in the opposite way, contribute in like manner to the general attitude of indifference or of scepticism adopted towards matters in Soviet Russia. Outside the circle of fanatical partisans, who are loaded up with misleading information and absurd evidence published specially in the principal European capitals under the direction of the Secretariat of the Russian Communist Party, no one can give credence to the miraculous accounts of life in the U.S.S.R. For the time, at least, conscientious readers have given up trying to acquaint themselves with the problem or to understand it.

It should be explained here, in parenthesis, how it is that the Press, which is known as the International Communist Group, is able to publish deceitful statements, even though the information is true enough in itself.

The usual method of procedure in force during the period dating approximately from Lenin's death to the present time, consisted in laying the greatest emphasis on the statistics relating to the increase in production over the previous year, expressed as a percentage. To the public, who were ignorant of the real value of this comparison, these figures seemed more than satisfactory.

But production had fallen very low during the civil war, as well as during the struggle to save the gains of the Revolution from reactionary attacks—to a level which was low even when compared to pre-war standards, actually to 18 per cent., though this estimate is not based on reliable data. On certain estates the level of production had fallen to zero, especially in the districts occupied by the Whites. When peace was restored within Russia and without, work was everywhere resumed and statistics show the progress made year by year towards the restoration of her industrial system. But it is quite evident that the most impressive percentages must be robbed of any significance if they are based on comparisons made with so low a starting-figure. A country might manufacture one motor-car one year, five the following year, ten the year after that, and so make, first, a 500 per cent. and later a 1,000 per cent. increase in production, without being able honestly to say that such "success" meant really anything at all. It is, however, this type of fact which the Press in question turns to such good account.

Nevertheless, it has been necessary to find a less debatable standard to satisfy people who are more exacting than the readers of the inspired Press, and the figures for production in 1913 have therefore been taken as a basis. That year is a very useful and interesting guiding-mark, because in the twelve months immediately preceding the outbreak of war, Capitalist development reached the highest point ever attained before the world crisis. But although important conclusions can be drawn from the statistics for 1913, these are much less significant than some people would admit, for Russia was well known to be one of the most backward countries in Europe, and her great industrial system was evolved only in this century. Capitalism has shown elsewhere, particularly in the United States of America and Japan, how rapidly it can develop a country which, though backward, is rich in natural resources and in labour supplies. But in Russia the mere fact of having exceeded the figure for production in 1913 does not allow of any claim to the superiority of the present system over the past.

If it were possible, a comparison made between modern output and the level attained by Capitalist effort, freed from the shackles of Tsarism, would indeed be significant. Though there are no statistics available, it would be easy to work out a minimum figure for production from a study of its rhythmic increase before the war and from a consideration of the impetus which any bourgeois revolution invariably gives to industry. This comparison has still to be made.

Failure to remember the increase in population may also cause deception. The census figures, in themselves, carry no significance, but must be considered in comparison with each other. Thus, where the output increases less rapidly than the population, production is, relatively speaking, on the down-grade. This is shown in concrete form if an average per head is taken. But the population of the U.S.S.R. is increased by three and a half millions a year, so that statements based on out-of-date demographic data would appear entirely misleading.

The real sign of progress is actually the average consumption per head. In 1927, the tenth anniversary of the October Revolution, the authorities at Moscow responsible for foreign propaganda announced that the level of production of 1913 had either been already, or shortly would be, exceeded. But the qualified institutions, charged with examining national economic questions, declared that in 1932 only would the pre-war average of consumption per head be equalled, an estimation differing from the one above in which the increase in population and decrease in imports had not been considered. This simple declaration is in itself enough to render valueless the claims of an optimistic officialdom, repeated parrot-like and expressed in every possible shape and form by thousands of agents appointed for this purpose in every country: they are enough to stultify the so-called "evidence" of ignorant people or of those easily deceived who could have ascertained the truth without going to Russia, simply by taking the trouble to read any of the documents issued by the Supreme Economic Council of the U.S.S.R.

That is not all: the quality of production must be

taken into account; to manufacture articles of which a quarter, a third, sometimes only one-half are fit for the rubbish-heap is not matter for self-congratulation. But this is what has been happening in Russia in many work-centres, as the official reports clearly show. It is also questionable whether results have not been obtained in a manner detrimental to the workers' welfare. The cost price of the article manufactured must be kept in mind, and, finally, the ever-increasing price of primary necessities, always greatly accentuated following upon great social catastrophes, wars and revolutions, must be included in the necessary calculations.

The propagandists of the Soviet legend ignore these various factors when making their pronouncements; they quote valueless figures in their discussions and indulge in three, four, or fivefold deceptions as it suits them.

Another way of abusing the confidence of the man in the street is to offer him apparent proofs which would seem, however, to an experienced person as conclusive evidence of lack of sincerity on the part of those who advanced them. The use of photographs which have no bearing upon the subject-matter is another of their methods. To quote only one example of this kind, chosen purposely from among numerous others on account of its freedom from political significance, let us take the photograph in the "Humanité" of September 23rd 1928 under the heading, "The Truth about Russia," and described below as follows: "*The Palace of Work at Moscow, formerly the school for daughters of the nobility.*" It depicts an enormous building well known in Russia, and the only one of its kind. The former school for the daughters of the nobility was not, however, at Moscow but at Petrograd, and the present Palace of Work is in reality the former almshouse. It is just as if a Russian newspaper published a picture of the Eiffel Tower and described it as the Bourse at Marseilles. La Fontaine's monkey thought the Piræus was a man; the "Humanité" mistakes Moscow for Petrograd, old people for young ladies of the nobility, and the Smolny Institute for an alms-house—and all this is found under the high-sounding title (entirely free from intentional sarcasm) "The Truth about Russia". This makes one wonder what liberties such papers will take next when they feel a political matter must be defended at all costs.

In another issue of the same newspaper, a very typical investigator, on his return from Russia, showed off his recently acquired knowledge by referring to the Emperor Alexander I and confusing him with Alexander the Great, thus committing one slight chronological error (not to mention others) of some twenty-two centuries. Reports made by this kind of traveller are chock-a-block with similar observations, always written in the same categorical strain, brooking no contradiction.

Only the objective verification of facts is treated above. With regard to their interpretation from the point of view of the programme of Revolution, the problem arises of how to ascertain if the economic system of Russia is developing in a Socialist or a Capitalist sense, or, in other words, whether the Bolshevist Revolution is moving towards its goal or is deviating from its course. The Russian Communist Party did not undertake a social revolution in order to set up a system of production and a way of living common to other bourgeois countries, even the most advanced. Their intention was to suppress the exploitation of man by man, to abolish privileges, and to work towards real equality by pooling the resources of production and exchange, by doing away with individual profit, and by the distribution of products according to the need of each individual member of society.

In order that Russia may develop *in this direction* the U.S.S.R. must be superior to Capitalist States as regards organisation, technical services, and steady, well-regulated production, while at the same time creating a new social order—a society without classes. I say in this direction, because a country as backward as Russia cannot be expected to realise Socialism by the means at its disposal alone; the essential point is that the effort made shall be properly *directed.* If Bolshevism fails to show its superiority, in the above respects, over all other systems, it will, quite unknown to itself, bring about nothing more than a bourgeois revolution and pave the way for the reintroduction of the Capitalist system.

To this question, the most important of all, the Soviet legend has no sort of answer. The object of this book is not to offer the reader a ready-made solution or to advance a thesis; the author's sole intention is to give an accurate sketch of the principal features of the condition of the masses in Soviet Russia and to present certain ideas that may assist the reader to form an accurate opinion. He shuns all doctrinal controversy, and as an antidote to the poison of contradictory fables simply offers his evidence as an unseen observer, strengthened by approved references in support of his statements.

No longer are hair-raising stories believed about Russia, and attempts to describe it as a land of enchantment would not merit more attention than the usual methods of humbugging advertisement if their continued abuse did not constitute a real and immediate danger to the Soviet Union by stifling all opposition, criticism, and liberty in the lands affected by the Revolution, in Russia and elsewhere, for reasons of State "justified" by sophisms. These descriptions must be treated once and for all as they deserve, for they are favourable to the new religion of Leninism with its orthodox rites, its mystical intolerance, its persecution of proletarian incredulity, and its dogma of the infallibility of the Secretariat of the Bolshevist Party. This last is a phenomenon which reflects the conservative interests of the privileged classes, now in the process of formation, and the nascent idealism of the bureaucratic aristocracy which would inevitably result in the restoration of Capitalism if it were ever to mature.

The Soviet myth does not disarm the enemies of the Russian Revolution, but on the contrary assists them to turn to ridicule every piece of honest evidence offered in support of the Soviet régime. It has a baneful influence in covering up its faults, digressions, and a tendency to degeneracy which healthy criticism would certainly check, if not eradicate; it is inimical to revolutionary interests, paralysing scientific study of the Revolution and deceiving the working classes in every country. The traditional libels published by the Bolsheviks, who profit by misrepresenting every critic as coming from the enemy camp, do not even require refutation. This hostility to criticism is kept alive, not by the writers who denounce its evil effects, but by the Bolsheviks themselves who have adopted and continue to adopt this attitude.

This book reveals the real truth, and for that reason neither exceptional circumstances nor the miscellaneous information which is found under striking headlines in Russian newspapers are taken as illustrations of the general situation, even though these are not without their occasional significance. The chief features of the life of the working classes are revealed either by accumulating enough facts to state a general case or by quoting cases sufficiently important to show the general characteristics. References will be made, not to occasional episodes, but to permanent, established conditions.

No evidence will be found to relate to the period of "war communism" or to the years immediately following upon it; of the facts disclosed, some date from the death of Lenin and a great number from the tenth anniversary of the Revolution. In such cases where the author does not give his personal experiences (he has lived in Russia as a Communist for a considerable period under all kinds of conditions), the facts presented are exclusively of Soviet origin. The reader must not forget that the Russian Press of to-day depends, without exception, on the Secretariat of the Communist Party, which is the very incarnation of political power. These newspapers, very naturally, tend to suppress events which do not show the Soviet Government in a favourable light in order to deprive the foreign and hostile Press of all grounds for criticism; they only depart from this practice in special circumstances when their pronouncements are even couched in over-emphatic language so as to arouse public interest, or in cases where exaggerated statements may serve a useful purpose in times of internecine strife.

The present leaders of the Soviet Union who have monopolised the dictatorship have recently introduced an innovation into the Communist system of government by inventing a special privilege, known as "self-criticism". Everyone can and must criticise himself.

"Self-criticism" is not only authorised but ordered to be used; it is a free gift, yet one that must be employed; it is not a secular privilege, being singularly reminiscent of a religious practice—that of confession—except that in this case it is made in public. The helpless unemployed, who live by begging and whatever they can pick up in the way of food, have the right to criticise themselves; poor peasants with no ploughs or oxen, burdened with families and with nothing but their wretched crops between them and starvation, are entitled to censure themselves for their shortcomings; starving, verminous, abandoned children have the right to blame themselves for their faults; unfortunates, outcasts, martyrs of social inequality are also entitled to criticise themselves. But the Chief Secretary of the Bolshevist Party can only be criticised by himself, and up to the present time he has deemed himself irreproachable. Also, the secretaries of the Chief Secretary, their secretaries and their secretaries' secretaries, are only open to censure from themselves or from their superiors. This "happy" system, which was evidently "discovered" by those who benefit personally by it and which is a distinct advantage to certain sections of the community, is an example of Soviet democracy working in just the contrary way to what was intended by the political programme of the October Revolution.

The time has come to ask a straightforward question: For how much are these secretaries responsible? At the top of this pyramid of officialdom are those who think themselves invulnerable; at its base, supporting it, lie the great masses who, though they are bowed down by burdens inherited from the past, yet owe much of their depression to the errors committed by their sham élite.

CHAPTER II

THE TRAGIC LIFE OF THE WORKERS (1)

In town and factory—The housing of the proletarian family—Workers' barracks—Housing problems—The new buildings—"Coffin dimensions"—Conditions of work—Protection and security—Medical supervision—Enormous increase in accidents—Remedial measures.

When the condition of a country's working classes is examined, it is possible to gauge its general characteristics by various facts. Tables of statistics with coefficients, percentages, and comparative estimates provide one avenue of approach to the question. But though there is certainly no intention to dispute in these pages the value of this method, it must be noted that only persons in a position to realise the significance of these data in relation to each other can duly appreciate their importance. For example, a knowledge of wages is only profitable when it can be compared with the price of primary necessities and with the demands made upon the workers.

It seems, therefore, that the best way of giving an idea of the daily life of the workers in the U.S.S.R. is to describe the conditions under which they live and work. Statistics will then assume their proper proportions.

It might be possible to quote from personal experience, but if the reader is to be spared the examination of all challengeable statements, it is preferable to have recourse to the properly authenticated reports found in the Soviet Press which, besides being supported by the necessary documentary evidence, are characteristic in themselves and provide illustrations of the general situation. It is as well to remember in this connection that the whole of the Press in the U.S.S.R. is directly or indirectly subject to the orders and under the control of the Secretariat of the Bolshevist Party.

The following passages are taken from "Pravda": "Not one family out of 150 has been able to find the accommodation allotted to it on legal principle; sometimes two or three families, eight or nine persons, live in the same room. Children are crawling about nearly everywhere; human beings are crowded together on top of each other in dirty, verminous surroundings. A putrid stench poisons the atmosphere" (March 26th 1925). These were the conditions in the Karl Marx factory at Vyazniki in the province of Vladimir. The same paper, on March 29th, mentioned the acute housing problem in the Ural province: "The number of workmen not provided with lodging now reaches 5,000 at factory N., and 1,000 in the district round P., 2,500 at Z., etc." In Sormovo, a town of 32,000 inhabitants, "more than 50 per cent. of the dwellings do not satisfy even the most elementary sanitary conditions" ("Pravda", April 3rd). In the province of Moscow, in factory L.: "There are rooms in the workers' barracks in which nine or ten individuals live together; people are forced to sleep on the ground; there is no ventilation, the atmosphere being thick and stifling" ("Pravda", April 17th). At K., in the province of Ivanovo-Vosnesensk, in the workers' barracks: "Two families live in nearly every small room; there are bugs and cockroaches." In other adjacent buildings: "The situation is even more lamentable; hygienic conditions simply do not exist . . . etc." ("Pravda", May 6th). On the same date and in the same newspaper appears the report on conditions at Kostroma: "The great scarcity of accommodation is very marked, more than one thousand families of workers are living amidst horrible conditions. . . ." In the textile industry at Moscow: "More than 75,000 workmen and employees still require lodging." Then in the gold-mines of the Lena district: "The workmen live wretchedly in big, dark sheds; families and unmarried persons being indiscriminately mixed. The more fortunate cram themselves into hovels, two or three families at a time. Many have no mattresses and sleep in their clothes. No ventilation at all: dirt and vermin" ("Pravda", May 27th). In the factory E., Moscow province: "It is doubtful whether anything could be worse than the accommodation there, the dormitories in particular. They are low, suffocating buildings with not even the smallest windows; there is a reek of stoves. . . . The beds are camp-beds, made of wood; everything is verminous and the lighting is of the most primitive kind ("Pravda", June 5th). In the factory, called the October Revolution, at Lugansk: "The housing problem has assumed incredible proportions. Some families of workers have found shelter in sheds, others in rooms, two families in each. A great many unmarried workmen have not even that, and spend the night at the station" ("Pravda", June 6th). At Kadievka (Donetz) there is accommodation for 2,400 out of 4,200 workers and their families. "Many lodgings have only one room, and the consequent overcrowding is appalling. Each room accommodates two families or five to six persons. Four hundred of these lodgings are unfit for human habitation . . . etc." In the factory known as the Red Rose, at Moscow: "People live with unweaned children in damp cellars, two families in a room, and sometimes more than that. The husband sleeps in the dormitories and his wife joins him there" ("Pravda", June 20th).

The following is an account of how the Moscow municipal workers are housed: "Three men sleep in two beds, placed side by side; some on the dirty floors, in the corridors, under the beds. Women with children at the breast live in this filth, in this heavy, smoky atmosphere. There is no system of lighting and the courtyard has been turned into a latrine. . . ." ("Pravda", June 24th). The workmen in the Profintern factory in the province of Bryansk live in sheds; "families of eight, twelve, or even sixteen persons, often occupy a room of 5 square archines or 27 square feet. This results in the spread of infectious diseases, particularly tuberculosis, from which 80 per cent. of the workmen are suffering" ("Pravda", July 11th). In the province of Nizhni-Novogorod, at the Stenka Razin glass factory: "The situation is very bad with regard to housing accommodation. There are bugs in the workmen's dormitories as well as dirt and dust. Many sleep in the woods, in the drying-room, or in the loft" ("Pravda", July 26th). At G.-K., in the province of Vladimir: "The workmen live in narrow, damp barracks, all in a ruinous condition, and some families which are stricken with typhoid and venereal diseases live in sheds. Living conditions in these barracks are dreadful beyond imagination. In winter the inmates are frozen; in summer rain falls through the roofs; everything is rotten, crumbling. They are not workmen's rooms but kennels" ("Pravda", August 26th). In the province of Ivanovo-Vosnesensk, at a certain factory Z.: "The Commission has established that there is an appalling lack of housing accommodation, and declares that the most elementary rules of hygiene have been violated. Sometimes two or three families, comprising twelve or fifteen persons, live in very small houses where the total living-space is 7 to 9 square archines (37 to 48 square feet), half of it being occupied by the stove and other utensils. A female worker and her three children live in a stinking lavatory of 3 square archines (16½ square feet). Many workmen live in sheds and cellars. One woman was literally thrown out into the street" ("Pravda", September 13th).

Such were the reports to be read in "Pravda" of Moscow alone, for just a few months of the year 1925. These various cases were noted during a hurried and very cursory reference to this paper. An examination of the five principal organs published in the capital and of hundreds published in the provinces and in the federated states would reveal a thousand examples, providing a striking picture of the workers' misery.

What further developments have there been with regard to this state of affairs? For the majority, matters have gone from bad to worse in face of the rapid increase in population, in cities and in industrial centres, compared with the almost negligible progress made with building operations. It will be quite worth while to scan the pages of some newspapers for 1926 and to give in a brief summary the chief characteristics of the situation. The reports could not be quoted at length on account of the unavoidable repetition of facts.

The "Trud", the Central Communist organ, is perpetually protesting against these miserable conditions. "In the tobacco plantations of the northern Caucasus, at B., the women actually sleep on the ground on thin palliasses on the same spot as they work; tobacco dust penetrates into their respiratory channels and causes much sickness. Lavatories are non-existent" (Number for March 25th). Generally speaking, in the metallurgical trades, the average living-space is 7 square archines ($37\frac{4}{5}$ square feet), or sometimes $4\frac{1}{2}$ square archines ($24\frac{3}{4}$ square feet) in certain districts. At K., in the barracks, where the workers belong to different gangs, there is one bed for every three workmen, who take it in turn to sleep in it. The new workmen, of whom there are a considerable number owing to the development of industry, sleep in the stations, near the blast-furnaces . . ." (April 14th). "In Moscow, casual labourers are piled up as many as ten to fifteen in corners where there is barely room for two; in one basement, twenty-six workmen sleep on the floor, lying closely together. The majority, however, spend their nights in the stations or on the street" (April 20th). "Miners in the Ural district sleep in barracks on the floor; they have no lavatories or drying-rooms. Many have to live two or two and a half miles away from their work, and this distance has to be covered sometimes twice a day on foot." (April 29th). On June 2nd the same paper stated in a general article that in the metallurgical trades the living-space per head was only 38 square feet and at Moscow 24 square feet. In the textile trade, 282,000 people lived in intolerable conditions; a number of railway-workers slept in tanks and wagons. . . .

The "Rabochaya Gazette" called attention to the situation in the turf-pits at T.: "The workmen sleep entirely unprotected from the wind on the scene of their labours and are worried by mosquitoes" (June 15th). At the Sparrow's Mount brickworks in Moscow, "workmen lie on bare boards, or on the ground without mattresses" (June 23rd). "In the Communist Vanguard factory, sometimes as many as fourteen workmen live in one small barrack-room; nearly every room is divided into two stories, like a ship's cabin. There is one family to each of the planks which act as 'stories'. Pregnant women and little children are continually falling off on to the hard ground" (June 23rd). In the L. manufactory province of Moscow, "the piling up of human beings, one on top of the other, is appalling; in the France barracks, 40 rooms are occupied by 80 families, comprising 250 persons". But these are really fortunate compared to 600 workmen who are forced to find shelter in the "isbas" of the surrounding district and live there "among bugs, fleas, cockroaches, in a damp and mouldy atmosphere, thick with smoke and soot, in the closest proximity to cattle". "People sleep on planks and tables as well as under them; at night it is impossible to get out of the room, for the whole floor-space is covered with human bodies" (June 24th). Marietta Shaginyan gives a picture in the "Zarya Vostoka", of Tiflis, of the housing conditions among the manganese miners of Chiatura: "There are about 2,000 workers living in dark, smoke-filled tents in groups of twenty; one-half of these sleep on planks, the other on the ground. There is no drinking-water, nor are there lavatories, baths, or ambulances; and the workmen's skins are eaten into by the manganese" (Numbers 1, 136 *et seq.*, March). In the Red Ray glass factory in the province of Pskov, the 500 workmen live in a town where all the buildings are worm-eaten and rain and snow fall almost straight through on to the occupants; there is living-space of 107½ square feet for ten or twelve persons ("Trud", October 30th). In the Ural district, at the T. factory, newly engaged workmen, as well as students from the trade school, have no lodging and sleep in the station: children sleep in the factory, under the turbines.

All these facts are taken quite at random from bundles of newspapers published in 1926; it would obviously be quite impossible to read them all. These examples of existing conditions will make for a better understanding of the general situation, at the same time giving life to the bald statements of figures as given, for instance, in connection with the miners in the "Vyestnik Truda" (Number 10, 1926). The writer of this report declares that the situation is growing worse on account of the increase in men available for employment: 30,000 workmen will be homeless in the Donetz region by 1927; in the oil-fields 40 per cent. will be without shelter at Baku, 25 per cent. at Grozny. Dwellings are small, insanitary, and in ruins everywhere in the Kuznetsk district in Siberia as well as in the Moscow basin.

Semashko, the People's Commissary of Health, wrote in "Pravda" on March 25th 1926 about the condition of young workers, and revealed the results of an inquiry which had been instituted two years previously. Thirty-three per cent. had no beds, and 40 per cent. lived six and even more to a room. (We shall see that the situation gets steadily worse.) In these conditions the health of young workers was deplorable. An inspection of 79 factories and works revealed the fact that out of 1,585 adolescents, 1,120 were ill. These figures were in no way exceptional, but in the words of the newspaper which reported them, "they are unquestionably typical" ("Trud", July 2nd 1926). At Yaroslavl, more than half the young workmen were suffering from tuberculosis or anæmia. In the Krasny Perekop factory alone, 600 apprentices were ill ("Pravda of Youth", October 1927). But time and space do not allow of quoting further extracts from the Press in this connection. It is quite easy to imagine the widespread demoralisation which would result from such conditions. Yaroslavsky, a high Government official, in alluding to one aspect of the question, made the following statement at a conference (The "Krasnaya Gazette" of April 15th 1926): "Is it possible to describe as Communist a state of affairs in which parents are obliged to satisfy their sexual needs in front of their children owing to the lack of space in their lodging?" It is easy to imagine the endless tortures suffered by the wretches forced to "live in these dormitories, barracks, cellars, holes, and hovels".

Assailed with complaints on this subject, the "Trud" gave a whole page to the housing problem on April 20th 1927. "Everywhere", ran the report, "one finds the same distress, the same cramped accommodation, dirt and diseases." Several examples were given of these dreadful conditions, and figures were quoted which showed that there were still not enough new houses to accommodate a greatly augmented population. At Tver, in the Proletarian factory, the workers had sheds in which were kinds of cages, each containing five beds, five trunks, and five ikons. One of these sheds alone provided shelter for 5,000 people. Damp cellars were used as lodgings and children fell ill; some of the workmen were obliged to walk from seven to eleven miles to their work. In the textile factory B., near Moscow, workers' town settlements were over-populated, and there was much sickness among the children. Many of the latter were corrupted sexually by witnessing the promiscuous intercourse existing between adults ("Trud", May 22nd). In the Moscow-Narva district in Leningrad, the living-space was 21½ square feet per person; fifteen houses were declared unsafe and 650 people had to be turned out at a moment's notice, though there was no other kind of accommodation available for them (The "Evening Krasnaya Gazette", November 28th). It was established by an inquiry carried out by the inspectors of peasants and workers in all the great industrial centres (Moscow, Leningrad, Sverdlovsk, Stalingrad, Tver, Yaroslavl, Ivanovo-Vosnesensk, Saratov, etc.), by the order of the Council of Commissaries, that everywhere habitable space was increasing less rapidly than the population ("Trud", July 7th).

Now to turn to some cases from the following year (1928). At Stalino, in the Donetz district, only 125 out of 2,500 labourers were housed at all, and these were literally piled up on top of each other in the dormitories; on each palliasse three men had to take it in turns to sleep. Everything was repulsively dirty and the noise of machinery deafening ("Pravda of Youth", January 5th). At the Red Weavers' works, on entering a workman's house, an indescribable, intolerable stench assailed one's nostrils caused by rotten cabbages, dustbins full of scourings, slops, the reek of stoves and appallingly filthy water-closets. Walls were worm-eaten and the floors dirty to the most repulsive degree. In the dormitories beds were pushed close up against each other and there was not room to put a stool down. People slept, played cards, smoked, cried, and quarrelled in them ("Pravda", April 1st). At the workers' barracks in a brick-works (province of Moscow) it was found that there was an insufficiency of accommodation in the dormitories, which were dark and filthy and where it was impossible to breathe. The same conditions existed at the Proletarian Victory factory near Moscow, and sleep was quite impossible. Nine four-storied barracks in the Rykov factory provided shelter for 5,000 people; some even lived in the cellars, which were crawling with vermin ("Pravda", April 3rd). The "Pravda of Youth" reported the facts revealed by an inquiry made into conditions at Leningrad where 45 per cent. of young workmen were found to be lodged in the vilest of dwellings; in the Ural district, 61 per cent. were crammed into overcrowded buildings and 58 per cent. slept on the ground. The situation was the same in the Donetz region (April 3rd). In the Krivoy-Rog basin, the workmen's settlements were not fit for human habitation; most of them lacked water, light, beds, and cleanliness ("Izvestia", April 18th). The delegates to the Miners' Congress gave a description of their comrades' miserable lives: the old buildings, they said, were falling down and the new ones already needed thorough repair. Workers were packed in "like sardines"; one story became three stories because people not only slept on the beds and underneath, but above them on planks stretched across the room. Everywhere there were vermin and parasites. "We are ashamed to describe the conditions", said one speaker. In some places the ground was cemented and the children fell ill: in others the streets were veritable sewers; there was a lack of water for drinking and washing, etc. ("Izvestia", April 27th).

Half of the 200,000 young workers employed in the Donetz slept on bare boards and in sordid hovels ("Pravda of Youth", May 11th). Two eminent official controllers, Soltz and Peters, denounced the authorities concerned for their failure to relieve the situation in spite of their ability to do so. Near a factory called the Red Echo, the workmen were piled into old and dirty barracks; at K., there were seventy people to every room, etc. ("Trud", August 2nd). Men employed on the Dargom Canal slept in unclean hovels which were infested with vermin and where the rain came through the roof; there was one wash-stand among 200 men ("Trud", August 10th). At M., the shed windows were broken, roofs had holes in them, walls were cracked, and there was an entire lack of wash-stands and stools. In many other places, principally at Ivanovo-Vosnesensk, the same conditions prevailed ("Pravda", September 23rd). From the platinum-mines in the Urals came the same story of sheds with cracked walls, cold, dirt, vermin, and of workmen forced to take it in turns to share the most disgusting bunks imaginable ("Trud", October 31st). At Makeyevka, in the Tomsky factory, the sheds were pestilential and rubbish was left lying about for months at a time. There were no wash-stands or clothes-rooms, and often no electric light; most of the windows were broken ("Trud", November 1st). "The workers' settlement in the Astrakhan fisheries is perpetually covered in dust; the sheds are dark and worm-eaten. They provide shelters for families, unmarried persons, and drunkards all mixed higgledy-piggledy together. One building, nicknamed the "tomb", though reputed to be uninhabitable, was occupied in 1926 by seven families. But after it had been decided many times to evacuate it, still more partitions were removed and a further batch of people was crammed into it" ("Pravda", November 4th). At the Eighth Trades Union

Congress many delegates denounced the housing conditions. One of them remarked that there could be no talk of a cultural evolution when as many as eighty to one hundred persons were crowded closely together in the dormitories. A railway-worker declared that he and his comrades slept in cellars, old trucks, or even in holes. In fact, the representatives of all the industrial regions, without exception, aired their complaints and grievances, each describing the particularities of their respective "prisons" ("Trud", and other papers, December 14, 15, 16, 18).

Finally, a few examples will be given for the year 1929. In the Don basin the same cry was heard. "We live so much piled up on top of each other that we are being suffocated." Dilapidated houses were overcrowded and newly constructed ones soon fell into the general state of disrepair; masons were forced to sleep under miners' beds, and *vice versa*. This resulted in the demoralisation of the workers, who promptly took to drink ("Pravda", January 22nd). At Leningrad, for only 1,245 out of 45,200 labourers engaged in building could accommodation be found. Houses were being built for approximately 4,000, leaving therefore 40,000 without shelter of any kind (The "Evening Krasnaya Gazette", March 22nd). In the previous year 120,000 casual labourers had entered the district round about Moscow, and this year (1929) 180,000 were expected. But there was only room for 2,000 in the night-shelters, so that the remainder would have nowhere to lay their heads ("Pravda of Youth", April 2nd). The Soviet authorities carried out an inquiry into the lot of these casual labourers. In one room, measuring 172 to 215 square feet, ten or sometimes twelve men were found crowded together, generally sleeping in their clothes, sometimes even on the ground. Many of them slept in the night-shelters, thus coming in contact with the off-scourings of the population. "It is impossible either to rest or to wash in our shed," wrote one miner; "there is not a single mattress and we sleep on the bare boards. You have to go 500 yards to find even a well. If it rains, well, you can always swim, I suppose. You are more tired when you get up than when you went to bed" ("Pravda of Youth", April 14th). In the same issue of this paper a description was given of a shed in the Donetz district: bedsteads were made up of planks, sometimes covered with rags in which vermin were swarming. Two miners slept together in each bed, giving up their places after a time to another couple, who in turn made way for two of their comrades. Throughout one winter some sheds had no window-panes at all; there was no water for drinking or washing. The "Trud" reported that according to information supplied by the board of the Central Council of Trades Unions, servants, of which there were 300,000, were obliged to sleep in corridors or in the most unwholesome nooks and corners (July 6th 1929).

Such is the lot, not of a few sections of workmen suffering under specially unfavourable circumstances, but of the great majority of the working classes in this, the first Republic in the world to call upon the name of Socialism. Those human beings to whose labours the creation of everything is due are penned up, millions of them, into foul hovels worthy of the Middle Ages, are sent to seek shelter under the stars, or left to the tender mercies of the weather. Retailers of the Soviet legend have not seen that side of the picture. They have allowed themselves to be shown round a few palaces and villas where a small number of specially favoured workmen live—a few hundred at the most. But these veritable sties in which a decent European peasant would not even keep his pigs, in Russia are crammed with thousands wallowing in filth. These they have not seen.

Once again the question arises whether the situation is improving or growing worse. The Gosplan, the State-Planning Commission, in its first five-year programme for the period 1926–27 to 1931–32, recognised that the situation would inevitably follow the latter course. Co-operative building societies have been formed, but it is difficult to see how this has benefited anyone. One of the best Communist political writers in the U.S.S.R., L. Sosnovsky, who has been deported to Siberia and is at the present time in solitary confinement at Chelyabinsk, writing on August 22nd 1928 in the "Proletarian" of Kharkov, brought the following facts to the notice of Leon Trotsky, who likewise had been deported: "In the capital of the Ukraine, 38 per cent. of the 40,310 workmen and members of their families who belonged to 800 of these co-operative schemes, were living in cellars; 62 per cent. of the available living-space was not allotted to workers." In a sub-head, the same paper made the following pronouncement: "By no law is a workman prohibited from living in good lodgings"—a remarkable discovery after ten years of "proletarian revolution". At a meeting of important Communist officials at Moscow on August 5th 1929 it was reported that "the housing conditions among the Moscow workers are still as *unsatisfactory* [*sic*] as ever. It is interesting to notice that in recent years Moscow has built enough houses to lodge 270,000 people, but that more than 800,000 have made their way into the Moscow province" ("Trud", August 6th 1929). According to recent official information, therefore, the situation in the capital of the U.S.S.R. and the surrounding district has been further aggravated by the unexpected addition of 530,000 souls, without counting the normal increase in population. One wonders

D

how the figure of 270,000 was arrived at; could it be by calculating on the basis of 21 square feet per person? On this point the report is silent. But since the statistical methods of the Soviets are well known (and Stalin, the Secretary of the Bolshevist Party and high-priest of all the secretaries of all the Russias, himself declared from the platform of the Thirteenth Communist Congress that they were entirely untrustworthy), it is inevitable that their figures should be received with caution and . . . divided, mentally, by two or three. It must be noted also that from each figure given for habitable surface must be deducted the area taken up by passage-room, corridors, antechambers, etc., as well as the space occupied by the enormous fire-clay or brick stoves traditionally employed in Russia. But what can be said of these new buildings that have recently made their appearance in statistics?

New workmen's houses were built near the T. factory in the Uralsk; they had not been up a year before they were worm-eaten, rain came through the roofs, and extensive repairs were necessary ("Pravda", November 20th 1926). At Zlatoust the greater part of the monies intended for the construction of new houses was misappropriated and the officials responsible prosecuted, but the most necessary adjustments could not be carried out ("Pravda", December 15th 1926). After a few months, houses became quite uninhabitable. At E., in the Donetz, buildings required a complete overhaul after two years, and at L. after only one year ("Trud", April 20th 1927). The inquiry carried out by the Workers' and Peasants' Inspectorate, which has been already mentioned in these pages, revealed that 90 per cent. of the new houses were built of wood and had one story, and that only 10 per cent. had two. They had been constructed for the most part by the workmen themselves without plans, technical advice, or the aid of any controlling hand

("Trud", July 7th 1927). At Kharkov, houses were built in groups of ten, but soon a whole section of these new buildings started to crumble away; there were cracks in the walls and roofs, planks became loose, doors and windows warped, and rain trickled in everywhere. The very ground under the buildings kept shifting, and the materials used in their construction were all rotten ("Izvestia", August 21st 1927). The factory of Nadejdin (Ural) built about twenty houses in which planks were rotten and stoves did not work: even the walls had cracks in them ("Pravda", April 1928). A house built by the factory Paris Commune in 1927 was reported to have become a complete ruin by the next year, the walls, ceilings, and floors all needing thorough repair ("Pravda", July 21st 1928). A three-storied house built on piles by the co-operative society of workmen and employees of the Electrobank entirely collapsed ("Pravda", July 20th 1928). At Kiev, the new houses were built by the co-operatives contrary to all rules of sanitation, the essential points being overlooked. At Vasilkov they were entirely unsupplied with water and quite unfit for habitation; the stoves did not heat the rooms and all the work had to be done over again ("Trud", October 18th 1928). In December 1928 the delegates to the Eighth Congress of Trades Unions denounced the muddle that existed with regard to building. There were no constructional plans or sketches, and often the fourth story was completed before the estimates had been passed ("Trud", *idem.*). Not only were the plans never prepared to time, but there was a shortage of materials, which were of poor quality and so badly distributed that in all undertakings the quantity required was miscalculated ("Pravda", March 29th 1929). The correspondent of the "Trud" telegraphed from Lugansk on July 25th 1929 that buildings were being put up for which neither estimates nor plans had been prepared; that materials, which were of poor quality, were lacking, and that houses were hardly completed before they required extensive repairs. All the errors of the previous years were being repeated ("Trud", July 26th 1929). A drawing appeared in "Pravda" of May 16th 1928 which showed a house constructed by the Textilstroy: the roof had been pushed up and the walls forced several yards apart by a big tree that had been left growing in the middle of the building.

The population of the U.S.S.R. is increased every year by three and a half millions, much more rapidly in the towns than in the country. The development of industry and the miserable conditions prevailing among the peasantry have resulted in the very rapid growth of the urban populations; many of the old houses are no longer habitable: all these facts give an idea of the vast needs that must be supplied before the U.S.S.R. can find themselves on a level with civilised countries in the matter of housing their people. There may, indeed must be references to the heritage of the past, but if any real effort is to be made along the path of progress the realities of the present situation cannot and must not be denied. According to a high official, Larin, the available living-space per head for the population of Moscow, in which he includes the higher grade functionaries, government servants, artisans, the middle classes as well as other privileged persons, is on an average 64 square feet, but in the case of students is as low as 32 square feet. This shows that the proletariat enjoys rather less than 32 square feet of living-space per person, and the question will be raised later whether students have even that allowance. Most people's accommodation falls below the average, and that is why in Russia it is said that the lodging-space available for each inhabitant is practically of the "same dimensions as a coffin".

Faced with these facts, the reader will wonder whether there can be any workmen in Russia who are decently housed or any houses fitted out with the most ordinary conveniences; whether, in fact, there can be even any modern, if not model, houses. There are certainly some, though very few, which answer these requirements, and it is precisely these that are shown to tourists who style themselves "delegates" or friends of the U.S.S.R. That is simply a proof of the existence in the Soviet States, as in Capitalist countries, of a privileged section among the labouring classes. In Germany, Austria, Holland, Switzerland, Scandinavia, even in Great Britain and in the most backward Latin countries, to speak only of Europe, healthy, comfortable workmen's houses are to be found. That does not, however, prevent Communists denouncing, and quite rightly, the hovels in which many unfortunates still live, or of taking up the cudgels on behalf of the outcast labouring classes. The important point is not to find out how privileged workmen enjoy living in properly appointed houses, which are, incidentally, few and far between, but to become acquainted with the daily life of the great masses. The reader is now in a position to form an idea of the condition of the proletariat in Russia and will have a better understanding of the next question to be examined—the relative value of wages.

After studying housing conditions it will be necessary to ascertain the conditions under which work is carried on in factories and elsewhere. Owing to their inevitably frequent recurrence, many repugnant details have been omitted from the passages quoted in full, as well as from the summaries. It should not, however, have been difficult to imagine the conditions prevailing in these filthy hovels in which the occupants sleep, get drunk, smoke, spit, quarrel, and sometimes fight; where children are crying, men play noisily at cards, drunkards stagger round, and the delirious cries of the sick are heard. (The evil effects of alcohol and the general corruption of morals will be studied later.) The same methods as previously employed will now be applied in the examination of the facts which characterise the problems of relief, safe working-conditions, medical care, social insurance, as well as certain other aspects of the worker's life.

But it is important at the outset to realise that though laws have been passed and decrees pronounced which establish, on paper, the most excellent principles, yet it is quite another matter to get them applied. The world of the U.S.S.R. is paved with the thousands of good intentions and decisions which still remain to be carried out, and which, perhaps, will never now be brought to mind. Facts, not vain texts, must be reviewed. But though there are many obstacles in the way of putting theory into practice, and it is always easy to criticise, yet that is all the more reason why the life of Russian workers should not be described in the garbled language of the official reports which give an entirely untrue picture of the real conditions. The following incident, taken from the many thousands available, provides a good illustration. The workman has, in theory, the right to a reduction in the charges made by the public health services, and in particular by the dental service, whose prices for the supply of false teeth are quite prohibitive. One workman who had eleven teeth missing went to the "Mosdravoldiet" (the sanitary service of Moscow) to obtain a new set at the reduced rate. But because, in order to benefit from the reduction, he had to be at least twelve teeth short, he was met with a blank refusal. "Must I sacrifice a healthy tooth so as to be able to replace the twelve that I haven't got?" he asked ("Pravda", July 30th 1925). It is worth quoting another incident which seems striking enough even though it is related in a semi-narrative style. It shows the obstacles daily encountered by the proletarian who chooses to stand on his rights.

"The situation as regards medical relief in the Donetz work-centres is extremely bad. At G., where there are 18,000 workmen, there is no clinic. Some of the mines, which are about six miles from a town, are visited by a doctor twice a week. At G., for example, as many as a hundred cases of all kinds are examined in a day—gynæcological, surgical, and venereal, as well as diseases of the eyes. There is not even a wash-stand in the surgery, and the doctor, after examining a case of venereal disease, puts his unwashed hands to the eyes or in the mouths of other patients" ("Pravda", February 4th 1926). Events of this kind are very commonplace and all very similar. The following is a much abridged account of the facts revealed in the course of an inquiry into the conditions in this group of mines: only 11 per cent. of those employing more than 1,000 men had first-aid outfits, and there was one sick-bed where, according to the regulations, there ought to have been thirty-eight: in many places even stretchers were lacking. Not one mine had the regulation bottles of drinking-water and often not even goblets. There were no baths in 20 per cent. of the mines, and those that did possess them had let them get into a dreadful state. Heating, towels, soap were non-existent; work was carried on in pools of water, from which from time to time the miners quenched their thirst. No water-closets, piles of excrement everywhere, no attempts at sanitation, diseases of all kind—such were the conditions ("Trud", April 2nd 1926). "The number of accidents has increased, and taking industry as a whole, the coefficient figure for 100,000 working-days has risen in one year from 21 to 33 per cent., and in the metallurgical and textile trades from 10 to 14 and 39 to 47 per cent. respectively, owing to faulty organisation" ("Trud",

April 8th 1926). From Kharkov it was reported that the number of accidents had increased by half over the previous year ("Trud", April 13th 1926). In the Donetz, between October and February, 10,763 accidents occurred, of which 61 were fatal; in the previous year there had been 17,000 accidents in the mines, and 23,456 throughout the whole basin (The "Kharkov Communist", April 14th 1926). At Stalino, 4,500 Tartars and 350 Chinese had to do extremely dangerous work, and were paid less and in every respect more hardly treated than the Russians ("Trud", April 28th 1926). In Georgia, woodcutters in the marshes worked twelve hours a day under very unhealthy conditions, and those employed in the building of the bridge over the Ingur were "completely deprived of all rights", suffered humiliating treatment at the hands of the engineer-in-charge, and did not even know the terms by which their work was regulated ("Zarya Vostoka" of Tiflis. Numbers 1, 133, and 1,162, March and April 1926). In the Ural chromium factory, workmen were forced to labour enveloped in clouds of mineral dust, of lime and soda, which affected the mucous membranes of the eyes and respiratory organs, causing profuse bleeding from the nose, bronchial troubles, and tuberculosis, thus sweeping off the personnel. Gas-masks were quite insufficient ("Trud", October 10th 1926). "Accidents are increasing in industrial concerns. For every 1,000 workmen there are 102 accidents *per annum*, chiefly among lumbermen and in the mining and metallurgical industries" (The "Rabochaya Gazette", October 3rd 1926). In a saw-mill, in the northern Caucasus, the employees sometimes laboured twelve hours a day quite ignorant of the exact wages due to them, and were paid at the ordinary rate for overtime, Sunday, and holiday work, being also obliged to clean the machinery and sweep out the workshops in their own time without any extra pay. The stokers were forced to come one hour and a half in advance in order to start the boilers—an extra labour for which they never received anything. There were no wash-stands, and the workers were without medical aid and dispensaries ("Trud", November 16th 1926). In the province of Tambov, near Uralstroy, 150 workmen who were signed on, having been promised good wages and lodging, were abandoned to a dreadful fate—all dying of hunger ("Trud", November 24th 1926). One workman with a family of five was incapacitated from working by an injury to his hand, and being without any resources spent six months applying for the miserable allowance of 10 roubles (8s. 4d.) due to him in the circumstances, and wore himself out completely by his vain endeavours (The "Rabochaya Gazette"). In the district of Krivoy-Rog there was a workman who had waited two months to have amputated a limb that had been crushed ("Pravda", June 9th 1926).

The report of the plenary session of the All-Russian Central Council of Trades Unions stated: "Workmen who are ill have to wait ten days before they can see a doctor; medical men are very scarce and there are no hospitals." "We consider", said Tomsky, "that the Health Services are not seriously attacking the problem; their efforts are confined to making declarations and framing high-sounding phrases, while the workman receives no sort of care or attention." "Comrade K. has given a series of facts and figures which show the enormous increase in accidents, and this has been confirmed by the local delegates in their speeches before the Council. The present system of economy in everything is reflected in the failure to ensure safe working-conditions." "The directors of factories belonging to the metallurgical trust have forced their employees to sign an undertaking to claim no damages in case of accident." "The Commissariat of Work does nothing"—a statement which was repeated several times. "As regards unsafe and insanitary working-conditions in industrial concerns, the situation continues to be unsatisfactory, and in some cases the workers' health is suffering and their lives are in danger. Much difficulty is found in working social insurance schemes. This has resulted in the suspension of pensions and of special grants in certain districts," etc. (The "Rabochaya Gazette", 9, 10, June 13th 1926). In view of the huge debts owed to assurance funds by economic groups in the Ukraine, payment of special grants had already ceased in certain districts ("Pravda", September 23rd 1926).

Now to pass on to the year 1927, the tenth anniversary of the Revolution. The "Trud" once more reported the increasing number of accidents, particularly in the Donetz and Kuznetsk districts. "Pravda" (April 13th) stated as a definite fact that there had been an increase of 60 per cent. on the total for the previous year. The "Vechernyaya Moskva" estimated that 45,000 accidents had occurred in the province of Moscow; one workman in ten had been injured and 3,500 in all incapacitated (April 29th 1927). The lumbermen in the Ural forests and in the districts bordering on the White Sea were as hardly treated as under the Tsarist régime ("Trud", May 31st and June 2nd). In textile industries, accidents had doubled in number in comparison with pre-war figures. One-half were not reported to the Inspectorate of Work. Seven factories employing 36,000 hands could not boast of one wash-stand or any soap, and there was dirt everywhere. Accidents were on the increase in all industries. One factory had no ventilation at all, and in another the workmen drank unfiltered water, with the result that a fearful epidemic of typhoid ensued ("Trud", June 16th). The central committee of metallurgical workers reported a considerable increase in accidents and industrial diseases due to the wear-and-tear of material and to working overtime ("Trud", June 16th). In Armenian and Georgian mines the measures taken to provide medical attention were quite ridiculous, and there was one hospital with 20 beds for 8,000 workmen ("Trud", July 8th). In a certain glass-works the men had to endure very high temperatures while at the same time cold draughts blew down upon them as they worked. They drank foul water, and the ambulances were packed with sick people. In some turf-pits the workers had to stand in water up to their knees; their sheds were unhealthy, drinking-water and baths were unobtainable, and they could not procure medical attention ("Trud", August 18th). Once more the same paper reported the enormous increase in accidents in the Moscow centre: 35,000 in the first six months of the year ("Trud", August 26th).

The following year the situation continued to grow worse, and the authorities, roused at last to take action, called various conferences and gave orders for an active campaign. "Pravda" of January 28th, having denounced the negligence of the economic departments and the weakness of the Inspectorate of Work, invited the Communist Party and the Trades Unions to use all the power at their command in dealing with the question themselves. A special conference, called in February, brought to light the multiple causes of these accidents and the effects of Soviet rationalisation. It was discovered that tools were worn out, regulations were not observed; that there was a lack of light and ventilation; that dirt, disorder, and overcrowding, failure to make use of the credits voted, inexperience on the part of the personnel, unpractical methods, and over-work—all militated against safety and success in industry ("Trud", February 7th, *et seq.*). Some workmen were found to be completely exhausted by "sweating" methods. At Stalino, mere youths each unloaded as much as 600 pouds, or 9·5 tons, of goods a day instead of the regulation 500 pouds (8 tons), a fact which seems hardly credible ("Pravda of Youth", January 5th 1928). The Inspectorate of Work often gave false figures for accidents, so as to give the impression that there had been an improvement in the situation. So at Lugansk, when the situation was reviewed it was revealed that there had been five or six times more accidents than the official figures allowed ("Trud", August 4th). In an electrical works, 28 out of the 125 workmen employed in the stamping-room had suffered injuries to their hands. No measures were taken to protect employees from dangerous machinery, etc., and the competent authorities remained quite unconcerned (Leningrad "Pravda", August 1st). At Artemovsk there was an increase of 18 per cent. over the previous year in absenteeism caused by sickness, and in the Constantinov metallurgical works the figure was as high as 27 per cent., while in some factories it was more than 50 per cent. above the previous year's total. The health services were unprovided with the necessary stores and medicines ("Trud", August 3rd). The Commissariat of Work was guilty of the most scandalous neglect, while the Inspectors were entirely incompetent and to a great degree responsible for the abuses and the chaotic conditions ("Pravda" and "Trud", August 5th). The construction of the Dargom Canal was carried out without the most elementary precautions being taken to protect the workers, and, in consequence, there were very many accidents caused by blasting operations and by moving trucks ("Trud", August 10th). For the second half of 1928 there were 26 accidents among every thousand workmen at Ivanovo-Vosnesensk instead of 18 as in the previous year ("Trud", August 29th). Thousands were injured at work in the Ural district where trust and factory authorities had not carried out the necessary protective measures. The figures showing the huge increase for the past three years were as follows: 14,430, 26,958, and 37,947. The question of safe working-conditions in industry was everywhere neglected in its technical aspect; the allotted funds and credits were only partially utilised ("Trud", October 30th). The second half of the year saw the number of accidents at Kiev double what it had been in the first; working-stock had become too dilapidated, and safety regulations were not enforced ("Trud", November 3rd). Workers in the Astrakhan fisheries were ill-treated by the medical staff ("Pravda", November 4th). Tomsky reported to the Eighth Trades Union Congress that "accidents are not diminishing but are on the increase" (December 1928).

These are the facts to which the false "friends of the U.S.S.R." have been anxious to shut their eyes and about which they desire to say nothing. Soviet newspapers are full of such information, all dealing with the situation as it is at the present time. In the Press of 1929 there was plenty of evidence to show how the proletariat is treated in the country governed by a "dictatorship of the proletariat". In the Siberian gold-mines, men were signed on without any steps being taken to provide them with bread, provisions, lodging, or tools, so that many in their misery tried to escape, but were prevented by the militia who, although there were 40 degrees of frost, took their boots away from them ("Trud", February 28th 1927). It is difficult for proletarians in capitalist countries to believe that such conditions are possible, particularly as the State, which is the abode of these horrors, flies the flag of Socialism. At Kiev, from among skilled shipbuilders who were engaged on a promise of high wages, some withdrew utterly disheartened on discovering the real terms of their contract, others simply found their services rejected and were obliged to sell their belongings to save themselves from death by starvation. They encamped wretchedly in the station, and were afforded no help of any kind whatsoever ("Trud", March 21st 1929). "A certain stabilisation of traumatism is now observable", "Pravda" reported, without meaning to be intentionally ironical, and went on to emphasise the great number of accidents which had occurred. In the heavy industries, injuries were as high as 30 per cent., giving a general average of 17·5 per cent. The same newspaper reproached the Commissariat of Work and the Trades Unions with not having roused the initiative of the masses—a subject which will be fully examined later. A recent inquiry into conditions in the Donetz district revealed that special safety measures were still unsatisfactorily applied in those mines, and in many did not exist at all. "The miners' lamps are in a lamentable condition, the effects of which are acutely [*sic*] felt in mines dangerous on account of fire-damp." Supervision of both technical and hygienic matters was extraordinarily weak ("Izvestia", July 12th 1929). The correspondent of this paper, accompanying this commission of inquiry, observed that attempts were made to show "villages *à la Potemkin*",[1] or, in other words, to camouflage the realities ("Izvestia", *idem*).

Such are the conditions under which the working masses of Russia live and labour. A thorough acquaintance with them is essential if other aspects of the Soviet régime are to be understood. "Our labour legislation is now so vast, so complicated, so incomprehensible that a member of the working classes has no idea where he is." "The provisions of a law may be interpreted in half a dozen different ways, and one is never quite sure which decision

[1] A field-marshal and favourite of Catherine II, whom he was often successful in deceiving.

will be accepted as the right one" ("Trud", August 30th 1929). The proletariat is as good as lost before it becomes involved in this labyrinth of bureaucratic methods. It has, on paper, so many rights that it is practically impossible for it to benefit from any of them.

CHAPTER III

THE TRAGIC LIFE OF THE WORKERS (2)

In town and factory—Wages—The average wage—Pre-war standard—Real and nominal salary—Secret reductions and subtractions—"Voluntary" shares and obligatory subscriptions—Delayed payment of wages—Forced "free loans"—Rest homes—The wage in roubles—Privileges of the wage-earner—Unemployment—Labour exchanges—Exploitation of women and children—"Nurseries"—The eight-hour day.

It is possible to gain a valuable insight into the standard of living of the labouring classes in Soviet Russia by discovering what the workers are paid in wages and what is the duration of their working day. It must be admitted that it is no easy matter to throw full light on these questions, but anyone who has seen how the proletariat is lodged, fed, and clothed, is in a position to judge approximately the true value of its wages. The worker, whose only lodging is a space of "coffin dimensions" in a shed or barracks, and who lives, as already described, in circumstances which recall the horrible stories of Dostoyevsky, is just as inadequately clothed and fed. He has generally nothing but the rags that cover him, and his worldly possessions are contained in a bundle, never in a trunk or chest. If he was told that in Capitalist countries the majority of workmen have each a little house all to themselves and their families, with pieces of furniture, a bed with sheets, a table and chairs, sometimes a wardrobe, often a bicycle (without even mentioning the superior living-conditions of certain specially favoured sections of the working classes found in some countries), he would not believe it. The newspapers and the official speakers (and there are no others) assure him that his foreign comrades are in much worse straits than himself, and as this is the only opinion which has the right to find expression, he therefore ends by accepting it. The Russian proletariat is proletarian in the strictest meaning of the word. His arms are his sole weapon and defence—and this only when the Soviet work organisation has not left him with an injured one.

It is well known that the Russian workman's wage before the war was a mere pittance, and therefore the mere assertion that the present average wage is the same as, or a little better than, it was before the war is not in itself a point in favour of the new régime. But even this statement is untrue in many cases and may lead the way to other deceptions.

For some time past the sham optimism of officialdom has thrived on the uncertainty concerning the real value of the rouble, while the workers have suffered from it. The pre-war rouble was worth twice as much as the paper-rouble of the present day; the gold rouble is worth less than the pre-war rouble on account of the fall in gold values. The commodity-rouble is a conventional unit fixed by the index figure of retail prices, which varies in each market and may even be arbitrarily calculated. It is quite easy to see how very profitable professional liars have found this complication and how it has aided them in their propaganda. But a stable point of comparison was essential for the State economic plans, and for several years this commodity-rouble has served this purpose in all trustworthy documents.

It will be well to pay no attention to the fantastic percentages which purport to show the increase in present wages over those paid in the days of civil war and military Communism, when uncertain payments in kind had replaced wage-payments which, so to speak, did not exist at all. The pre-war level certainly offers a more valuable point of comparison, but only as a criterion of poverty. All the same, the meaning of the current expression, "average wage", must be understood, and only the smallest effort is required immediately to discover its fraudulent nature.

At the International Economic Conference at Geneva in May 1927 the Soviet delegate, Ossinsky, who was also Chief of statistical services in the U.S.S.R., when questioned concerning the duration of the working day in Russia, coolly replied that it was one of "7 hours and 57 minutes". This airy statement was not, however, allowed to pass unchallenged, and he was asked to explain how this figure had been reached. The Chief of Statistics showed that he could not answer this question and had to telegraph to Moscow for the necessary information. After a delay of some days—for no one even at Moscow knew any more about it than he did, and inquiries had to be made—it was learnt that the average was arrived at by including part-time workers in the grand total. In other words, the "normal" average was obtained by taking working days which were either too short or too long, thus adding two evils together, and dividing by the number of workers! But this average was in no way a real one. Over-work on the part of some and a lack of effort on the part of others, both signs of complete inequality in social status, contributed between them in providing this so-called average. This deception about averages hid two brutal truths. It is just the same as if the number of healthy people computed by statistics was made to include anæmic and apoplectic persons. This is a remarkable example of Soviet statistical methods, hardly calculated to inspire confidence in the economic science of the new Bolshevist school. Therefore the figure for the average wage is reached in the same way as the average working day: the wage total is divided by the number of employees, or, in other words, an entirely fictitious figure is arrived at which in no way tallies either with the relatively excessive payments made to some or the insufficient wages paid to others, and gives no exact idea of the wages actually earned by the masses. (At any rate, these were the facts disclosed concerning the "average wage" after investigation had been made in reliable quarters at Moscow.) This miserable average, which has not even the excuse of being a presentable figure, since it is approximately on a level with the wretched standard of Tsarist days, is once again the outcome of the twofold manifestation of social inequality which, from the Socialist and Communist point of view, is entirely inadmissible. This very marked inequality in wages is one of the most striking anomalies in the life of Soviet workers: skilled workmen have been found earning five or six times as much as the ordinary labourers employed in the same factory. This glaring example of injustice is swallowed up in crafty calculations which give the "average wage". It has been impossible to discover if the high salaries of directors, managers, engineers, and technical experts are included in the grand total from which the "average" is calculated, and whether, in consequence, they contributed to a marked increase in the average wage, thus levelling up on paper the unfair, disproportionate payments made to certain privileged members of society, as compared to the miserable pittance given to the great majority. This question was examined with the greatest patience, but owing to the complete ignorance of the Communist leaders and other high officials consulted on this point, the truth could not be ascertained. It would not, however, be surprising if this method were, in fact, employed.

Whatever actually does happen, what is commonly known as average wage must not be confused with the wage of the average workman or of the great masses. Here another complication arises: the mean average of various average earnings, which are established by the easy-going method described above, is in its turn obtained by the addition of separate percentages by which the total is then divided. It is a case of deception heaped upon deception, and to such a degree that the tricksters themselves end by becoming entirely lost in their calculations. Of this it will be possible to judge later: already in 1926 the alleged pre-war average had been "generally reached or exceeded", but according to the statements of official representatives in the Trades Unions the average wage was definitely lower in comparison with the pre-war level. Taking industry as a whole the figure was 89 per cent.; in metallurgical trades, 75 per cent.; in mines generally, 65 per cent.; in coal-mines, 61 per cent.; in salt mines, 63 per cent.; in iron and other metal mines, 64 per cent.; in naphtha mines, 76 per cent.; and on the railways, 67 per cent.: in the textile trades the average wage was 80 per cent. On the waterways and in the postal service the percentage was still lower, but it was given in roubles and not as a percentage ("Trud", July 21st 1926). How, then, was it possible for all these averages, which concern every industry and the proletarian masses, which indicate conditions in metallurgy, mines, transport, and textile trades (and building, which is on a still lower level, might be added)—how can they, being so markedly below the pre-war standard, have reached and exceeded it as a general whole? Simply by the absorption into the grand totals of those figures which referred to a few sections of privileged people. But the average earnings of the great majority still remain as much below the miserable pre-war level as ever they have been.

It would be impossible to make use of data which might be called "general" without giving particular instances as well. There are still signs of the gross inequality in wages which has been already noted. In mines the wage figure was 65 per cent. of the pre-war standard, which, expressed in roubles, came to from 31 to 49, according to the district. But certain grades of postal workers were earning 14 to 18 roubles a month, though the average salary in their service was probably 55 roubles. On the railways a locksmith received 73 and a plate-layer 43 roubles. All these figures were taken from the same article in the "Trud". Though they are presented with no attempt at method, they convey much more meaning than complete tablets of statistics from which no trustworthy information can be drawn; they pierce the cobwebs of sophistry that surround the average wage and throw light upon the everyday comparisons made with pre-war conditions. Although these figures relate to the year preceding the tenth anniversary of the Soviet Republic, yet they are a great aid to the understanding of the most recent statistics.

In 1924 L. B. Kamenev, one of the three leading directors of industry, made the following pronouncement in "Pravda" (December 5th): "No, comrades, to reach the pre-war level is not our aim and object. Our workmen did not bring about a revolution only to receive as much as they did before the war; their needs are greater than that, and they brought about this Revolution so that they might enlarge their means of existence, educate their children, and satisfy their desire to become a cultured people." In the twelfth year after the Revolution, and the ninth year after peace has been restored within and without, it is interesting to study the situation in the light of this statement. Official statements may even provide useful evidence, provided that they can be read correctly. But before coming to that point still further precautions must be taken.

The average wage, with all that it implies as regards inequality, is calculated from unstable indications;

moreover, certain special advantages, on which payment in kind are supposed to be based, are also taken into consideration—the index figure of living, rent assessments, group services, and social insurance. It is necessary, therefore, to distinguish *real* from nominal wages. The former may fall while the latter rise; but it is the actual wages earned that must be kept in mind. They decrease, in fact, when the index figure of living does not correspond with the actual prices. This index figure is based on the prices at which, in theory, provisions should be sold in the co-operative stores; but the latter generally sell goods either at higher prices or of inferior quality, and cannot often supply certain products, which the buyer is forced to purchase in the private market, paying twice or three or four times as much as the official price. Thus the *real* salary will suffer a very marked decrease. It will also fall when there is a general rise in rents, which happens three or four times a year, and is bound to fall continually in view of the rapid dilapidation of real property due to the lack of funds available for upkeep. Something has already been said about medical relief, which is a kind of payment in kind, and some mention will later be made of convalescent homes.

Piece-work is still generally employed in industry. As early as 1926, 68 per cent. of metal-workers, 64 per cent. and 63 per cent. of those employed in chemical industries and in mines respectively, were paid by the piece, etc. ("Ekonomicheskoe Obozreniye", July 1926), and since then this proportion has continually increased. This vast number of workmen cannot hope to earn anything approaching the average salary unless they work with an intensity that comes near to break them physically. In cases where the wage is calculated on a fixed basis multiplied by a coefficient figure varying according to what category the workman in question belongs (and there are 17 of these sections representing the various degrees of qualification), the nominal average salary may remain stationary, whereas the real salary falls when the coefficient changes. In cases, also, where workers are bound to produce a certain quantity of material, etc., in a given time, an increase in the amount of work required reduces the actual earnings and is not shown in the theoretical average wage. Without being able effectively to voice their own opinions, workmen find group-contracts thrust upon them which often reduce the real salary in spite of all attempts to hide it, and it is no longer a matter of any consequence if the terms of work agreements are violated. The wage-earner has suffered yet another loss by the abolition of free tram-tickets, and the money thus appropriated has been reserved for use by the various group-services or paid into the public funds, only to be squandered by the executive, etc. But this reduction is not shown in the average wage. It must not be forgotten that it is obligatory to subscribe to newspapers, even to those which the subscriber does not wish to read. "In spite of the resolution of the Third Soviet Congress, the Executive Committee of the Kharkov province enforced the payment of subscriptions to the 'Visti' under penalty of fine—in this case 3,000 roubles; but as it was written in Ukrainian, Russians could not even read it" ("Pravda", June 19th 1925). This is a good example of the importance attached to the would-be resolutions of these so-called Congresses. A decision taken by the Kiev Executive Committee on the "limitation [*sic*] of obligatory subscriptions to newspapers" freed "private persons" from their obligation and abolished the fines ("Pravda", August 11th 1925). But a decision is one thing and its application is another. This abuse continues, disappears to reappear again; it lingers in places where control is lax and is found once more in different forms. In many towns, comrades are forced to buy "portraits of their leaders" (*sic*) or sometimes red flags, even if they are already provided with them. Wages are subject to manifold hypocritical reductions which often take a most unexpected form.

That is not all. From the real wage, already reduced to miserable proportions, further deductions must be made. From time to time workers are called upon to sacrifice a considerable portion of their wages in the payment of donations and subscriptions, though it has even been definitely stated that membership of organisations and associations of the voluntary type is free. But what actually happens is that workmen are enrolled in a mass, without being consulted, or only after some staged consultation in which they take no part—a procedure which is described later in the chapter on the "Dictatorship of the Proletariat", and which shows how impossible it is to go against decisions taken "in higher quarters". This system of obligatory enrolment is the equivalent of impositions or camouflaged taxes which amount to a considerable sum in comparison with the miserable proportions of the real salary. The author, who was once working in a Soviet institution in Moscow, found that he had been made a member of eight organisations or societies without ever having consented to belong to one, for the very good reason that the Soviet citizen cannot possibly hope to procure a hearing, even if he does voice his own opinion. The author was, in spite of himself, a member of the pseudo-professional Union, the "Mopr" (the International Revolutionary Aid Society, called in the West "Red Aid"), of societies of Children's Friends, of Aviation, of Chemistry, of the Society for the Suppression of Illiteracy, and of two others, since forgotten and by this time probably extinct. Subscriptions were deducted on pay-days in the pay-office without there being any opportunity of protesting, and in the same way other reductions were made from time to time in aid of abandoned children, the Leningrad flood victims, etc., but the bulk of the money, almost constantly deducted from wages, went to permanent funds, such as education, and to mutual aid organisations of various kinds. The fact that the number of Union members revealed in statistics is now higher than the total of those available for membership gives an idea of the extremes to which this arbitrary system may be pushed! Its abuses have been so glaring, so intolerable, that the Central Government has several times been forced to interfere and curb this excess of zeal. Official instructions have appeared in the Press fixing a limit to voluntary subscriptions, a singular confirmation of the subscribers' liberty. "Pravda" of August 2nd published a resolution of the Council of People's Commissaries which forbade the higher administrative authorities, the so-called general assemblies and the co-operative housing societies, to bring any pressure to bear on wage-earners. It was stated in "Pravda" of July 31st 1926 that "the request [*sic*] that there should be a cessation [*sic*] of these automatic [*sic*] enrolments in mass [*sic*] of members for voluntary [*sic*] associations and a reduction in number of staff appointed, etc., *has not been carried out*". Such requests, made on behalf of the workers, who were being systematically robbed, were never willingly fulfilled, for their execution would not have been in the interests of those who benefited from the spoils, and of course the victims themselves had no alternative but to keep silent. When after some years this policy of spoliation had decreased in intensity, its principal features still remained and the abuse still existed in another form, much stronger and much more widespread, and the responsibility for this rested with those who issued these "directions".

The instructions in question were issued only with the intention of allaying the exasperation of the workers, so that by avoiding a storm over a few copecks it might be easier to extract at one fell swoop a respectable number of roubles. At first the system of issuing public challenges was much in vogue. Two industrial concerns would be asked to compete against each other in a race to subscribe to the flotilla "that was to be Russia's answer to Chamberlain", or to the tanks upon which the "conversations" with Chang-Kai-Chek would so much depend. Naturally the proletarians in neither of the rival establishments were consulted as to their wishes in the matter; everything being decided by the secretaries or executive of the "cells" on an order from high quarters—but it was they who had to pay. That was nothing, however, beside the blow that struck them in the shape of loans which were also supposed to be voluntary, but were, in reality, forced upon the workmen, and sometimes represented approximately as much as a whole month's wages. The third of these loans has just been realised (1929). Could it be natural that the ordinary Russia proletarian, earning a wage very much below the wretched average and living in a corner of "coffin dimensions", would of his own initiative willingly subscribe a month's wages to the loan? How this sum is extorted from him will be seen later in the chapter on the "Dictatorship of the Proletariat". It will now be shown that the value of the real wage is still further diminished by another cause.

An examination of the wage question would not be complete without reference to the delay in payment of wages, an evil which has for a long time weighed down upon the majority of workers, though at the present time it is no longer of frequent occurrence or of great importance. Until a few years ago it was quite common to find the wages had not been paid for several weeks or months. In the meantime, the purchasing-power of earnings was falling fast, the workers were getting into debt with the shopkeepers, who were promptly doubling or tripling their prices, etc. Certain classes of wage-earners suffer from its ill effects, and even when a wrong which is deeply rooted, as in this case, is in process of being righted, its consequences still weigh heavily on its victims. In a certain district N. there were delays of two to four months, and in February workmen had just been paid for October and clerks for September ("Pravda", February 7th 1925). School-teachers in the province of Ekaterinoslav had yet to recover money due to them as far back as 1923 and 1924 ("Pravda", May 20th 1925). The Central Committee of the Teachers' Union complained of the increase of the delays in question ("Pravda" February 17th 1926). "In nearly all the provinces of the Union salaries are owing in institutions which depend on local budgets" ("Pravda", March 25th 1926). Salaries were never paid up to date in the majority of industrial concerns, and some were three or four months overdue. In some cases workmen had not received their wages for 1924 ("Trud", March 23rd 1926). In a glass-works in the province of Vladimir, payment had been delayed for a week or two, and for some days in a factory at Tula and in one at Moscow (The "Rabochaya Gazette", June 9th 1926). In a glass-works in the province of Chereopovetz, wages had been owing for two or three months, and in another, in the Donetz, complaints were made that because of the delays in payment workmen had had to buy on credit and pay double for that privilege (The "Rabochaya Gazette", June 12th 1926). In the same issue of that paper, three other cases were cited. In the Vyatka region, by the end of May, the wages for March had only been partly paid; at the T. sugar factory, in the province of Tula, wages were overdue and payment was made by coupons on the co-operative stores, where, however, there was a lack of provisions (The "Rabochaya Gazette", June 17th 1926). A delay of from five to seven days was reported general throughout the metallurgical trades (The "Rabochaya Gazette", June 20th 1926). While Moscow workmen waited for the wages due to them, they were forced to buy provisions on credit, so as not to die of hunger, paying three times the proper price (The "Rabochaya Gazette", June 23rd 1926). Several similar cases were quoted in the same paper (June 24th, 25th 1926). The Supreme Economic Council reported "the non-payment of wages at the proper time throughout a whole series of trusts; the practice is beginning of carrying over the accumulated debts from month to month" (Press of July 21st 1926). The representative of the Trades Unions stated that there were "numerous cases" of delay, "causing the deepest dissatisfaction among a vast number of workers" ("Pravda", July 29th 1926). "In spite of the strictest instructions," the Central Council of Trades Unions reported, "delays are not diminishing but increasing" ("Pravda", August 18th 1926). In the principal factories in the Uralsk, wages were paid twelve days late, and there were cases of two months' delay in smaller concerns and one of six months in the province of Perm ("Trud", September 1st 1926). In sixteen provinces alone the debt owing to teachers exceeded 500,000 roubles ("Trud", September 24th 1926). Workmen employed in the glass-works in the Pskov province had to wait two or three months, sometimes even longer, for their pay ("Trud", October 30th 1926). Some of the workmen started litigation in an attempt to recover their money, and proceedings which lasted several months finally accomplished nothing. In the province of Orel, masons had received no wages for nine months ("Trud", October 9th 1926). Workmen employed in the Ural province had not been paid for one hundred days, and if they made any complaint were forcibly expelled from their sheds without receiving the money due to them ("Trud", June 2nd 1927). In the Lenin glass-works workmen were paid . . . in glass, which they had to sell as best they could ("Trud", August 18th 1927). Wage-funds were often spent in other ways; workmen were refused credit in the co-operative stores, and at V., in the province of Nizhni-Novogorod, they had received no wages for three months, and at R. and G. (Donetz) there were further delays in payment ("Trud", August 27th 1927). At Bryansk, where wages were paid every five months, some workmen, who were owed 400 roubles, received payment . . . in flat-irons made in their factory! ("Pravda of Youth", November 24th 1927). Workmen employed on the Dargom Canal were paid after a delay of two or three months ("Trud", August 10th 1928). Even by August, teachers in the middle Volga district had not been paid their salaries for April ("Trud", August 10th 1929). The following series of examples, which are a few out of the thousand available, covers, generally speaking, a period of three years, and makes for an understanding of these group-contracts, which may be called "scraps of paper" quite as much on account of the manner in which they are drawn up as the way in which they are respected. The President of the Economic Council of the Northern Caucasus demanded that all these group-contracts which were so harmful to industry should be annulled, to the great indignation of the Union officials ("Trud", March 23rd 1926). An official inquiry revealed that, practically speaking, the terms of every group-contract were violated by the authorities, particularly clauses referring to engagement and dismissal, overtime and wages, safe-working and housing conditions, and to the prompt payment of wages or indemnities. "Economy was effected at the workers' expense", and Union and factory committee officials were neglecting their duty ("Trud", November 2nd 1928). At Moscow, group-contracts were constantly violated, and casual labourers who did not work on an agreement were signed on in the place of regular workmen. This has been noted to be of common occurrence in textile and metallurgical trades, printing-works, and in industrial concerns generally. The same thing happened at Leningrad, and there was also a complete disregard for clauses that had reference to safe-working conditions ("Trud", December 2nd 1928). Group-contracts have now been in existence for seven years, but it has not yet been possible to secure their fulfilment and there are still some plans that have yet to be carried out ("Trud", March 14th 1929).

The mountebanks of the Soviet legend and sham "friends of the U.S.S.R." have said a great deal about the payment in kind provided in the shape of free accommodation in rest-homes, sanatoria, etc. Something must here be said about them, too. The author, who had been sent to an establishment of this kind at Kislovodsk in the Caucasus, found on the evening of his arrival that it had been decided, at a meeting of the patients, to declare a hunger strike as a protest against the uneatable food provided. Russians are not generally particular what they eat, but they could hardly be expected to keep body and soul together indefinitely on rotten eggs and putrid meat. It was the same in other sanatoria in the district, at Pyargorska and Essentuki. Such was the state of affairs soon after Semashko, the People's Commissar of Health, had made his tour of inspection; while his visit had been in progress the food had shown a marked improvement, but immediately afterwards the same putrid filth once again made its appearance at table. In the dormitories beds were put so close together as to touch;

sick persons and convalescents had to endure the ceaseless hubbub of conversation and their neighbours' noisy movements, their spitting, and an atmosphere thick with smoke. They spent hours on end in queues waiting for anything and everything; for registration, distribution, medical examination and re-examination, medicine, and even, perhaps, a glass of curdled milk. And to think that this was called "rest"! Even a strong, healthy man would not emerge from such a place without suffering from some nerve complaint. The following year, in the Crimea, conditions were the same; in the Marino [1] Hotel at Yalta, the distribution centre, the negligence of the authorities defies description. This establishment, by a cruel irony of fate, was indeed aptly named, since its wretched inmates were destined to be "pickled" there! Invalids who had been already obliged to spend ten days out of their month's rest in travelling, waited a week or more for the privilege and pleasure of being crammed into an insanitary dormitory and of ruining their digestions by eating unrecognisable foods, only to be told in the end that they could not be taken in. From every resort along the coast, from Alupka to Simeyis and Eupatoria back again, came the same story of this deplorable state of affairs. The author, after an unfortunate personal experience at Gursouf, hurriedly fled. In the "home" where he spent a few days there were some patients strong-minded enough to make formal protests and demand an inquiry, which revealed that three-quarters of the available funds were squandered by the staff.

It is said that princely palaces and sumptuous villas have been socialised for the use of the proletariat, but have the details of this transformation been closely enough examined? What are the results of this socialisation? The houses in question can accommodate a few thousands

[1] *Mariner* = to pickle.

or tens of thousands of patients in rotation; they were not planned, built, or fitted out for the use to which they are now put. An admirably constructed and comfortable family residence is most unsuited for conversion into a sanatorium. Now, all vestiges of anything "rich" or "princely" have long since disappeared and only bare, unsuitable buildings remain. But who are they who benefit from such of these rest-homes as are habitable? Once more, not the proletariat, but certain privileged sections of the community; first of all, the officials of the Communist Party and then those belonging to the Soviet and Young Communist Parties, to the Trades Unions and co-operative societies—all those who are, in general, specially favoured in matters of wages and housing. Anything worth having is monopolised by the top-dogs and "the upper grades of society".

A few thousand genuine proletarians have been sent to these homes, a fact duly noted in the falsified statistics, but that will deceive nobody into thinking that the great masses ever benefit from these advantages. It has been found a great aid to propaganda to house peasants in the Imperial Palace at Livadia, thereby giving three or four weeks' pleasure (if such it be) to a few hundreds out of 120 million peasants in Russia. But afterwards, to what dreadful conditions do these "happy" hundreds return? It is false to talk about rest-houses for workers while they still have no proper living-houses with separate rooms and with lighting and water laid on; where things are clean and they can find peace and quiet, books to read, and good food to eat, and live untroubled by pestering authorities and plaguing bureaucracies. But that happy state of things is a long way off yet.

Every year the newspapers are obliged to publish the protests and complaints of those who are bold enough to voice their sentiments after a stay in these sanatoria or rest-homes. At the Proletarian Sanatorium patients could find no one to listen to their complaints and were neglected by the medical staff. The food disgusted them, and there were no books ("Pravda", May 8th 1925). At the Vorovsky sanatorium (Gagry), neglect by the medical authorities was reported, as well as a plague of bugs, cockroaches, and rats; the cats, dogs, asses, and oxen belonging to the employees of the establishment howled and bellowed day and night: no linen or clothing was provided. A "rabcor" (correspondent of a labour newspaper), having composed some verses in an ironical strain at the expense of the management, was expelled from Gagry, gagged and bound hand and foot by the armed police ("Pravda", May 10th 1926). The rest-house O., near Moscow, was described as a "house of fatigue"; the convalescents were all made ill by drinking the water. In a narrow corridor, where the beds touched each other, so close were they together, thirty or forty sick persons had to sleep ("Izvestia", August 13th 1927). A Commission of Inquiry denounced the trickery, the prevarications, and the yearly increasing extravagance of which the public health services were guilty. The staff made away with money intended for the patients. Managers and high officials invited and entertained their friends in such a way as to interfere with the treatment of the sick and to neutralise hygienic conditions ("Pravda", June 30th 1928). A correspondent, writing from Leningrad, related how he had to wait several hours in a queue to show his papers; another day he spent several more hours in the same way before he could obtain his certificate, and after that he had to queue up again at an office window as well as for the doctor's visit. Every day it was necessary to wait in a queue for a bath (The "Evening Krasnaya Gazette", July 19th 1929). References to the above conditions have been confined to one *per annum* for the last five years in order to show that they are indicative, not of exceptional conditions or circumstances, but of the general situation itself, which shows but the smallest signs of improvement and favours only certain privileged members of society. It would be possible to give many more examples, but it seems hardly worth while to examine in detail thousands of newspapers to confirm such a commonplace truth in Russia, of all places, where the watering-places, health resorts, etc., commonly provide a theme for bitter, time-worn jests. A newspaper recently published a photograph depicting an emaciated, gaunt individual returning to work after being in a rest-house, and meeting plump, cheerful-looking friends who say to him: "Well, you were able to sleep?" Aphorisms like the following are heard everywhere. "It is hard to work, but it is harder to take a rest." "Sick people and nervous cases are forbidden to enter sanatoria", etc. In a recent article headed "Lights and Shades of the Health-resort Question," Semashko described their miserable conditions. He found them burdened with debts, uncomfortable, badly managed. "The situation was just the same under the old régime," he said, "and that is why our middle classes used to go abroad to find repose and take the cures." But then, I say, there must be an end to this hiring of paid apologists and this deception of simpletons who, in their turn, spread false tales about the Soviet houses of rest. He agreed that the types of patients treated in hospitals unequally represented the various social classes and that this state of things left much to be desired. Latterly the proportions had been stabilised as follows: workmen, 33⅓ per cent.; officials, 40 per cent.; peasants, 10 per cent., with various others. But even this arrangement was only reached after the endless scandals caused by the invasion of these establishments by bureaucratic parasites who made away with everything. How many of this 33⅓ per cent. of these workmen are genuine members of the labouring class, and how many are ex-workmen who have now reached the lowest official grade, is a question that may well be asked. Semashko does not say, but he certainly suffered no illusions on this point ("Izvestia", September 8th 1929). Of the 222,787 cases treated in hospitals in 1928 (the figure given by Semashko), there were probably 75,000 genuine or alleged workers, but of these quite one-half were, in our opinion, deserters hiding in the lower committees of the Party and the Trades Unions. The rest, after twelve years of the proletarian dictatorship, are piled up into corridors, made to swallow mouldy food, and to wait in queues for the smallest attention. It is quite understandable now why the "chichki" (the gods [1]) of the Bolshevist aristocracy prefer to visit Vittel, Carlsbad, Baden, Biarritz, or Sorrento.

This, then, is the real truth about wages, stripped of its masking figures. Besides, Soviet statistics are so confused and contradictory that only real experts can understand them. References will be found below to the opinions expressed by some of the great revolutionary leaders whose competence to judge cannot be questioned. They are Trotsky, Zinoviev, Kamenev, Radek, Preyobrajensky, Smilga, and others. Their views, which were based on strictly official evidence, are to be found in the documents known as "Arguments against the Five-Year Plan" (*International Correspondence*, No. 124, December 11th 1924). This revealed that in 1927, the tenth anniversary of the October Revolution, the average wage among the labouring classes was 3½ commodity-roubles or 61 paper-roubles (48s. 10d.) and a few copecks. "It is clear that

[1] *Manitous* (French), J. J. Rousseau's word for North American Indian gods.

wages and the average living conditions found among *certain* groups of workers in *certain* districts, in particular in Moscow and Leningrad, are undoubtedly higher than the average given. But, on the other hand, the standard of living found in *certain very large grades* of workers is *considerably lower* than even these average figures", as has been explained earlier in this book. The question at once arises as to the actual value of the rouble, but this is not easy to calculate. It has no actual quotation in any money market, and is given an entirely arbitrary value in foreign currency by the Soviet Government, which, having a monopoly of exchange, is able to refuse the conversion of the chervonetz (paper-rouble) into foreign money. Its real value is to be found in Russia on the secret, free market or "Black Exchange". If the conventional, but really bogus, rate puts the rouble now as being worth two shillings, the current quotation for 1927 was 10d., and is now below that, in the neighbourhood of 6d. or 8d. The nominal average wage *per mensem* in 1927 was 60 paper-roubles, or 50s., the rouble then being worth about 10d.; in July 1929 the nominal wage figure had altered to 74 roubles 73 copecks ("Trud", September 6th 1929), the rouble being worth from 6d. to 8d., making the English equivalent between 37s. to 49s. 6d. Taking the present value of the paper-rouble even at 8d., which is too high a rate, the above reasoning is tantamount to saying that the average monthly salary of the Soviet workman was in 1927 equivalent to 50s., and in 1929 to 49s. 6d., figures which certainly over-estimate its true value. The great majority of wages are infinitely lower than these estimates, and are still further reduced in the manner already described.

In the light of these incontestable facts and figures the reader is now better able to visualise the forbidding picture of the workers' misery presented by the evidence already given. But there still remain many vital truths to be examined.

The *real* salary has fallen during the last year in spite of the rise of the nominal salary. This was reported, not only by the ex-president of the Commissaries' Council of the Ukraine people, Christian Rakovsky, who has now been deported without trial, in a letter of April 1929 (*Opposition Report*, No. 3–4, p. 12), but also in the official Press. Its fall is due to the marked increase in retail prices. "The co-operative stores have nearly everywhere put up the price of primary necessities, which has resulted in a considerable rise in the index figure of living and a decrease in the *real* wage" ("Trud", March 30th 1929). But the rise in price in the co-operatives is nothing compared to the rise on the free market, to which the consumer is bound to have recourse in view of the scarcity and even of the complete lack of most provisions. Another important point to notice is that the wages always lag behind the intensification of work and the increase in productivity. "The intensity of working-conditions increases, the strain on the workers' physical powers becomes more severe, and unemployment is directly or indirectly a drain on the wages due to them." Those schemes of rationalisation which have already been carried out inevitably aggravate the condition of the labouring classes when they are accompanied by developments in industry and transport on such a scale that dismissed employees cannot be reabsorbed in the new organisation. The living conditions of skilled workmen, casual labourers, women, and young persons are particularly hard." This was the view of Trotsky and his co-signatories in the document previously mentioned. All these observations still hold good.

It is by finding the consumption figure per head that it will be possible to compare the present miserable lot of the masses with their wretched pre-war condition.

But according to the Five-Year Plan drawn up in 1927 and criticised as being too modest by the Bolshevist politicians and economists, whose names have already been given, individual consumption is still lower than the pre-war figure and will remain so till the beginning of the financial year 1931–32. The Gosplan (State-Planning Commission) states this fact with authority. A parallel drawn between Soviet trade forecasts for 1932 (the fifteenth anniversary of the October Revolution) and the present level of prosperity in Germany and the United States of America shows that in that year the U.S.S.R. will probably consume five times less cotton goods, seventeen times less coal, four and eleven times, respectively, less pig-iron, three and seven times less electric power, etc., supposing that the consumption does not increase during the five years in those two countries. It is true that this Plan was drawn up for a limited period, and that another one was established to embrace the period 1928–29 and 1933–34; if this new Plan can be realised, the situation will improve during the next few years. But how can any hopes be placed in a scheme of which discussion is forbidden in the U.S.S.R. and which A. Rykov, the President of the People's Council of Commissaries, considers to be unrealisable?

In Russia at the present time there are approximately eleven to twelve million wage-earners, excluding four or five million casual labourers; there are also a certain number, very difficult to estimate, of daily agricultural workers of about two or three millions, and, finally, the unemployed, of whom we shall speak later. It is these great masses, together with millions of poor peasants, who are suffering the unspeakable miseries that have been outlined; only a few hundreds of thousands of officials and skilled workmen escape these dreadful conditions. But the privileges enjoyed by some and the great misfortunes of others provide a striking contrast and cannot be too greatly emphasised. Only by specially studying the question would it be possible to enumerate the specially favoured categories of urban populations —officials, technical experts, artisans, specially skilled workmen, and to indicate their standard of life. It is possible, however, to gain an idea of the increasing inequality in the Soviet Republics if it is understood that the wages of these privileged persons range from 200 to 800 roubles and more a month (£6 13s. and £26 12s.). Writers and journalists who are members of the Communist Party are obliged to pay a special tax, levied on high salaries exceeding 225 roubles (£7 10s.). A circular from the Central Committee fixed this payment at 20 per cent. on the first 225 roubles above taxable minimum, at 30 per cent. for salaries between 450 and 675 roubles (£15 and £22 10s.), and at 40 per cent. above 675 roubles. No special percentage was payable on salaries up to 500 roubles (£16 13s.) if the appointments were not guaranteed as permanent ("Pravda", June 12th 1928). But it was found practically impossible to check the salaries earned by individuals, and anyone who has lived among the Bolsheviks knows how far this system is applied. In any case, this shows the salaries earned by privileged persons and how different they are to what was envisaged by Lenin, who cherished ideas of making the salary of a public official equal to that of a good workman, imitating what was done in the Commune of 1871. This theme was developed by Karl Marx in his *State and the Revolution*, and in all the writings of Lenin between March and October 1917. Even death does not put an end to inequality. On reading, for example, in the "Izvestia" (May 20th 1928) that a monthly pension of 225 roubles (£7 10s.) has been awarded Tsyrupa's widow, one might be pardoned for asking how much is paid to a widow of a workman killed at his work when her worth (?) and needs are just as great as any high official's widow in the Party.

Having examined the lot of the privileged classes we will turn to those who have been deprived of their wages—the unemployed. Here, perhaps, Soviet statistics reach the height of their incoherence, not only on account of vastly divergent figures, but also of seemingly inexplicable contradictions which, however, may be cleared up if they are subjected to a careful and critical examination. The unemployed are registered at the labour-exchanges; but every town has not its labour-exchange, and there are certainly a number of ignorant folk quite incapable of registering themselves. Further, the exchanges do not register unemployed who are not of proletarian origin (and these are legion since the Revolution and since the almost complete abolition of private commerce), nor the great majority of young people who have not yet been in receipt of wages. This example shows how the number of unemployed in the towns must be calculated at more than double the figure given in official statistics.

As regards the figures for unemployment in country districts, which are in themselves vast reservoirs of manual labour and from which a great number of workers pour yearly into the towns, they show the most improbable variations.

According to Kalinin, the country districts have fifteen million workers over and above the number that can be employed ("Izvestia", August 28th 1926). The Deputy Commissary of Work, Tolstopiatov, stated: "We have an enormous surplus agrarian population with an excess labour-supply of more than twenty-five million individuals" ("Trud", November 27th 1928). If it is remembered that the general population increases by 3½ millions a year, it is possible to understand the gravity of the problem.

The figures for towns, although not so enormous, are very vague. Concerning the unemployed who are not registered at the exchanges, the President of the Trades Union Council made the following pronouncement: "Comrade Tomsky returns to the 'vicious circle', to the old but ever painful question, what is to be done with the non-Union unemployed so that they may find work? They are not admitted to the Trades Unions because they are not working in factories, and they are not allowed to enter factories because they are not Union members. For the same reason they are not registered at the exchanges. Something must be done to put a stop to this abominable situation. Above all, it must be made easier for young workers and the children of Trades Union workers to start work. In some way or another they must become workers and begin work, having been made members of the Trades Unions" (The "Rabochaya Gazette", June 9th 1926). According to the "Trud" the number of registered unemployed on May 1st 1926 (1,070,900), included 127,700 young workers instead of their real total of 500,000 ("Trud", July 28th 1926). This discrepancy between the correct and the registered figures gives a clue to the considerable number of unregistered adolescents, certainly more than one million if the normal movement of the population is kept in mind. The "Trud" (December 1st 1927), in reporting the fall in the numbers of unemployed from 1,477,000, the figure for April 1st, to 1,025,000, at the same time pointed out that a great many were not registered. "Pravda's" expert declared that the increase noted up to April 1st (and his figure was 1,455,000) was due to the obligatory registration of unregistered non-Union persons. Thus it appears that the number of unemployed on the lists has increased from 514,000 to 772,000: how many still remain unregistered it is impossible to guess. The same writer found that on May 1st 1927 there were 141,399 adolescents registered, whereas the "Trud" reported that one year before that there had been 500,000. He noted that only 600,000 received unemployment relief, which ranged from 12 to 18 roubles (10s. to 15s.) on an average, according to the different categories ("Pravda", June 7th 1927). As stated by the Trades Union leader, Guinsburg, there were 1,500,000 unemployed on October 1st 1927, and two millions on January 1st 1928 ("Trud", June 15th 1928). On September 20th 1928 "Pravda" gave the total for January 1st 1928 as 1,352,000, and for April 1st 1928, 1,598,000. The average rate for unemployment relief was 14 roubles (11s.) a month. The "Trud" (December 12th 1928) said that on October 1st 1927 the number of unemployed was 1,040,000, and 1,274,000 on October 1st 1928, and announced an inevitable increase for 1929. The "Izvestia", quoting Dogadov, the Trades Union leader, reported the "present" number as being 1,812,000 (December 14th 1928). The "Ekonomicheskayazhizn" (No. 107 of 1929) gave 1,700,000 for May 1st 1929, and of these only 800,000 were in receipt of relief, 900,000 being in consequence deprived of assistance. The "Trud" (July 6th 1929) reported the total as being 1,800,000 on May 1st 1929, according to the Central Council of Trades Unions. But the important document to which we have already referred, written by Trotsky and others, and based on data provided by the Gosplan, with the necessary supporting evidence, revealed that there were 2,275,000 registered unemployed in April 1927; and it is also known that the total is continually increasing and that the masses who are without work cannot obtain registration (adolescents, women, old people, and peasants who have left the land). Unemployment has been continually on the increase during the last few years, though latterly the movement has been greatly slowed down. The turning-point will be reached next year (1931): according to "Pravda" (September 1st 1929), unemployment will be reduced by 10 per cent. The salient features, however, of the situation as a whole are that in the towns 4 to 5 millions are unemployed, and that in the country 15 to 25 millions are without work; that there is a tendency to increase which will be slightly checked by the gradual application of the seven-hour day and the "uninterrupted week". As regards relief, every trust can be placed in the word of certain critics whose names have already appeared in these pages. They declared that the "average relief payment was approximately 5 pre-war roubles (12 paper-roubles (8s.) of the present day) and was only available for about 20 per cent. of unemployed Trades Union members". The peoples of Western Europe can only with the greatest difficulty imagine the indescribable misery of these millions of human beings.

These dreadful conditions have already caused trouble in the labour-exchanges, particularly at Odessa, Moscow, and Leningrad. Tired of their hopeless wait and exasperated by the officials, some of these wretches thrashed their tormentors and sacked the offices. The military intervened and "calmed" the angry crowds with their rifles. The newspapers did not hesitate to announce in the same breath that there had been hooligans in the ranks of the unemployed and that the latter were themselves to blame for the disorders ("Pravda", June 2nd 1928). This incredible explanation, made in defiance of the very principles of Communism, and written in the very same spirit that inspires the extremist organs of the reactionary Capitalist Press, acquitted the exchange officials of all blame, laying the responsibility on the victims of social injustice; but this explanation would not do. The evils of these exchanges were at last discovered. "They are cess-pits", said Melinchansky, a Trades Union leader. They were teeming with abuses; an inspection revealed that thirty-one officials had committed crimes. Favouritism was rampant everywhere, and the officials were plagued with requests for special permits and privileges. The exchange premises were in an abominable condition. Drunkenness and hooliganism developed among the wretches who encamped there; women suffered grave insults and were sometimes even publicly outraged. Corruption was rife among the officials; the Commissariat of Work knew all about the conditions but did nothing. Schmidt, the Commissary, defended himself by laying the blame, in his turn, on the Trades Unions" ("Trud", June 15th 1928. Minutes of the Central Council of Trades Unions). At Serpukhov, not far from Moscow, the labour-exchange consisted of two dirty, dark rooms, in which the crowds struggled savagely and people were crushed in their wild efforts to reach an office window, where often no official was in attendance. Resigned to their fate, the unemployed waited, sitting amidst the filth on the floor. Here they remained unprotected, helpless, and quite unable to obtain anything they might require. The only bed the young women could find in which to sleep was the director's. Seven thousand poor devils suffered oppression and insults at the hands of the director and his deputy ("Trud", May 13th 1927). A whole week's waiting was necessary to obtain registration. The women were brutally treated by the "kuligans" (hooligans) and, further, suffered from the exactions of officials, who forced their attentions "in kind" upon them ("Pravda", June 15th 1928). For several weeks the Press was ordered by the authorities to denounce the abuses and scandals in the labour-exchanges, and then once more lapsed into silence. What changes have there been since? At the next ebullition of discontent the same report as before will appear in all the newspapers, with only the slightest variations.

Women and children also suffer great hardships under the new régime. The classic formula demanding "*Equal work and equal wage*" is heard on the lips of Socialists and Communists throughout the world; but in Russia it is not heard. In 1927 Trotsky, basing his statements on official figures, described the female labour conditions of the previous year as follows: "In many branches of industry the wages earned by women workers in March 1926 were 51, 61, and 83 per cent. of the men's. The necessary measures have not been taken to protect female labour in such branches of industry as the working of turf-pits, lading and unlading, etc. In comparison with the adult wage the earnings of adolescents are continually decreasing. In 1923 they formed 47 per cent., in 1924 45 per cent., and in 1926 40 per cent. of the adult wage" (*Review of the Economic Situation of Adolescents in 1924–25 and 1925–26*). In March 1926, 49 per cent. of these young people were earning less than 20 roubles (16s. 8d.) a month (Central Bureau of Statistics). Explanations of what men's wages really represent have been given earlier in this chapter, and the same considerations naturally apply to the women and children's earnings, for which Trotsky gave the figures in 1927. Two years have passed without it being possible to do anything. Soviet newspapers are full of stories, descriptions, and reports—all of them clear evidence of the heart-breaking condition of proletarian working women and children.

"Pravda" of March 20th 1925 described the plight of female workers at Tula: "Investigations reveal a gloomy picture. The low level of education and almost complete ignorance, the absence of any qualifications for work and the consequently low wages, the expenses of feeding their families—all weigh heavily upon them and hamper their social and cultural development." Nearly all had three, four, some five and six mouths to feed, and wages corresponded to the third category and were worth, at that time, about 10 roubles a month (8s. 4d.). When she was away at work a woman had often to leave a child of three in the care of another one hardly any older. "Housing conditions are intolerable." Out of 42 who were questioned, 5 women could not send their children to school for want of material needs of various kinds; 11 had no boots or underclothing either for themselves or for their children; 14 could not always provide one hot dish a day; 12 were illiterate. (Tula is a town close to Moscow.) In the Astrakhan fisheries, women workers had for a long time been forced into immoral intercourse, and, "above all, received no payment for their services". So weak were they from want of food that they could not refuse the advances made them by the foremen. Even the most courageous of them lost their means of livelihood. "Morals have hardly been altered at all by the Revolution. Just as in the old days, the directors of the concern run after the women on to the rafts and into the rushes and catch them, and not only the responsible chiefs but even the humblest of the employees make this a practice." Newspaper labour correspondents called attention to numerous cases of this sort, but the Unions only dismissed those who were caught in the act. "That was no remedy at all", for their victims would not dare to give evidence against their seducers . . . ("Pravda", May 10th 1925). In the Caucasian tobacco plantations women worked, squatting on mattresses in an atmosphere thick with acrid dust, from six in the morning till nine at night. There were many cases of occupational diseases. The group-contract, which in one of its clauses limits work to eight hours a day, was not respected. "Marriages for the duration of the season only" were contracted, bringing in their train venereal disease and abortions of the most foul kind, etc. ("Trud", March 25th 1926). Serafimovich wrote that in the Crimea the girls who were employed in the tobacco plantations and in the vineyards were forced to sleep with their employers. Diseases of every kind and wholesale abortion were the result. Female workers were badly fed, housed, and treated "worse than in a convict prison" (The "Krasnaya Gazette", March 21st 1926). "Unemployment among women and the lack of housing accommodation have caused a great increase in prostitution, particularly of young children. There is a rapidly increasing number of prostitutes only fourteen years old" (The "Communist", Kharkov, April 15th 1926). In workshops, offices, in the shops as well as in the universities, the general complaint made by women is that they cannot find or keep their jobs, or avail themselves of any of their rights without having to pay "in kind" for the help of the men with whom decisions rest. In no other country in the world do the great majority of women suffer such cruel, intolerable oppression; and this shameful moral state is an undying reproach to the Party in power, whose members, moreover, chiefly profit by the abuses resulting from it. Many suicides can be attributed solely to this cause, and a great number of instances could be given.

In connection with one of these cases of suicide, "Pravda" said: "People like K. ruin these young lives too heedlessly and at too small a cost to themselves. Murder and suicide are not necessarily inevitable in these situations, but morality is very frequently struck death-dealing blows. That a girl student should be forced to sleep with a person like K., who holds a post at the university, in order that she may obtain leave of absence, a scholarship, a railway ticket, or some other favour, surely that is moral assassination? Facts of this kind are, unfortunately, not exceptional, and what makes the matter all the more serious is that all this takes place openly" ("Pravda", June 5th 1926). As a matter of fact, people in Russia have long ago ceased to be astonished at these daily events, and, as for showing indignation, their better instincts have been blunted by the dreadful sights they have witnessed during the last ten years. "We must tell the truth; since the Revolution, the conditions prevailing in many trades in which women are employed have not improved. The young actress cannot obtain an engagement without spending most of her time as the theatre-manager's mistress. A girl has often only one alternative—a life of prostitution or this method of gaining her livelihood" (The "Evening Krasnaya Gazette", October 1st 1926). A Communist factory manager sent for a girl worker and made her perform a task quite outside her proper work, and then, to boot, proceeded to force himself on her; the same individual insulted and ill-treated his women workers ("Pravda", March 3rd 1928). At Yaroslavl, the directors of the alcohol distillery, together with the Secretary of the Communist nucleus, availed themselves of their right to outrage the women in their employ and then dismissed them, to be rid of them; no one dared to criticise such actions for fear that they might be treated as a "Menshevik" or "Soviet enemy" ("Trud", May 11th 1928). In the peat-bogs of the province of Vladimir, women worked 10 or 11 hours instead of 8, in the rain, with water up to their waists, carrying burdens weighing as much as 88 lb. Twenty-four little girls worked in the marshes, though this was expressly forbidden by the law. Workmen dared not protest for fear of losing their places ("Trud", July 1st 1928). In the Volga fisheries at Astrakhan, of which mention has already been made, the director's staff and syndicate employees forced young working women to sleep with them and persecuted those who refused ("Pravda", November 4th 1928). In the Nikopol manganese mines, women were continually molested and harshly treated, and had to endure the unreasonable demands of the workmen, for whom they kept house and did the cooking. The "Izvestia" of July 6th 1929 cited various cases in which female workers, nurses, and teachers were at the mercy of their "superiors", who used them to satisfy their carnal desires. As a general rule, women who were in this manner turned into prostitutes, in spite of themselves, felt humiliated, defenceless, and did not dare to say anything, for they felt their shame bitterly and were afraid that they might be dismissed. Sometimes facts came to light in anonymous letters. Throughout the long succession of cases of corruption which have been discovered during the last three or four years, in important centres as well as in the most remote places in the U.S.S.R., and which involve hundreds of Communist and Soviet leaders as well as minor officials, sexual offences play a very prominent part. It is these defenceless women workers who have been the victims.

Like many other things in Soviet Russia, maternity and child-welfare services certainly exist . . . but only on paper. The proportion of those who in any way benefit from them is so small that the newspapers are careful not to boast about it. Official inquiries reveal that aid for expectant mothers hardly exists at all, and that maternity homes, of which there are ridiculously few, are much too crowded, and that there is an extreme scarcity of linen and other necessities. There certainly are some model maternity hospitals and crêches which visitors, tourists, and the "sham friends of the U.S.S.R." are taken to see. But surely these are totally insufficient for a country embracing "one-sixth of the globe"? Capitalist countries also have model maternity homes and crêches, and they are better and more numerous than those in Russia, but they cannot completely hide the evils of Capitalism. In the U.S.S.R. the maternity homes create less illusions than in other countries. It still remains, therefore, to apply the excellent principles formulated before the death of Lenin. Neither the causes of the war nor the responsibility for this state of things have been sought in the following pages; it is the facts that have been given.

On paper there are also laws and decrees for the regulation of child labour, but they are never put into force. The "Pravda of Youth", which recently began to take up the question, has revealed the most scandalous facts. In the province of Vladimir, children become agricultural labourers at the age of nine or ten, and, working fifteen or sixteen hours a day, are cruelly beaten by their parents when they try to escape from this prison life. Some, aged ten to thirteen, who mind the herds, shiver with cold the whole winter through, being clad only in rags. Little girls sleep with the cows, work from early morn to dewy eve, and are beaten for their pains. In Karelia, children are hired out by their parents for the whole summer for a cask of dried fish and five roubles. On the "sovkoszy" (Soviet estates) children of thirteen or fifteen are exploited and made to work from 13 to 15 hours a day for 40 or 50 copecks (3½d. to 4½d.). *Half of the young agricultural labourers are not given the ordinary weekly rest;* 130,000 little girls work 10 to 18 hours a day ("Pravda of Youth", June 19th 1929). A representative of the Union of Communist Youth said that of the 5,400,000 persons employed in agriculture, there were 2,000,000 young people, which included 1,300,000 less than 18 years of age and 638,000 of between 11 and 14; and this in spite of the law forbidding the employment of children under 14. Adolescents received on an average 13 roubles, or 8s. 8d. (boys); and 11 roubles, or 7s. 4d. (girls). Adults earned 21 roubles (14s.). The paper-rouble, it must be remembered, is worth now about 8d. The great majority of young workers laboured 10 or 12 hours a day, and sometimes more than 12 hours. No one opposed this cruel exploitation of children ("Pravda of Youth", June 26th 1929). At the fourth conference of Communist Youth a delegate said in his report: "Painful though it be, the fact is that no one troubles about the amount of work done by children. At first sight it seems impossible to believe that the conditions revealed in their letters really do exist in the U.S.S.R. Members of the children's organisations ("pioneers") are unanimous in saying that children are obliged to work 14 to 16 hours a day for a monthly salary of between 5 and 10 roubles (3s. 3d. to 6s. 9d.)" ("Pravda of Youth" in the same report). An article written in the same paper a month later painted the picture of child-exploitation in even darker colours. The same abominable conditions, such as exist in Eastern countries like India and China, were reported. Thousands between the ages of seven and twelve were employed in making mats and in the unhealthy leather industry. Artisans ("kustari") put babies of four or five to work; children of eight were occupied in winding woollen threads, a very exhausting process. Little girls in their tens of thousands worked as nurses and general maids, and worked like slaves. Absence of education, harsh treatment, deplorable sanitary conditions, were frequently reported ("Pravda of Youth", July 25th 1929). But what can be said about those children who are received into the special "homes", which form one of the favourite themes of the so-called "friends of the U.S.S.R." who write about Russia? It has often been pointed out that children are continually escaping from the State institutions where they have been sent, to become vagabonds, and that time after time they have to be brought back. The reasons for this will be given below.

According to the Soviet of the town of Tula, children's homes throughout the province present a sorry picture; sanitation is non-existent, children are crammed in, one on top of the other, the food is appalling, the instruction given is beneath contempt, and the personnel immoral. In several houses children were beaten and terrorised, and there were even cases quoted of little girls being outraged and one of a general mutiny ("Pravda", May 19th 1926). In the Vorovsky children's colony even worse conditions prevailed. Everything was repulsively dirty; there were lice, piles of filthy rubbish, and a stinking smell. Children were literally piled in, two and three into one small bed; in the rooms there were slop-buckets and excrement. They had no baths or warm winter clothing, and in only six months there were 3,096 cases of illness among 3,952 children ("Pravda of Youth", No. 149, 1926). Zorich, in an official report on the Yaroslavl children's home, related how the dirt and filth was indescribable, and how the beds and kitchen were verminous; blackbeetles were found swimming in the food and water ("Trud", September 2nd 1926). At another establishment in the neighbourhood of Moscow, in the depths of winter the children were hardly clothed at all. They were covered in eruptions and sores. Those who were ill slept on the floor. There was no doctor or chemist, no water; dirt and rubbish everywhere. For three weeks (in December) the house had not been heated. Everyone slept fully clothed; the children went hungry and the teaching staff got drunk, wasted and stole the public funds. Those in charge were Communists ("Pravda of Youth", No. 303, 1926). Bugoslavsky, a much esteemed and prominent Communist, who has since, like so many others, been deported to Siberia, in his general review of the question wrote that there are a few well-organised, well-managed establishments, but that the *majority* are in a sorry state because the buildings are damp, cold, dirty, small, and insufficiently supplied with bedding, and that many of the children who are accommodated in them are sick. He quoted the disclosures made by inquiries into local conditions. At Novocherkassk, nearly all the institutions were infested with vermin and full of children suffering from itch, ringworm, and typhus. The ravages of ringworm were particularly severe. At Rostov, the boys' homes would, he said, rapidly become nurseries for young robbers if order was not restored (The "Krasnaya Gazette", November issue for August 1927). At Vechniaki, near Moscow, children were beaten and literally tortured. "We are treated like human rubbish", wrote one group of these victims when an inquiry had been instituted after some particularly scandalous events. The personnel was proved to have been bestially cruel. The children lived in dirt and filth, were hungry and cold, and for the smallest peccadillo were stripped of their clothes, whipped, and cruelly beaten ("Pravda of Youth", August 30th 1927). It is quite easy to see why this paper gave such prominence to the following: "The abandoned children run away from these homes and distribution centres. Little ones are beaten, humiliated, and punished. Instead of acquiring a liking for work, they are made vicious and spiteful. This is not the first time that we have published evidence concerning the odious administration of homes in the control of the Moscow Health Service." In 1927 there were 1,852 refuges for 160,250 children. Financially, these homes were in sore straits, some of them only being able to expend four roubles (3s. 4d.) a month on every child. The chief points that emerge from this mass of general information are that children are cold and hungry; that they learn nothing, and, too often, are badly treated. The children's colonies in the Kazan district were in sore need, lacking linen, clothes, and shoes. In one home there were 20 to 30 beds for 120 little creatures, and not all of them had mattresses, and this was by no means an isolated case. The teachers lived in the greatest misery ("Pravda of Youth", January 22nd and 24th 1928). On January 5th 1928 the children in the Life and Work colony near Moscow revolted and sacked the institution, which had been formerly a count's palace—not that this fact made the children's lives any the more beautiful. The management received 3 roubles 60 copecks (2s. 11d.) a month for each child, and the paper reported that this was the case in many other homes. In the abandoned children's Institution both boys and girls got intoxicated, and it was the staff of the establishment who had set them this bad example, as well as treating them disgracefully. One child hanged himself and two little girls tried to commit suicide ("Izvestia", June 30th 1928). The "Youth" newspaper, having received "hundreds of letters" on the subject, once more denounced "the veritable horrors that were happening behind the scenes in these children's homes"; they were due to the lack of all necessities and to the incompetence of the qualified staff ("Pravda of Youth", August 9th 1928). The same paper took up the question again the following year more vigorously than ever, demanding that education officials responsible for the negligent administration of children's homes should be prosecuted and a general commission of inquiry set up. The Odessa children's refuge was a "school for thieves", a place of corruption, of drunkenness. The little inmates slept on the bare boards in damp, dark rooms. The girls' dormitory was a hot-bed of prostitution. From a whole series of places, whose names were given, came reports of children being cruelly beaten, a circumstance of which

Communist and local authorities were well aware, though they did not attempt to interfere. There were stories without number of bloody brawls, theft, pillage, and debauch. In the province of Tula there was another case of general mutiny. The reason why children prefer to live as vagabonds in the streets is fully explained by the description of general conditions above ("Pravda of Youth", April 17th 1929). On leaving these homes girls found themselves alone, helpless, and friendless, and the result was that many became prostitutes: this was notably the case at Odessa ("Pravda of Youth", May 9th 1929). Anyone who has lived in Russia as *a Russian* and not as a mere visitor will find these remarks entirely superfluous, but, on the other hand, they are necessary to convince those who would be tempted to believe the so-called "evidence" of certain eye-witnesses incapable of either seeing, hearing, or seeking the truth.

Then privilege, unhampered by these sinister realities, plays the same part in the lives of these little ones as in those of adults. For example, the Malakhovka institution in the suburbs of Moscow is excellent in every way, and there are others like it. But the happy lot of a few privileged children cannot compensate for the veritable martyrdom of a great number of these little unfortunate ones. The object of the October Revolution was surely not to create a few model institutions like islets in an ocean of injustice. Putting aside all thoughts of progress in Socialism, the removal of the glaring evils, which are the legacy of the past or the fruit of modern conditions, will not be accomplished except after many long and weary years, and then only after the difficulties are properly faced and the policy of self-deception shunned for ever. The illusions which are propagated by the Soviet legend help to prolong the existence of these evil conditions.

Some particularly striking contrasts of material and

social inequality are to be found in the ranks of industrial craftsmen where the "heritage of the past" seems very carefully preserved. These "kustari" (artisans) occupy an important place and compose 60 per cent. of the labour employed in industry, furnishing 30 per cent. of the total production ("Trud", April 16th 1929). There are more than four millions of them, and of these 200,000 have been organised into co-operative societies ("Pravda of Youth", April 24th 1929). The workers' code does not exist for them. "They do not recognise the eight-hour day; even in the artels (associations for invalid workmen), whose members are almost exclusively cripples and ailing persons, the working day is often from twelve to fifteen hours. In 1927–28 half the artels worked systematically more than eight hours, and in 1928–29 already more than 60 per cent. of industrial workers had become members. Their wages, in certain cases, were between 200 per cent. and 1,000 per cent. more than those paid in State industries. An instrument-maker earned on an average 826 roubles (£34 8s.) a month, a locksmith 300 roubles (£12 10s.), a fitter 220 roubles (£9 3s.), and an unskilled workman 134 roubles (£5 11s.). In one of these artels (though it is possible to discover if the same conditions prevailed in all of them) there was "complete absence of any health or sanitary arrangements in these trades and of measures ensuring safe-working conditions. No attention was paid to the legislation regulating child and adult labour." "The "kustar" exploits his own children, eight or nine years old, and makes them work 12 to 14 hours a day, sometimes on holidays; rewards them generously with thumps and raps on the head, and does not send them to school" ("Trud", August 31st 1929).

A description of the most down-trodden social categories is not complete when the lot of the townspeople has not been discussed. Proletarian teachers and students will have a chapter to themselves later, but a few words may be said here about servants, of whom there are 300,000 registered. A certain number receive *no* money wages, only their board and lodging, and quite a quarter of them are paid the minimum legal wage. They have no eight-hour day, the majority working from early dawn till nightfall: there is also plenty of information as to how they are lodged ("Trud", July 6th 1929). Then mention must be made of another category of proletarians, which is quite unique in the world—unpaid workmen. One must go to Odessa to see them; they come four times a day to the factory at the end of each shift and are taken on if there are any absentees. They receive no salary, but have a right to one pound of soap a month ("Trud", August 30th 1929). With regard to the question of the length of the working day it is necessary to collect certain information which is indispensable for the completion of this picture of the workers' life. The constant violation of the eight-hour day law has been pointed out in the accounts already given of conditions affecting women and children. Many men workers are not better protected.

The eight-hour day was decreed by the leaders of the bourgeois democratic Revolution of March 1917. It was incumbent on the leaders of the Soviet Revolution to carry it out. The question is, How far has this been done? On the railways, contraventions of this law are very numerous. On the Baltic line, for example, the men are on duty for twenty hours at a time. In 1925, there were 8,200,000 hours worked overtime ("Trud", March 20th 1926). Semashko reported that young workmen laboured generally longer than the legal limit ("Pravda", March 25th 1926). "Labour regulations are not applied with us on any estates. Even commercial employees and chauffeurs, who seem particularly favoured as regards their occupation, work under very hard conditions. The former have a working day of from ten to eleven hours" (The "Rabochaya Gazette", June 16th 1926). A brick-makers' delegate told a building conference that in his district the eight-hour day had long been a thing of the past, and that the working day always lasted ten hours or more (The "Rabochaya Gazette", June 25th 1926). Overtime was commonly worked in the majority of institutions and industrial concerns in contempt of the Inspectorate of Work ("Trud," October 9th 1926). In a certain saw-mill in the Caucasus the working day was as long as twelve hours; overtime, as well as Sunday and holiday work, was paid at the ordinary rate. Workmen were forced to carry out the cleaning of machines, etc., without extra remuneration ("Trud", November 16th 1926). Registered overtime greatly exceeded the limit imposed by the regulations, and there was also overtime that had not been registered. In the great industries more than one-third of the men worked overtime, even though unemployment was very rife ("Trud", April 29th 1927). The Moscow Inspectorate of Work found that in one year there had been 53,000 violations of social legislation. Various institutions and industrial concerns applied for permission to work 1,826,000 supplementary hours during one year, and were successful in obtaining official sanction for more than half of what they had asked for, and of course no one knows how many millions of unregistered hours were worked overtime throughout the country. For the following six months nearly four times the amount of extra hours were demanded, two-thirds of which were granted ("Pravda", June 8th 1927). In the peat-bogs of Ust-Tosna, the working day was one of ten hours, without counting supplementary time, and the men slaved from four in the morning till eleven at night ("Trud", August 18th 1927). At Bryansk, they were at work from four or six in the morning till eight or ten at night ("Pravda of Youth", November 27th 1927). In the Donetz, "the eight-hour day has been stamped underfoot"; at Stalino, 1,000 workmen, of whom 300 were youths, worked more than eight hours unloading wagons: some of them were completely exhausted, having worked for twelve hours ("Pravda of Youth", January 5th 1928). In nearly all the peat-bogs the employees were shamefully "sweated"; the working day for men was twelve, for young persons ten to twelve, and for women ten to eleven hours—and this in the marshes. Following upon a mining disaster at Chakhty (Donetz), an inquiry revealed that the miners who had perished had been working for thirteen hours without a relief, as was very well known to the Unions ("Trud", August 3rd 1929). A ten-hour day was introduced at Stalingrad in order to speed up the construction of the tractor-factory ("Trud", August 20th 1928), and many similar reports received confirmation. That is the reason why the various anti-Communist political parties have given such prominence in their programmes to the need for strict adherence to the eight-hour working-day and for the suppression of unpaid overtime, etc.

On the occasion of the tenth anniversary of the October Revolution the Soviet Government issued a manifesto promising the workers a seven-hour day, a reform which would have been comparatively easy to carry out in a country where the unemployment question was acute and wages were of the starvation order. Two years have passed and the seven-hour day is in force only in a few hundreds of industrial establishments, and the great masses do not yet benefit from the eight-hour day. The Commissary of Work promised to bring in the seven-hour day for approximately 450,000 workmen by the end of September 1930, which would bring the number working under the new arrangement to one million only, and this three years after the manifesto of 1927 ("Trud", August 31st 1929). But how many hours overtime will be worked in addition, and when will the law be applied to the twelve million wage-earners? At the rate of one million a year, not for thirty-six years, without counting the increase in proletarian populations. It is easier to issue decrees than to carry them out. Once more, care must be taken not to confuse what is still on paper with what is an accomplished fact.

CHAPTER IV

THE TRAGIC LIFE OF THE WORKERS (3)

Country districts—Peasant classes—"Kulaki", "bedniaki", and "seredniaki"—Taxes and the "bedniaki"—Country sanitary conditions—Peasants' houses—Illegal imposts—Forced "voluntary loans" —The proletariat on the "suvkhoszy"—Local authorities' abuse of power—Confiscation and arbitrary arrest—Signs of revolt.

Of the one hundred and fifty million inhabitants who, roughly speaking, make up the population of the U.S.S.R., more than one hundred and twenty millions are peasants. Every day, to this vast total, ten thousand more are added, and while this book was being written and printed half a million Russians were born. Of the remaining thirty millions, many are really peasants, for the reason that a great majority of proletarians divide their time between town and country and because places which are described as towns are often nothing more than big villages. Most of them, therefore, are working peasants, and it is their lot which will be examined in this chapter.

The October Revolution had, as everybody knows, given the peasant masses the usufruct of all the lands in Russia. That is what the leaders of the movement had desired, but they were quite unable to see that "property", on the one hand, and "usufruct", on the other, were not at all one and the same thing. The area handed over to the communes has, therefore, been increased by the addition of property belonging to the Crown, to the Church, and to the nobles. But in some districts where there was no property to confiscate, hardly any change in the size of the peasant holdings has taken place. Another important factor has been the very rapid increase in population in many places which has effectually reduced the peasant holdings to their original size. The granting of plots to landless peasants has sometimes absorbed all the confiscated properties available for distribution, and in some cases has even diminished the original individual share. According to Kalinin, "in Tsarist Russia there were 16 million small-holdings, to-day there are between 25 and 27, or, in other words, each plot is now half as large as it used to be and consequently produces half as much" ("Pravda", May 28th 1929). The working of small individually owned holdings, which was in force under the old communal system (*obchchina* or *mir*) and which is incorporated in the Soviet régime, has the great defect of splitting up to a very great extent the land under cultivation. The head of each family has, in fact, a right to several plots of land of varying worth, often a long way distant from each other. As the family increases, so does the share diminish; it is not possible to work these holdings with modern agricultural machinery, and the system of crop rotation which was created according to the abstract principles of justice does not tend to improve the soil. This division of land into fractions and its general poverty leads to cultivation on an extensive system which gives a very inferior yield. Intensive farming with the use of powerful machines and rational manuring processes is only possible on the vast estates suitable for collective labour or for Capitalist or Socialist development. At the present time, Capitalism plays no part in agriculture except in certain limited undertakings; Socialism does not exist as yet, the Soviet estates representing only a mere fraction of agricultural organisation. The consequence of this is that global production is insufficient, that it is impossible to export cereals, and, on the contrary, it becomes necessary to buy abroad and ration the population.

The aim of this book is not to analyse the economic development of Russia, or to discuss the problems that would inevitably present themselves during such an examination; nor is there any intention of putting forward arguments for their solution or of championing a policy. The writer's sole object is to show how the workers are situated and to try to provide a clear picture of what the near future may hold in store for them. Thus it will be possible to avoid too frequent references to statistics in this short study of rural organisation and to proceed at once to an examination of the social classes.

Russian peasants are generally divided into three principal groups: the rich, the poor, and the medium class ("kulaki", "bedniaki", "seredniaki"). This is a somewhat vague method of classification, but an examination of their various resources at once makes a more careful gradation possible. According to a book published in 1928 by the Communist Academy, entitled *Social Differences in Soviet Country Districts*, it is possible to divide the peasant population into five categories, as follows:

1. Proletarian families who hire out their services for more than 50 working days.

2. Semi-proletarian families who hire out their services for 20 to 50 working days, or who hire ploughing-oxen for more than 20 days, or implements for more than 10 days, to till their own land.

3. An intermediary group of families who hire out their services for less than 20 days, or hire the services of others for the same period; who hire out their own oxen, or employ on their own land those of others for less than 20 days; and the same with implements for less than 10 days.

4. Another intermediary group of families who have the means to cultivate their holdings and who hire the services of others for periods of 20 to 50 days; who can employ other peasants' oxen for more than 20 days; who let out implements for more than 10 working days;

or who farm more than four acres of plough-land or ten acres of pasture.

5. Small Capitalist families who employ outside labour for more than 50 working days.

The periods given above denote the balance between the number of days on which peasant families have hired themselves out and those on which they have hired outside labour; the majority of peasants work their oxen and implements on each other's land in the ploughing season and at harvest-time, or let them out for use. The same writers gave the following figures as representing the average value of productive property in the possession of families examined in 1925 and corresponding to the five categories above. (This figure included oxen, produce of farm-yards, materials, farm buildings, machines and tools, as well as stores apart from food-stuffs.)

1. From 220 roubles in the Northern Caucasus to 310 roubles in the Ukraine (£9 3s. 4d. to £12 18s. 4d).

2. From 280 in the Urals and in Siberia to 400 in the Ukraine (£11 13s. 4d. to £16 13s. 4d).

3. From 510 in Siberia to 850 in the Ukraine (steppes) (£21 5s. to £35 8s. 4d.).

4. From 920 in Siberia to 1,200 in the Northern Caucasus (£38 6s. 8d. to £50).

5. From 940 in Siberia to 1,680 in the Northern Caucasus (£39 3s. 4d. to £70).

Having made the necessary reductions for working expenses (sowing, labourers' wages), the families' yearly incomes were given as follows in the report:

One hundred and sixty-three to 276 roubles (£7 15s. 10d. to £11 10s.) for those whose productive property was less than 200 roubles (£8 6s. 8d.); only one-half of this income was earned by farming alone, the remainder coming from payment for personal services or rent of lands.

Families whose productive property was worth between 200 and 500 roubles (£8 6s. 8d. to £20 16s. 8d.), had an income of between 234 and 329 roubles (£9 15s. and £13 14s. 2d.), this being to a great extent the profits from farming and from wages paid to them for labour on neighbours' farms.

Those who had productive property between 500 and 800 roubles (£20 16s. 8d. and £33 6s. 8d.), received in the Ukraine an income of 345 roubles (£14 7s. 6d.), and at Smolensk 455 roubles (£18 19s. 2d.), three-quarters of which came from farming. (There was a direct tax of between 25 and 39 roubles—20s. 10d. to 32s. 6d.)

Incomes ranged from 482 at Tambov to 685 roubles at Smolensk (£20 1s. 8d. to £28 0s. 10d) in cases where productive property was worth between 800 and 1,400 roubles (£33 6s. 8d. and £58 6s. 8d.). There was a direct tax of 31 to 62 roubles (25s. 10d. to 51s. 8d.).

In cases where productive property was above 1,400 roubles in value (£58 6s. 8d.) the income ranged from 502 in the Ukraine to 1,007 roubles at Smolensk (£20 19s. 2d. to £41 19s. 2d.), with a direct tax of 55 to 111 roubles (45s. 10d. to 92s. 6d.).

This apparent masterpiece of statistics may certainly conceal errors and deceptions of every kind, but in this case it is more probably in connection with the richest categories—those who have something to hide—that faked figures and misstatements will be found. It is relatively an easy matter to work out the income and property values of the poorest classes which alone in this case hold any interest for us, and the figures given for them may, therefore, be taken as approximately correct. In the foregoing pages the lot of privileged persons in the towns—officials, technicians, small traders, shop-keepers, "kustari" (artisans), of which there are four millions—has not been examined, and in the same way, in dealing with conditions in the country, it is the situation of the most impoverished classes only that has been subjected to a careful study. It is quite useless to proceed before giving a summary of the official statistics for the combined peasant populations. The most important fact that emerges is that a proletarian family has to live on a yearly income of between 160 and 275 roubles, approximately (£7 15s. and £11 10s.), and a semi-proletarian family on about 235 to 330 roubles a year (£9 15s. and £13 14s.). If the leaders' opinion is shared that 40 per cent. of small-holdings have to be worked without horses, and if the six million daily labourers, whose wages are almost identical with those above, are included in these categories, then the proletarian and semi-proletarian classes must comprise nearly half the rural population. But if they are permitted only to include the "bedniaki" (poor) and the "batraki" (daily labourers) to the exclusion of all types of farm-workers usually placed in the intermediary group, then they will constitute a little less than a third of the total. But with the addition of the third category in which the annual income ranges between 345 and 445 roubles (£14 7s. 6d. and £18 19s. 2d.), these proletarian and semi-proletarian categories, without any question, include the great majority of peasants—more than three-quarters of the whole. The reader knows full well the real value of the rouble, and is therefore able to get a clear idea of the miserable condition of one hundred million peasants.

The poorest among these hundred millions would, according to the learned treatise already referred to, earn 160 roubles (£7 15s. 10d.) a year *per family*, or 12s. 11d. a month; the income of families not quite so poor would be 455 roubles (£18 19s. 2d.) per annum, or 31s. 7d. a month. And it must be emphasised that these are the yearly wages of the *whole family*. Only by eating pulped buckwheat (cacha) from one year's end to another can wretched peasants keep body and soul together. Of course, it is true that country people have much simpler needs than town-dwellers, and it must not be forgotten that Russia's evolution resembles that of no other country and has caused her people, only freed in 1861 from the shackles of serfdom, to be the most backward in all Europe. But after fifteen years of war and prolonged privations, these peasant workers are still lacking even the barest necessities of life, and it should have been the task of the Revolution to raise them to a higher level of living. Kalinin, in his reply to complaints from the country districts, wrote: "Have I ever denied that the lives of poor people are hard? No, they still suffer anguish. It is not our fault, it is our misfortune. Socialism alone can save them" ("Izvestia," August 1926). That being so, let there be no talk of misery in Russia while people are paid to misrepresent it abroad as the abode of happiness.

It is this state of "peasant poverty", as it is called in Russia, which begets the millions of unemployed that are attracted into the towns, the millions of labourers who become factory drudges, the millions of casual labourers whose lot is precarious to the extreme, the thousands of little children that stray about the streets—all that vast lower strata of humanity, often workless, often homeless, whose working and living conditions have provided such a sinister picture in these pages.

If one may judge from the lot of unskilled workmen in the towns, the situation of the country workers, scattered throughout the vast Russian and Siberian plains, cannot be a very enviable one. In the towns there are organisations, institutions, and newspapers which can at least be expected to save appearances and to intervene in cases of extreme ill-treatment, if only to save the authorities the trouble of righting the wrongs themselves. But in the country there is nothing of that: the proletariat is almost defenceless, even puzzled as to what really is its exact status. It is ignorant of its own rights, as it is about everything: how, then, can it learn about them, to whom can it look for protection and for an attentive hearing to its complaints and claims for justice?

It is useless to approach the Soviet [1] assemblies—we shall see later their true worth. Zinoviev, who in 1924 was one of the three leaders of the country, wrote in a moment of frankness that "in the country the only 'work' that the Soviet does is simply confined to collecting the taxes" ("Pravda", October 11th 1924). Then, to see why it is likewise futile to ask the aid of the Communist Party, one has only to read a book written by two Communists, Rydin and Truntayev, entitled, *The Communist Nucleus and Soviet in the Village*, officially published in the State editions of 1924. It reveals that Soviet power is entirely devoid of any significance in the country districts; the old forms of administration still linger on and new systems do not count at all except in so much that they oppress the villagers; the poor or fairly prosperous peasants are at the mercy of the first Communist or Comsomol (member of the Communist Youth) who comes along. Elections for places in the Soviets are nothing more than obligatory ratifications of a list of candidates drawn up by the local Communist nucleus; no one wants to be a member. Under pressure by the Communists, it is arranged that everyone shall in his turn discharge this distasteful duty. Once the Soviet is elected (!) under these conditions, it gives no further sign of life, not even meeting once a year. In spite of his own feelings in the matter the President has to collect the taxes and compile a list of defaulting taxpayers. All matters of importance are discussed by the peasants in their tradi-

[1] Soviet means "council."

tional assemblies (skhod). The Communists consider themselves to be the masters, but instead of guiding they command, and where there is a Communist nucleus it usurps the functions of the Soviet. Such were the statements made by conscientious Communists who knew their facts: and they would not dare to reveal the whole truth. Their views on this matter are shared by all intelligent and honest individuals who have lived in the country in Soviet Russia. "All the work is carried out by the presidents and secretaries. . . . The Party committee does everything, and not only takes the place of the Communist groups in the Soviets, but of the Soviets themselves" ("Pravda", August 4th 1928). These Soviets and village Communist nuclei devote all their energies to the maintenance of order and to the collection of taxes, and it is therefore not surprising that none of their members bothers to see that the rights of millions of "batraki" are respected. From time to time a newspaper has described how their condition savours of the Middle Ages, but nothing is done for them, and for a very good reason.

In the course of an inquiry into the administrative work of the lower Soviet grades, some of the highest officials must have remarked the dreadful misery of the daily agricultural labourer. "It is time", wrote one of them, "to establish a minimum salary, if not for everyone, at any rate for certain groups of 'batraki'." In an overwhelming majority of cases the wage of the daily labourer makes it quite impossible for him to provide himself with food ("Pravda", August 14th 1925). Nothing could be clearer, and it is quoted word for word: "*The wage of the daily labourer makes it quite impossible for him to provide himself with food, in an overwhelming majority of cases.*" It is useless to juggle with statistics, to quote misleading percentages and fallacious figures: The daily labourer is dying of hunger, and that "*in an overwhelming majority of cases*", and in spite of anything "friends of the U.S.S.R." may say to the contrary. The same article stated that "in the Don district, shepherds' wages have been reduced by two-thirds and still continue to decrease". A shepherd, therefore, cannot earn enough to feed himself, and even so his wage is further reduced by two-thirds. The report went on to say that owing to his extreme ignorance the labourer was quite unable to agitate for an adequate salary, and therefore State aid was indispensable. It seems incredible that a blacksmith, for instance, could force the "batraki" in his employ to work sixteen, and sometimes more, hours a day, in the eighth year after the Revolution. And now, twelve years after the great event, the same medieval conditions prevail. Life in the depths of the country in Russia has not been perceptibly affected by social changes, and sudden movements, like the October Revolution, can only change outward appearances unless some intelligent, resolute action is taken on behalf of the poor, slave-minded "batraki."

According to the "Trud" (May 26th 1927), the wage of the daily labourer had not yet reached the famous pre-war level, and even if it did, life for him would still be one of unutterable misery. The same paper reported that the wages of skilled agricultural workers, who had a special trade and understood machines, were 30 per cent. above the pre-war figure. But that still meant a life of misery for them. As the value of such statistics has been shown in connection with town workers, in the case of agricultural labourers it is not even worth while to show their absurdity. Farm labourers in the Ukraine, which, is, relatively speaking, the best-developed agricultural district in Russia, work on an average 13½ hours a day during the three months that they are engaged, and they are paid in kind. The mean average is 12·4 hours for men and 11·9 for women, and half of them are paid in kind. Conditions are the same in the Caucasus. Among the most hardly treated are the men and women employed on the tobacco plantations; they are crammed into huge sheds, where they work and sleep, and are obliged to eat standing up without ceasing from their labours, dipping their spoons into wooden utensils which are shared by everyone ("Trud," July 5th 1927). If the "mean average" is twelve or thirteen hours a day, it is not difficult to imagine the plight of those who work more. Ossinsky has settled once and for all the real significance of these "mean averages". "Save us, comrades, we are perishing", has long been the cry of workmen's delegates from the P. marshes. When they emerge from the mire of the peat-pits, wet, tired, and dirty, they seek repose in their huts, where they lie on straw bedding thinly strewn over the damp ground. "If they would only give us a plank or two," they say; "it is quite impossible to sleep on the damp earth." Promises are given, but nothing is done; the Communists get drunk and play cards, hardly differing in their behaviour from non-party men ("Trud", August 27th 1929).

Such is the lot of millions of proletarians employed in agriculture, and one wonders under what conditions the tens of thousands of poor as well as "medium" peasants live out their lives: and "medium" spells poverty rather than riches. One sure way of discovering nothing in this connection is to examine statistics, for no distinct, concrete idea of the daily life of the masses can be gained by contemplating their sterile figures. Yet there is abundant living testimony in the shape of statements made by Communists who, thanks to the authority conferred upon them by their party, are in a position to tap the most reliable sources of information, and have besides a deep knowledge of agriculture and of the peasantry. Even to Russian town-dwellers the country remains a complete mystery; entirely unexpected developments are suddenly revealed which surprise even the most vigilant observers; and these require investigation from time to time. Yakovlev, the well-known Communist, issued in pamphlet form an account of what was literally an exploration into the conditions prevailing in the province of Kursk. So great was the interest aroused by this short work, *The Country as it Really Is*, that he continued his inquiries and published the results in a fuller treatise entitled, *Our Village*. It is not easy in a few words to summarise the contents of works of this kind, but the main sense of Yakovlev's remarks may quite shortly be noted. Throughout the country districts there has been no change since the Revolution; manners and customs, the peasants' miserable conditions, and the productive value of their labours—all remain unaltered. The germs of the new life will develop or wither away, according to the strength of the ties that bind town and countryside. Another Communist, Leon Sosnovsky by name, who is the editor of "Pravda" and the "Byednota" (the poor peasants' paper), together with the chief Soviet publications, and an accepted authority on peasants' affairs as well as being a most intelligent, talented man, has published some remarkable articles, far more instructive than heavy year-books of statistics, graphic extracts, or economic theses only comprehensible to the "initiated" who are capable of mentally transforming figures into tangible realities. The following extracts, taken from one of these articles, are most illuminating.

An inquiry into conditions at Nizhni-Novogorod contrasted the amount of labour expended by various social groups of peasants and the large share of produce appropriated at the end of the year by the so-called

Soviet State. In one case a poor peasant who had a family of five to feed and was himself the only bread-winner, possessed a horse twenty years old, a goat, three hens, and wooden agricultural implements; he borrowed a plough from a neighbour for 50 lb. of flour. His annual harvest was 30 bushels of rye, 70 lb. of flax, and 23 cwt. of potatoes. The tax imposed upon him amounted to 29 bushels of rye, or the equivalent of his entire grain harvest. In this case, therefore, it must be supposed that five people can live for a whole year on 23 cwt. of potatoes and the price of 70 lb. of flax. Of course the unfortunate wretch could not pay.

Another peasant, B., who again was the only wage-earner in the family, had eight mouths to feed. His livestock consisted of a horse, a ewe, and a lamb. His annual harvest was 51 bushels of rye and 4 tons 3 cwt. of potatoes. He was allowed a reduction in taxes which amounted to 4¼ cwt. of produce because he had lost two horses, one after the other. This payment represented a huge percentage of his crops, which were intended to feed eight persons. It is also important to realise that in the province of Nizhni, peasants are not so poor as in the majority of districts: the two cases cited above show poor peasants each in possession of a horse.

The "medium" peasant, Z., had a family of six to feed and there were two breadwinners. He owned a horse, two sheep, three lambs, six hens; his crops for the year were 59 bushels of rye, 38 cwt. of potatoes, and 70 lb. of flax-seeds, and, considering that there were six mouths to feed, the tax of 30 bushels of rye was a heavy one. Of this, 18 bushels was paid to buy shares in the corn-loan, which is briefly discussed in a later chapter.

In another case, in a "kulak's" or well-to-do peasant's family, there were six people to feed and three earning wages. His son was a student at Nizhni. His livestock consisted of a thoroughbred mare, two foals, a cow, a ewe, seven lambs, two Yorkshire pigs. He was found at stock-taking to possess one sower, one threshing-machine, two ploughs (one with double shares). His yearly harvest was 140 bushels of rye, 2½ cwt. of flax, 5½ tons of potatoes, and 1 4/7 tons various. He obtained a reduction of 2½ cwt. on account of land improvement. He had, besides, 42 bee-hives producing 13 cwt. of honey, which was worth more than all the rest of his crops put together, and was not taxed. He paid his taxes with shares in the corn-loan and bought others, making a profit of 90 pouds (28 cwt.) (in the voucher the sum was specified in pouds), and thereby covering all the imposts to which he was liable. His tax percentage was therefore *nil.*

Another "kulak" had a family of three, all earning wages. He owned a horse, a cow, and a calf. The total for crops raised on his land is not given, but in any case, with three people able to work and the stock available, he must have harvested *at least* twice as much as the poor peasants mentioned above. But his economic resources did not end there: he possessed a mill with two grindstones able to grind 31 cwt. when the wind was strong, for which he paid 35 roubles (29s. 2d.) in rent and licence. On every 100 pouds (31 cwt.) he made a profit of 10 roubles (6s. 8d.). If his actual gain is taken as only 5 roubles (3s. 4d.), and if there are 150 productive working-days a year, then his minimum profit is 750 pouds (11 5/7 tons) and his expenses 35 roubles (23s. 4d.). But that is still not all: there was a little brickworks run by his family and two paid labourers, which produced 60,000 bricks a year. On this the Treasury imposed a tax of 22 pouds (6¾ cwt.); therefore, even including the sum paid for the mill, he was not taxed more on his whole earnings than the "medium" peasant Z., who had to rely on the cultivation of his land alone for a livelihood.

The conclusions reached are quite clear: at the time when Sosnovsky was writing his articles ("Pravda", August 27th 1924), the State was grievously spoiling the poorest and at the same time asking nothing of the richest. This roused Sosnovsky and certain other members from the Communist ranks, who knew full well what was going on, to protest against the fiscal policy adopted, quite unconsciously, by the Party in country districts, but carried into practice by the machinery of an officialdom fully conscious of its evils and influenced by well-to-do peasants. The Communists who made these disclosures have been thrown into prison or deported to Siberia, but it has, nevertheless, been found necessary to pay heed to their warnings and to cease from plundering poor peasants, auctioning their tools and furniture, and even throwing into prison those of them who could not pay their taxes. Certain other articles are worth quoting:

A peasant whose home was near Leningrad came back from the Red Army, having been duly lectured and indoctrinated, an atheist and a Soviet of the most advanced type. He had six in his family and farmed one dessatine (2½ acres) of ploughland and one dessatine of meadow. Being an industrious person he courageously cleared 1¼ dessatines (3 acres) of wooded land after a year's work and had harvested the first of the rotation crops on three-quarters of a dessatine (1⅘ acres) of this new land. According to the law, reclaimed land was exempt from taxes for several years, but nevertheless he had to pay an impost on it of 23 roubles 75 (19s. 9d.), "a sum which only in a nightmare would have seemed credible to him". Though he made representations to the Soviet, "all his wealth was seized" and a chest of drawers and a grindstone, provisionally left with him, were finally sent away to the cantonal authorities. Becoming anxious, he made inquiries and received a promise that nothing would be sold till some explanation was forthcoming. Two days after, the chest of drawers was sold, but no purchaser was found for the grindstone. Then followed an endless succession of inquiries, interviews, committees, and at last it was suggested that an agricultural surveyor should be sent to make his examination at the peasant's expense. To this the peasant agreed and paid the costs. The surveyor reported that he should be exempted from taxation for five years. Months passed: his furniture had been sold, the grindstone shortly would be; and yet the peasant kept on hoping, hoping . . . ("Pravda", April 22nd 1925).

Another article by a different writer in the same paper described how statements of taxes, applications for relief, etc., passed through five or six stages of inspection and were months in the process. In the meantime taxes were collected, creating situations similar to the following: A soldier serving in the Red Army, and, consequently, a servant of the Revolution, received a letter from his family as follows: "Vania, we shall soon be sold up, our last loaf of bread has gone and we shall be hungry. Vania, we received your certificate of service, but they would not read it or take any notice of it. We are going to sell our 16 pouds (529 lb.) of barley, our 10 pouds (6 bushels) of rye, which will only bring in 15 roubles (12s. 6d.), and we have 30 roubles (25s.) to pay in taxes. When you come back, you will find your home deserted" ("Pravda", April 22nd 1925). As a matter of fact, the family in question should not have had to pay any taxes at all.

Such incidents, which are characteristic of the general situation, are only too common, and it would be easy to give thousands of them. But the moment that the State realised that there was a shortage of corn it discovered that the sympathies of every peasant had been alienated from the movement: the poor and certain of the "medium" classes because they had been oppressed, plundered, and hardly treated; the rich and the rest of the "medium" peasants because they could not procure food-stuffs in exchange for their corn, or because they considered themselves defrauded by the low taxation-prices paid them for that commodity. This is not the moment to reveal the fortunes and vicissitudes of the economic policy applied to the country districts by the Communist Party: the main object of this book is to give a true picture of the labouring masses, and no allusion should be made to other matters unless they are necessary to the understanding of the question under review. The State, that is to say, the Party, has therefore been obliged to grant concessions to these poor peasants, not in order to conform to the principles upon which, as we have seen, its officials set so little store, but in the hope of making allies of the cultivators and of obtaining their corn supplies. Rich or well-to-do peasants buried their corn; the poor had none at all and could find none to buy. Then the State, hard put to it to revictual the towns, adopted brutal methods of confiscation and repression, and caused corn supplies to disappear from the markets, once more antagonising the whole peasant population. Thereupon the poor found direct taxation greatly reduced and even entirely abolished as far as the poorest classes were concerned—not that in any case they could have paid their dues. But this did not provide them with corn, which was rationed in the towns and at the same time sold in the open market and in secret, at four or five times the official price. Moreover, though now freed from the nightmare of direct taxation, poor peasants are still mulcted in indirect taxation. Not only is the Soviet Budget based more and more on indirect imposts, which are directly contrary to accepted Socialist and Communist principles, but the high prices of manufactured products are also evidence of camouflaged indirect imposts. These high prices, approximately three or four times greater than in Western Europe, would not be so serious if they were genuine. As a matter of fact the shortage of goods has been so marked and production so inadequate in proportion to the demand that the few commodities thrown on the markets have only served the ends of speculators, and, passing from hand to hand, have fetched exorbitant prices. The poor peasant has always been robbed in one way or another. Driven into a corner by the misery he endures, he is obliged to borrow from the "kulak" to save himself from dying of hunger, only to become the slave of his usurious creditor. Vodka and drunkenness complete his downfall.

According to official statements concerning health conditions in the country, "sick people in the province of Gomel besiege the hospitals to the number of 2,000 a month. Turpentine is measured out in teaspoons, and only twenty quinine cachets *per mensem* are forthcoming when hundreds are down with malaria." "Syphilis is the scourge of our canton", ran a report from the Nizhni province. "There are some villages where half the population are suffering from syphilis." In the Orel province, Dr. P. found villages in which the work of schools was entirely interrupted, the children being infected with syphilis. "In the Kalouga province half the inhabitants of certain villages are syphilitic." There must be certainly many cantons and districts where similar conditions prevail. Naturally the country people are always in the hands of quacks and bone-setters, who take advantage of their obscurantism and poverty. Ghastly descriptions followed of the practice of sorcery, which takes the place of proper medical assistance ("Pravda", April 7th 1925). Since then no improvement has been effected. On the contrary, newspapers report that there is an increasing scarcity of doctors and nurses in the country, as well as a serious shortage of medical requirements. "The 'batraki' are entirely deprived of medical assistance"; "medical relief is organised in such a way that only rich or well-to-do peasants can benefit from it. The country doctor is without any means of transport, and if called to examine a patient has to ride the horse sent to fetch him; if the sick person is poor he cannot, therefore, have any medical attention" (The "Rabochaya Gazette", September 14th 1929).

In a certain number of villages, "peasants' houses" have been built to accommodate peasant visitors. The winter saw the establishment of one of these at Moscow, which, however, had never been occupied, at least not till 1924. It was well appointed and clean, doubtless because it was never used, though the beds were too close together in the dormitories (they were touching) and the washing arrangements were entirely inadequate. This establishment, of course, was on view to foreigners, bourgeois, and workmen, as well as to the various false "friends of the U.S.S.R." and to all those whom it was thought worth while to deceive. But the real "peasants' houses" which are actually in use, in many respects closely resemble the "children's homes": in the Soviet Press they are described as "absolute stables". It is enough to read "Pravda" of June 6th of the same year (1924): "These houses are filthy and are used as taverns." Krupskaya referred, as an example, to one at Tver, where the propaganda bureau is always closed (except for the visits of high officials) and where the tea-room is used as a vodka saloon.

It is impossible to talk of the life of peasants without mentioning the thousand acts of unbridled tyranny to which they fall victims. The manner in which the local

Soviets are forced upon them (and there are other points in this connection to be treated in a later chapter) makes one wonder if there can be any limit to the oppressive treatment of these defenceless peasants by Soviet, or, more particularly, by Communist officials. The poorer he is, the more open is he to attack. The writer lived for some time at an important centre in Southern Russia in an artel of agricultural workers, who, though specially privileged in various ways, were at the same time subject to the strict control of the Moscow authorities. Even in these conditions illegal taxes fell so thick and fast upon them that any agricultural venture, in fact any undertaking whatsoever, was doomed to failure. The mildest resistance, even an appeal to a court of law, would have brought confiscation or, perhaps, imprisonment in its train. A Russian "citizen" has no chance of seeing justice done unless a combination of really exceptional circumstances reveals a particularly scandalous situation which is of sufficient interest to some prominent Communist official to cause him to give it the necessary publicity. But cases in which attempts are made to protect the oppressed peasant are very few and far between in comparison with the untold number of unjust and irregular practices which are crushing the life out of him. "Illegal taxes continue to be levied"; "much has been said and written concerning the extraordinarily large number of duties and taxes levied upon the country districts"; "certainly, at the present moment, they are not so numerous as they have been during the last few years, but the evil is still a long way from being entirely eradicated" ("Pravda", March 3rd 1926). Official declarations in this strain have appeared repeatedly in the Press, condemning the illegal impositions which have been added to legal taxes, and Rykov himself was particularly prominent in this connection; but these pronouncements have had no effect. Circulars were despatched from the centre to the surrounding districts, but they were submerged beneath thousands of other circulars to which no attention was ever paid, and which could not even be read.

The method of extorting supplies from the peasants by the means of forced loans has become a matter of everyday occurrence, in spite of official condemnation no less frequent. It is the same in the towns as in the country districts: the "citizen" is not free to refuse to subscribe. Workmen and employees often find that their subscriptions, of which the amount has been fixed without their knowledge by the Communist officials, are deducted from their pay. An official list of subscribers (all entirely "voluntary") is drawn up by Soviet officials accustomed to fiscal methods and to the assessment of individual means, and it is left to them to determine how many shares are to be purchased by each peasant according to the number of which they have been ordered to dispose. A special loan, or "corn loan" as it is called, drawn up in terms of pouds of rye, was issued some years ago; it was payable and redeemable in kind or in money, and the vouchers were accepted in settlement of taxes due. But as its operation was governed by special circumstances and could not be renewed to advantage, peasants are now obliged to take up their share in these so-called agricultural and "industrial development" loans. To offer resistance to this system of "voluntary obligatory" subscriptions would be to risk denunciation as an enemy of the Revolution and to lay oneself open to reprisals which were well worth avoiding. "It must be said that in many cases [*sic*] the methods permitted in the floating of the loan are only calculated to destroy the confidence of the peasant masses in State credit. It cannot be too often repeated that confidence can only be restored by persuasive measures and by the establishment of the principle of voluntary subscription" ("Izvestia", April 25th 1928). This paper took up the difficult task of saying enough without revealing too much, and that is the reason for these euphemistic expressions of which the purport is really perfectly clear. In the same issue appeared some significant reports concerning the methods employed at that time of obtaining subscriptions to the loan; in the Uralsk, a local executive committee *summoned* the inhabitants from twenty-five miles round and suggested that they should buy debenture shares. Was it possible to decline the proposals of those who had the power to summon them? Near Kherson, the peasants tried to get out of paying big subscriptions by asking for vouchers worth 5 to 10 roubles (4s. 2d. to 8s. 4d.), but the official "offered" them those worth 50, 80, and 100 roubles (41s. 8d., 66s. 8d., and 83s. 4d.); if the peasants declared that they could not afford to buy them, the representative of the "dictatorship of the proletariat" drew up information against them and referred the matter to the tribunal so that their goods might be confiscated. The Soviet delegate in the Stavropol district received debentures worth 800 roubles which he himself allotted to various groups of peasants and cultivators. Even the "batraki" were imposed upon without being in any way consulted; when the time came for the distribution of flour to the poor, the "batraki" were summoned and ordered to make their payment for shares within three days, otherwise they would have no flour, which was, practically speaking, tantamount to threatening them with death. In the Uralsk, a delegate declared that he had to choose between instituting proceedings to recover losses on his investment or being prosecuted for refusing to subscribe to these forced loans, and of the two the latter course was preferable. There is an endless variety of abuses of this sort which would, if such a thing were allowed, fill ten columns in the "Izvestia's" daily issue.

Burdened with shares which they did not want and spurred on by necessity, bond-holders in town and country alike endeavoured to get rid of their holdings, either by re-selling them at a great loss or by using them to pay their debts or taxes. The State was then threatened with having to "call in" the bonds, to use the expression employed on stock exchanges when companies buy back their stock in order to prevent a general collapse of the market-rate. Fresh pressure had to be brought to bear on those who held back and the Press set in motion so that the slightest inclination to sell the bonds might be interpreted as an act hostile to the Revolution. Even stricter measures were applied in towns and factories where the disposition of labour organisation favoured their enforcement: the general councils of Soviet institutions and industrial concerns passed resolutions (or rather accepted the motions dictated by the Communist nucleus and district officials) enjoining all shareholders to put their vouchers in the safe keeping of the banks in order to escape the temptation to dispose of them. In the country this idea was quite impracticable.

For some years now a new category, consisting of workmen and daily labourers employed on the "sovkoszy" (Soviet estates), has been in the process of formation. These estates are intended to serve as models of agricultural development and are to be imitated throughout the length and breadth of Russia, taking the place of the old individual, or family cultivated, farms. With regard to the treatment of proletarians on these estates, Antselovich, a Union official who was forced upon the Agricultural Workers' Union, stated that "they are suffocating from want of air in narrow, dirty barracks, where refectories and co-operatives do not exist. Complete chaos reigns on the estates, technical skill is of a very low order, and production very poor; wages are not up to the pre-war level and are only paid out once in six months" ("Trud", May 26th 1927). "Our accommodation is worse than a prosperous peasant's stables", declared a delegate at the Agricultural Workers' Congress ("Trud", December 6th 1928). On a "sovkoszy" in the Crimea, workmen engaged in winnowing are shut up for a whole day in a barn and their food is handed in to them; they even have to use a pail, which is also passed in to them, as a makeshift closet ("Trud", March 23rd 1929). Some "sovkoszy" women labourers in the province of Poltava, unable to obtain payment of their wages, crowded round the pay-office; a mounted militiaman charged and dispersed them. Two days later another crowd assembled and the militia, once again summoned, drove them away, arrested several, and threatened them with their weapons. The director was prosecuted, but as the "Trud" said, "there are plenty more of these mischievous people about". ("Trud", August 16th 1929). It is worth noticing that the Communists are in a very great minority on these Soviet estates, which are models of future collectivist organisations. They prefer to remain "seredniaki", or even "kulaki", to the doubtful honour of being encumbered with Soviet agricultural methods, or of serving as the pioneers of new development schemes. There are even very few Communists on the "kolkoz" (collectivist farms) which have been established under the ægis of the State; only 7,200 of the 100,000 agricultural members belonging to the Party were working on the "kolkoz" at the beginning of 1928 ("Pravda", November 9th 1928).

It would be a grave omission from a chapter dealing with the condition of poor country workers to withhold any reference to the frequent abuse of power by the local authorities, which results in extortionate, if not criminal, practices. The point is that these are not isolated cases of petty oppression, but indications of a widespread evil engendered by the vestiges of peasant barbarism and favoured by the political régime. The Soviet is not the creation of the pseudo-electors, but a "machine" which has been forced upon them, a fact of which even official evidence gives conclusive proof. The number of office-holders in the Soviet is limited to a president, one or two secretaries, a few officials or departmental chiefs, according to the size of the commune and of its population. In certain cases the men who occupy such positions are perhaps honest, but incapable muddlers; in others they are only seekers after personal gain who make a pretence of being true Communists and loyal supporters of the Soviet cause in order to cover their selfish deeds. These innumerable petty usurpers are able to indulge safely in all kinds of dishonourable practices, unless the peasants of the district happen to be intelligent enough to obtain the intervention of the authorities or can find some shrewd "selcor" (country correspondent) who will report their oppressors' misdeeds to the newspapers. But in the back-of-beyond, in the "gluchi" (depths), as it is called, of the Russian country districts, it is something of a luxury to find a "selcor" or a peasant of the progressive type: besides, it is easy to corrupt the one and get rid of the other. In short, during the last four years the unbroken succession of scandals of varying magnitude has revealed the defects in the Soviet governmental machine: theft, peculation, extortion, tyranny, the persecution of the helpless, debauchery, and sometimes even murder—this has been the record of the Soviet rule. Whenever the lower grades of the bureaucratic mass were thoroughly purged, village tyrants were unmasked in their hundreds and thousands and brought before the tribunals.

The details of a typical case are given below. But in

important towns also, similar incidents occurred of incalculable significance; so great a commotion did they cause that they deserve even more attention than parallel cases in the country. Weak excuses were offered for the scandalous régime in remote rural districts, but nothing could justify a state of affairs which permitted dishonest administrative methods, at least in towns where the wheels of the Soviet governmental machine revolve one upon another; where innumerable organisations rival each other in complicity or in shortsightedness, and where proletarians live in great numbers and, though supposed to play their part in the dictatorship, silently endure corruption, tyranny, and the practical jokes of their rulers—a situation which has no parallel in any countries, as distinct from colonies, organised on the Capitalist system. The Smolensk affair, which is the best known of all, is narrated more conveniently in a later chapter, but in the meantime it will be well worth while to see what occurred at Kherson.

This town is not a little isolated place in the steppes of Central Asia; it is something more than that as it has a population of 100,000 souls and is near Odessa. The attention of Sosnovsky, the journalist, was drawn to certain statements in which charges were preferred against officials in the Soviet administration. He thereupon published an article which resulted in an inquiry being held, and this led to the arrest of sixteen local chiefs and their officials, among whom were several Communists; one of them was even a member of the order of the Red Flag. For some years past these men had been terrorising the district, and no one had dared to report their rascality for fear of paying too high a price for their daring. The Commission of Inquiry promised that all complaints would be granted a secret hearing, and in consequence people stampeded towards the building where the case was to be heard, and a queue had to be formed outside. Chlikhter, the People's Commissary, who was president of the Commission, declared: "*It would be a mistake to imagine that this state of affairs is in any way exceptional owing to its special character and the great number of abuses that had been revealed; in this case, thanks to a whole series of reasons, our social maladies have been revealed more clearly than ever before.*" Nothing could be clearer than this, and no further examples need be given. One of the accused, the chief official, had been appropriating enormous sums, organising debaucheries, forcing militiamen to amuse him by dancing, and persecuting those who denounced him in the Kherson newspapers. As a member of the Winnowing (!) Commission appointed by the Soviet Government, he had obliged his female collaborators to become his mistresses under threat of dismissal. By his orders, police officers and officials outraged women and stole quantities of wine—escapades in which he played a prominent part himself. Yet he was called a "Communist". The second was also a member of the Party, an accomplice of the first and chief of the militia; he had misappropriated public funds, forged official documents, silenced the protests of his conscientious militiamen, killed persons who had been arrested, and concealed the thefts committed by his mistresses. The third, another member of the Party, had been an accomplice of the first two. The fourth stole and seduced. The fifth—a Party man and decorated with the Red Flag—had committed the same crimes; he arrested peasants for no reason whatsoever. All of them robbed the official funds, ransomed the inhabitants, outraged women, forged accounts, and wallowed in the filthiest debaucheries ("Pravda", June 5th and 10th 1925). It is not the writer, but the People's Commissary conducting the inquiry who declares, "*This is not an exceptional case.*" The Central

Committee of the Communist Party in the Ukraine supported this statement in a long resolution, in which they emphasised the *demonstrative* character of the affair and declared that "the Kherson case has not settled the question of the Party's struggle for legality in revolutionary methods; the chief features of the Kherson affair have been found in other cases of abuse which were afterwards discovered" (Tultchino, Kiev militia, and others) ("Pravda", September 24th 1925).

A few weeks earlier the Revisionary Court, in the small Caucasian Republic of Nakhichevan, ordered the arrest of the People's Commissaries of the Interior, of Agriculture, of Finance, and of Justice; the President of the Co-operatives and of the Court; the People's Assistant Commissary for Education, and the President of the Syndicates were also taken into custody. There were in all twenty-five important officials arrested on charges of oppression, embezzlement, extortion, and despotic rule, etc. Communism played an important part in the country. "The arrests have created a very favourable impression on the people and they cannot hide their satisfaction" ("Pravda", April 9th, 10th, and 11th 1925). And this makes one wonder how "all these Commissaries of the People" came to be elected. . . . A few weeks later a regular gang, which for two years had been terrorising the district, was thrown into prison. Among those arrested were the President of the Soviet, a former agent of the Ogpu, the chief of the militia, the judge, and the Committee secretary of the Communist Party, etc. "There were no bounds to the fear in which this gang was held and to the public mistrust of the Soviet power." A certain witness, Ch., declared on his way to the inquiry: "Let them cut my throat, but I will not tell the truth. The 'selcor' Moroz has put an end to this shameful silence and widespread fear." Moroz, who was an intelligent youth, had come quite by chance to his wife's native district; there he discovered what was going on and, not without great difficulty and at the risk of his life, sounded the alarm at Odessa. The gang in question had, to put it quite simply, made an armed attack upon the peasants, murdering them and plundering and burning their farms. "The people were firmly convinced that the militia was no more to be trusted than the robbers themselves, and that in consequence all the authorities were untrustworthy" ("Pravda", July 16th 1925).

Near Vinnitza, the ex-President of the Executive Committee, his deputy, the secretary of the Party Committee, the chief of the militia, and "a number of local government officials", all had to be arrested. They were charged with various abuses, as, for example, with having imprisoned fifteen peasants who asked for a delay in the payment of their taxes, as well as the "selcor" (reporter) who had communicated the facts, etc., to his paper ("Pravda", May 12th 1925). The conduct of all these departmental officials at Vinnitza is not an unprecedented occurrence; similar cases are to be found in almost every district. But it is seldom that anyone manages successfully to bring the facts to the notice of authorities who are continually bombarded with complaints, demands, and protests. These accumulate in pigeon-holes, ledgers, and drawers, and are doomed to oblivion. The Vinnitza affair has assumed the aspect of a commonplace event in Soviet life. Three years later the "Izvestia" reported that the Soviet officials in a district near Semipalatinsk had seized for their own benefit tens of thousands of cattle and had made wholesale arrests among the peasants, many of whom started to flee across the Chinese frontier. The centre was informed of this and a Commission of Inquiry was despatched to the district. As a result of this, 140 prisoners were set at liberty and the cattle restored to their rightful owners. But the central authorities are not always able to intervene and can only make amends for acts of injustice in a very limited number of cases.

The Ukrainian People's Commissary had every reason to emphasise the typical character of these incidents; their gravity and frequence have revealed the thoroughly corrupt state of all Soviet organisations. The scandals of the following years have strengthened this point of view, demonstrating their widespread character in a way that even the bitterest enemies of the system would hardly have dared to think possible. But apart from these overt acts of injustice that have, by their violence, aroused antagonism on all hands, there are innumerable cases in which peasants are daily subjected to persecution, petty annoyance, and to mean oppression, and to such an extent that all classes in the country have become exasperated by this accumulation of wrongs. A short-sighted, imprudently conducted policy may easily cause social groups with divergent interests to unite in resisting the demands which the State makes upon them. That is what occurred when the authorities resorted to brutal methods in order to obtain corn. Though in principle directed against the big peasant monopolists, these aggressive measures made way for a struggle between the Soviet administration and peasants who were suspected of holding back corn. The uncertain reaction from these attacks caused the great majority of peasants to combine against the Soviet power. Under these conditions the poorer classes were not the last to take part in the struggle: they were bound, in their misery, to fall into the clutches of the "kulaki", who knew full well how to make them their innocent tools. In addition to the passive resistance offered in the form of curtailed sowing and in the concealment of corn supplies, during the last few years there have been threatenings of rebellion and active, sporadic outbursts, resembling guerrilla warfare. During this period many government agents, real or suspected, perished, stabbed from behind, and Soviet crops were burnt in the general commotion. In 1928 there were approximately 24,000 anti-Communist outrages (arson and armed attacks), according to the "Izvestia" of December 8th 1928. The total for 1929 has not yet been published, but hardly a day goes by without some mention in the newspapers of these manifestations of discontent. The chiefs of the U.S.S.R. attribute all these disorders to revengeful "kulaki" who, they say, are fighting against the "progress of Socialism". But would this for a moment convince anyone that one infinitely small class, scattered throughout a vast land and swamped by masses of other human beings, could engage in an unrelenting struggle (which nothing seemed to render propitious) unless the great stricken multitudes gave their tacit consent to it and took an active part themselves?

CHAPTER V

THE POWERS OF DARKNESS

The powers of darkness—The illiterate mass—Relapses into illiteracy —Half the children uneducated—Soviet schools—School-books, etc.—Teachers' lives—Proletarian students—Standard of teaching—Pre- and post-school instruction—Clubs and "Red corners"—Vestiges of barbarism in the provinces—Religious sects—Increase in alcoholism—The vodka deluge—The drink bill—Workwomen's lives—Anti-Semitism.

The peoples of Russia are as miserably endowed with culture as they are with worldly goods. The great majority of the 150,000,000 inhabitants are still entirely illiterate, and vast numbers are in hardly better case. In recent official statements this depressing fact has been freely admitted. Soviet statistics give the striking figure of 60·4 as the percentage for illiterates in the population as a whole ("Izvestia", July 11th 1929). But in the remaining 40 per cent. there is a large proportion of illiterates who are counted as having been "discharged", but who in reality have once more relapsed into illiteracy. "As he has absolutely nothing to read and is even obliged to give back his lesson-book, the peasant can only just scrawl his name after a year's study, and, twelve months later, has completely forgotten all he ever knew" (The "Rabochaya Gazette", June 24th 1926). This remark was made about the Ukraine, but it holds good for any other part of Russia. The number of those who "relapse" in this way has not been verified, but all the evidence goes to prove that they form a large majority in the category of former illiterates who are now deemed to be "educated" persons. Then among the 40 per cent. in question there are the "malogramotni", who can only just spell out the alphabet, read words in big letters on signboards, or write their names with great difficulty.

This class cannot, however, write a letter or read a newspaper. Something must now be said of the quality of the instruction received by the remainder under the Soviet system.

In certain districts of the Union sometimes 90 per cent. are illiterate, according to the "Izvestia". The entire Soviet Press, in fact, keeps repeating, as a kind of password, Lenin's pronouncement to the effect that Socialism cannot be established without the organised instruction of the masses. Even if Lenin had himself forgotten to make this statement, it would, nevertheless, have been attributed to him. The decision taken to suppress illiteracy before the tenth anniversary of the October Revolution, like so many million others, has never been carried out. On the eve of the twelfth anniversary, all the high-sounding declarations made on former occasions had to be withdrawn, and the authorities were forced to admit that the problem was still unsolved. After claiming that "illiteracy had been stabilised" ("Pravda", September 2nd 1928), the Bolsheviks are now obliged to recognise that the tide of ignorance has advanced under their dictatorship.

Only those who have not troubled to examine the evidence emanating from Soviet sources will be in any way astonished at this situation. For alongside the loud, hollow-sounding, deceitful statements that have appeared in the newspapers concerning the so-called cultural revolution, the Communist Press has been obliged to publish the real facts and figures—for internal use only. "At the present time 65 per cent. of the rural populations are illiterate. If a new system of life is to be introduced, first above everything, ignorance must be swept away" ("Pravda", June 23rd 1925). "The complete suppression of illiteracy will only be effected by a system of general education by which 100 per cent. of the children receive instruction in elementary schools." This was the conclusion reached by Lunacharsky, the People's Commissary for the Suppression of Illiteracy ("Pravda", September 22nd 1925). "Our elementary schools only provide instruction for half of the children" (The "Rabochaya Gazette", June 10th 1926). "Relapses into illiteracy, forgetfulness of knowledge already acquired, at the present moment greatly exceed the pre-war level" (The "Rabochaya Gazette", June 15th 1926). Here, at any rate, is a pre-war level greatly exceeded! After a few months 60 to 70 per cent. of the women forget almost all they had ever learnt (*idem*). The "Crocodile", a Communist paper, famous for its sarcasm, depicted "the suppression of ignorance" as a snail (Number 28, July 1926). "We have ourselves organised an army of illiterates by granting insufficient subsidies for education, and we are now starting to tear our hair to find ways and means of instructing them" ("Pravda", September 25th 1926). "Fresh instruction must be given to a great number of illiterates who have already had some teaching but have now forgotten the essentials of what they have learnt" (The "Rabochaya Gazette", October 9th 1926). "The percentage of children who have not been admitted into the schools, despite the efforts of their parents, is increasing. There are cases in which the teacher has three groups of pupils in the same class, making a total of one hundred children in all. Under these conditions, school-work becomes a kind of convict-labour and gives very poor results. The principal defect in our teaching system is the amount of instruction given to children in their fourth school year; it is of an illusory nature, not only because there are no fourth-year pupils in certain districts, but because approximately 70 per cent. of the poorest peasants' children do not even reach their third year: and this is a most distressing fact." In 1913, 30 roubles in modern currency (20s.) was the expenditure *per annum* on every pupil, and now the amount is given as 16 to 18 roubles (12s. 4d. to 12s. 6d.), while in New York the corresponding figure is 34 dollars, and in London 104s. A teacher only receives two-thirds of a workman's average wage, hardly more than half the miserable pittance he earned in Tsarist times. This statement occurred in an interminable, inconsistent, complicated, *optimistic* article, written by Lunacharsky, quite in his usual style ("Pravda", September 29th 1926). It must be pointed out that the figures for London and New York show the expenditure per head on all children, while in the U.S.S.R. they only refer to the grants per head to scholars alone, or approximately half the children. (Further, the Russian figures must be taken as being very much higher than their real value, for public funds are being continually squandered and embezzled, as will be shown later.) "There is an insufficient number of schools, of materials, as well as of teachers, whose salaries are quite inadequate. The children are short of clothes and shoes; their food is bad and they leave school before their time is up. Sometimes one teacher has to instruct a class containing 120 to 160 pupils. There are fewer schools than in Tsarist times and 30 per cent. more scholars. Teachers are burdened with social obligations outside their ordinary work and are deprived of their most elementary rights" ("Trud", November 13th 1926). "Free education only exists on paper, and schools are kept up on the funds provided by frequent deductions from the wages of workmen, who contribute a half or even three-quarters of the necessary money" ("Trud", May 22nd 1927). "After a year or two, sometimes even after a few months, an illiterate person forgets what he has learnt in a three months' course at the instruction centre" ("Trud", September 29th 1927). "In the Uralsk, no accommodation can be found for 70 per cent. of the children in the schools, and the situation is more or less the same in all industrial centres. This shortage of school premises makes it imperative to work the class-teaching in shifts. School-buildings are small, dark, and cold; three-quarters of them require repairs. A great number of children are obliged to sit on the ground, for there are no benches. The lighting of these school-rooms is absurdly inadequate; disease is rife among these badly clothed, badly fed children" ("Trud", August 9th 1928). "Fifteen million children do not benefit from any instruction" ("Pravda of Youth", July 30th 1929).

The dilapidated state of these schools and the wretched conditions under which children and teachers are condemned to work are great handicaps to progress. In the province of Stalingrad, 447 out of 988 schools needed repair. There were only 520 teachers and only half the children could gain admittance to the schools, which even then contained twice their proper number (The "Rabochaya Gazette", June 19th 1926). It was the same, or even worse, in nearly every district. In the province of Samara there was no firewood, and teachers had to go daily and ask for logs from the local Soviet. In the province of Voronezh the wood intended for the schools was kept sixty-two miles away, and as there was no means of transporting it the children were nearly frozen. Broken windows, terrible cold, a scarcity of benches, and children sitting on the ground in the depths of winter—these were the conditions nearly everywhere, even close to Moscow ("Pravda", February 26th 1927). But still more dismal conditions were to be revealed. Not only was the number of schools insufficient, but those that did exist were in an indescribable condition. In some cases sheds, where sometimes the temperature was as low as two degrees below zero, were used as classrooms; in others, old dilapidated barracks, quite unsafe for the purpose, were employed as school premises. In the provinces of Vladimir, Penza, Yaroslavl, Tambov, in the Uralsk and in the Donetz, at Ivanovo-Vosnesensk, and at Sverdlovsk, it was the same. Generally speaking, children had to be divided up into three groups, working in relays, which made it quite impossible to clean or ventilate the rooms, and even then millions of children were still without a school. Workmen found themselves obliged to leave the factories where they were employed because their children could not obtain instruction in the local schools ("Trud", April 10th 1927). In Moscow, nine-tenths of the scholars had their lessons in relays; in workmen's districts there were three shifts a day ("Vechernyaya Moskva", June 22nd 1928). At Sormovo there were elementary schools in basements, and at Chakhty in sheds, where the air-space was 44 instead of the regulation 230 cubic feet.

The insufficiency or complete lack of school supplies was on a par with the condition of the buildings themselves. Exorbitant prices were charged for the few products manufactured in Soviet factories. In the province of Gomel, an *Outlines of Russian History* cost three pouds (1¾ bushels) of rye; in the Saratov province there were only 25 grammars and 7 other books among 45 children. In a canton of that district, among 1,600 pupils, there were 707 arithmetic books written by 23 different authors and published in the majority of cases before the Revolution. A pencil cost 10 and an exercise-book 6 pouds (3½ bushels) of rye. The children used to write on the tables, floor, and walls; 40 per cent. of the schools were so dilapidated that they could not be used. In winter, there was a shortage of coal and "tulupe", "valenti", and bonnets had to be worn by the pupils and their teachers—if they possessed them. Pedagogic reviews and all political literature were luxuries unobtainable by the teacher ("Pravda", August 22nd 1924). The suppression of illiteracy in the country was being checked owing to the shortage of spelling-books. "The Special Commission has given an order for these books to be supplied to the country districts"; "the Commission is appealing to all the workmen", etc. ("Pravda", December 25th 1924). The results of this method of distributing supplies may well be imagined. . . . "Incapable of providing illiterates and children with a miserable spelling-book, the State relied on the good will of the unemployed or workmen earning a famine wage and with a living-space of 'coffin dimensions' in which to sleep. There were no spelling-books, but millions of unwanted, illegible books were printed." On January 1st 1926, in Moscow and Leningrad alone, there were 65 million unsaleable books, representing a "value" of 12 million roubles (£500,000) ("Trud", April 10th 1926). Rykov reported that school-books were written for a type of child which exists nowhere on this earth and were made from an unmentionable substance (The "Evening Krasnaya Gazette", May 11th 1928). "Bookshops and depots are crammed with books, but popular works are unobtainable by country people, besides being exorbitantly dear" ("Trud", July 1st 1926). Text-books and other teaching materials were almost good for nothing at all (The "Rabochaya Gazette", October 9th 1926). Here is an example of the worth of Soviet products: A multiplication table published at Odessa contained the illuminating statement that 4 times 8 are 30, 4 times 9 are 26, etc. ("Pravda", October 14th 1926). "Everyone is clamouring for school-books, of which there is a shortage everywhere; in these conditions no cultural development is possible" ("Izvestia", October 4th 1928). "Only one-quarter of the books published by the State are legible and they are very dear, being quite beyond the reach of most would-be purchasers" ("Pravda," November 16th 1928). "The school year has begun and the first obstacle which faces pupils is the shortage of exercise-books. Children and their parents spend days on end searching for these books in shops and co-operatives, etc." (Leningrad "Pravda", September 6th 1929). In Moscow there was the same scarcity, and it was worse in the provinces.

The condition of Soviet teachers has already been outlined, but a more accurate account of their life and work must now be given. Until the first Teachers' Congress met in 1925 they were, as intellectuals and "therefore" as agents of Capitalism, deprived of all rights of citizenship. But in the Congress held in the eighth year after the Revolution they became—on paper—electors and eligible for election. It is not difficult to picture the type of "intellectual" as represented, for instance, by schoolmasters in the Uralsk and in the Caucasus, in the tundra and on the steppes, those who can only just read, write, and perform the four simplest operations in arithmetic. In 1925 teachers were permitted for the first time to hold a Congress (though in reality it was the authorities who summoned it), and from that time onwards their condition has to a certain extent improved. Rykov told the Congress that "their salaries had risen from 6 roubles 33 copecks (5s. 3d.) in October 1922 to 28 roubles (23s. 4d.) in 1925; it was quite true that this was entirely insufficient and that it would have to be augmented as much as was found possible and as far as the means at the disposal of the authorities allowed" ("Pravda", January 16th 1925). There were cases, however, of delays of months in the payment of salaries. Teachers were therefore earning 4s. to 8s. a month up to 1924—when they were paid at all. Their dreadful misery has been the theme of many speeches; Bukharin, in particular, reported to the 1924

Congress that teachers were reduced to begging in the streets. Lunacharsky had on a former occasion called attention to their shocking poverty, the many diseases from which they were suffering, the high mortality among them, and to the life of prostitution which women teachers were often forced to lead. Since the Congress of 1925 the condition of teachers has shown no change. On June 27th 1925 the "Pravda" gave details of a case which was described as being a *characteristic*, and not an exceptional, occurrence. Although a female teacher in the province of Samara was literally starving, she had been unable to obtain payment of her salary (18 roubles a month, or 15s.), which was long overdue. Thus prevented from any longer obtaining milk on credit, she had not sufficient strength left to resume her work. The writer of this article mentioned that there were teachers who were living "on the charity of peasants", and, "harassed by hunger", were leaving their posts. It must be noted that the monthly salary in June 1925 was 18 roubles 50 copecks (15s. 5d.), whereas Rykov officially quoted it as being 28 roubles (23s. 4d.) in January. This method of exaggerating the value of the average wage, which has been analysed in an earlier chapter, is of very common occurrence. An inquiry was instituted in February 1926 into the teachers' financial condition, and an examination of eighty-eight separate cases revealed that the average monthly earnings were 37 roubles (30s. 10d.), of which 68 per cent. came from the professional salary, the rest being profits from farming and money earned by the family. In order to receive payment of his salary the teacher was obliged to go six miles on foot, or to spend two or three roubles on the hire of a horse ("Pravda", March 25th 1926). Salaries amounting to one thousand million roubles (£41,666,666) had not been paid by March 1926. Teachers had not been paid since September, and they had to teach in unheated rooms without any school-books ("Trud", March 25th 1926). Among the Kirghiz, teachers were starving; from October 1st 1925 to February 1926 they had received only two monthly payments of 26 roubles (21s. 8d.) ("Pravda", March 28th 1926). "The teacher in our midst must be raised to a level in bourgeois society which he has never before reached, nor, perhaps, will be ever able to reach." The truth of this statement needs no proof. After quoting Lenin's words, "Pravda" once more denounced the delays in payment of salaries. Teachers were literally suffering from hunger and were lacking both boots and clothing ("Pravda", May 18th 1926). There was a shortage of teachers, but 82,000 were unemployed—surely a sign of excellent organisation! ("Pravda", March 16th 1927). The teaching profession was subjected to annoyances of every kind from the local Soviet authorities. In one place teachers were forbidden to dance the mazurka; in another, women teachers were forbidden to marry, so that they should not bear children and have to be granted leave in consequence ("Trud", March 17th 1927). Women teachers were persecuted to such an extent by Soviet officials that a series of cases of suicide followed ("Trud", December 29th 1928).

The condition of proletarian students is no better. In spite of some improvement their lot was, in 1925, "extraordinarily hard"; what, then, could have been their original condition? A medical inspection disclosed that a large percentage of students were ill and completely exhausted through overwork and under-feeding. They held bursaries worth from 8 roubles 50 copecks to 20 roubles (7s. 1d. to 16s. 8d.) a month as a general rule, but not all of them received assistance in this way ("Pravda", July 31st 1925). Lunacharsky wrote: "The efforts made by us to succour the students are not only insufficient in the extreme, but directly threaten their well-being." The student's minimum monthly allowance, exclusive of his many subscriptions and of what he spent on clothing, personal and bed linen, boots, and books, should have been 27 roubles (22s. 6d.), but the value of the average bursary was not more than 23 roubles (19s. 2d.). Medical examination of 198 students in the Institute of Technology revealed that only two were not ill; in other establishments only two or three were found to be in good health. Students suffered from overcrowding and under-nourishment (The "Krasnaya Gazette", March 18th 1926). Statements of this kind were common currency. "The great majority of students live in the most abject misery; their living-space is, on an average, 4 to 6 square archines (21 to 32 square feet)—when they manage to find any lodging at all. Hostels are full and many cannot gain admittance. Students are burdened with public duties which take up much of the time that ought to be devoted to study. They take posts as night-watchmen, porters, coal-heavers, road-sweepers in order to gain their daily bread. What real cultural progress can they make under these conditions?" ("Trud", September 9th 1926). "In towns in the Ukraine, only 30 per cent. can be certain of accommodation. At Odessa, some sleep in the corridors and water-closets of communal dwellings, others in the street, stations, and on the platforms" ("Trud", October 9th 1926). At Moscow "the students live in a filthy, crowded condition, in some cases almost in the street". "So dismal is this spectacle of student life that it calls for immediate intervention on the part of all State educational organisations. Students are fainting for want of food, their lodgings are cold, disgustingly dirty, and overrun with vermin, making any study out of the question. Some have to travel as much as twelve miles a day to the Agricultural Institute; many have no mattresses and sleep on the ground. Without a proper roof over their heads, 1,500 of them spend their nights in the stations and on the streets. In the end, these wretches become sodden with drink and generally demoralised" ("Pravda of Youth", October 23rd 1927). "At Leningrad 3,000 students have no lodgings" (The "Evening Krasnaya Gazette", November 26th 1927). "Young healthy students become worn-out old men within three years; many workmen who have been sent to the universities give up their studies on finding that it is physically impossible to eke out an existence; 90 per cent. of students take up employment which, exclusive of the time they give to study, gives them fourteen hours' labour a day in their third year. The standard of their intellectual work is naturally affected by this system and some spend ten years on a course which ordinarily lasts five. In one big technical school alone at Moscow 4,000 workmen, or sons of workmen, prematurely abandoned their studies" ("Pravda of Youth", July 4th 1928). "Students attending technical night-schools are workmen till four o'clock in the afternoon, then students from six till ten at night; they work fourteen to sixteen hours a day and are worn out by their labours; they have not sufficient time for sleep or for study, and they fall ill before they have been able to assimilate any knowledge" ("Ekonomicheskaya Zhizn", May 21st 1929). "The students in the Uralsk Agricultural Institute live in a damp basement, eternally cold and dirty—a veritable tomb. From among its 136 occupants, 102 are seriously ill and four have died within a year; for six years this basement has been declared unfit for habitation" ("Pravda of Youth", June 20th 1929). At Leningrad, "owing to the scarcity of lodgings and dormitories, there are some students who sleep in lecture-rooms and amphitheatres, and others find shelter in the stations, the porches of houses, and in night shelters" (The "Krasnaya Gazette", October 9th 1929).

The standard of learning among the rising generation is on a par with the condition of the school and university buildings, and teaching methods and opportunities for study are equally unsatisfactory. There are frequent allusions in the Press to the examinations, which reveal in its true light the intrinsic value of knowledge acquired by candidates. After five years at school one student included Africa in the Soviet Union: another described the eye as being part of the brain; several did not know the date of the October Revolution, although they continually referred to it; all of them thought that the main aim of Trades Union workmen was to obtain free railway passes for the supporters of their organisation (The "Rabochaya Gazette", March 17th 1926). After four years' study children could neither read nor write, nor did they know the most elementary rules of arithmetic. There was a shortage of books and a need for quiet, ordered methods. Entrance candidates for the great schools were lamentably ignorant ("Narodnoe Prosvyestcheniye", January 1926). The general standard of learning in secondary classes was falling perceptibly; only 11 to 25 per cent. of adult candidates successfully passed their entrance examinations. The majority of students had not heard of Pushkin, Ostrovsky, Saltykov, Uspensky, Tourgueniev, or Tolstoy. One candidate was under the impression that China and Persia were included in the Soviet Union ("Izvestia", November 3rd 1926). The following answers were given to simple political questions at a proletarian students' Congress: Ford was described as the Dictator of Spain, Hindenburg as the President of the Internationale, Aristide Briand as Emperor of America ("Trud", March 29th 1929). Many children were half illiterate when they left school

"(Pravda of Youth", May 10th 1929). Most of the pupils from high-grade schools were ploughed in their examinations. At Moscow, 250 out of 700 candidates who applied for posts as Government engineers failed at the start in the written paper on mathematics. The examiners at the School of Mines stated that if they had required the usual standard of knowledge asked of candidates, 90 per cent. of the candidates would have failed to pass (The "Krasnaya Gazette", August 13th 1929). Nowadays a rapid glance through any newspaper, even the so-called reliable Soviet publications, reveals how vertical has been the fall in the general standard of culture.

Infant and continuation schools are even worse organised than the schools themselves. Although reports have gone abroad to every country and in every language concerning the wonders of crêches and children's gardens, etc., in Russia, the brutal truth must be admitted. "Millions of workmen's children of pre-school age are growing up uncared for and totally deprived of the necessary teaching. The organisation of infant schools is carried out on a very limited scale and provides for only 58 per cent. of Russian children. The little creatures are either left to themselves to grow up in the gutter, or, in cases where their parents look after them, do not usually benefit from supervision, but, on the contrary, are entirely corrupted by it" ("Trud", July 10th 1929). In other words, very few receive any attention at all. This remarkable figure of 58 per cent. has appeared in other newspapers. Clubs, "Red or Lenin corners" which are intended to encourage reading and study after the day's work is done are worthy of all other Soviet establishments. They are small and dirty, unprovided with sufficient books, or supplied with illegible ones; in an atmosphere thick with smoke and with the reek of alcohol, the members play cards, quarrel, and indulge in drunken debauchery. Reports of this kind frequently appear in the Press. But one feature of the clubs that newspapers do not describe is their decoration. Tinsel emblems, the portraits of the leaders, hollow-sounding texts, and formulæ printed on bills and strips of calico, all these adorn the walls—a useless and unsavoury method of ornament which not only means the squandering of precious copecks taken from the workers and of millions of roubles taken from the local public funds, but encourages an unhealthy predilection for stage-effect, at the same time strengthening the sad illusion that outward appearances alone matter. A Socialist club need not be fitted out as if it were the resort of uncivilised "blacks", but sufficient air-space, good artificial lighting and ventilation, tables and chairs, writing materials, papers to read, a well-filled, well-kept library, clean, well-lighted rooms where quiet is assured—these are the things that count. Moreover, a club should not be a sanctuary where workmen can come and worship before the picture of a leader, neither should it be shown to high officials and foreign visitors in order to deceive them into thinking that it is a hot-bed of culture.

In a "Red corner" at Baku there were no books at all, only a highly coloured portrait of Lenin costing 2,000 roubles (£64). This formed part of an "altar" where respect could be paid to the memory of the departed leader. "Like all our Red corners", this club was locked. "Factories compete with each other in squandering large sums on the purchase of red cloth, picture-frames, electric lamps for these "corners of the dead"; very rarely was it possible to study in these "Lenin corners" ("Pravda", April 3rd 1925). In one club umbrellas had always to be used as the building had no roof; once or twice a week there was a cinematograph entertainment, but the films were generally damaged and quite incomprehensible;

the club was always full of drunkards abusing each other and fighting ("Pravda", October 27th 1925). Yaroslavsky wrote in 1923 that hardly 15 per cent. of Union members belonged to workmen's clubs ("Pravda", August 22nd 1924). "There are still too many, rather than too few, of these clubs." "These dirty, dilapidated Lenin's corners, always situated a long way from workmen's lodgings, ornamented with tattered bills covering their walls, with draped busts of Lenin, and supplied with a few out-of-date books which lie about in the dust—they do not in any way answer the purpose for which they were intended" ("Zarya Vostoka", May 19th 1926). "Clubs are only a means of squandering money; conditions are chaotic in them, and this drives away the more serious-minded workmen. The infinitesimal subscriptions given by workers is the surest sign of their disapproval ("Trud", July 31st 1928). "The clubs become hotbeds of corruption and robbery"; the much-vaunted cultural activity only existed in theory: any self-respecting Communist did not go to the club ("Pravda", August 13th 1928). According to statistics, a huge advance has been made in culture—but still only on paper. In reality, nothing of the kind is apparent. At Tula, a big workers' centre, the clubs were extremely small. There was a hall which could only hold 180 out of the 14,000 workmen using the building. A big factory ran two clubs which were only large enough to provide for hardly one-tenth of the employees, exclusive of their families. "Red corners" were dirty, dark, and empty; if a visiting committee was expected, then only were they hurriedly supplied with newspapers, so as to give them a presentable appearance for a few hours. Nevertheless their upkeep cost a great deal of money ("Izvestia", May 30th 1929).

Libraries were likewise in a most unsatisfactory condition. Yakovleva, Deputy Commissary for Education, herself admitted that, as in the case of "children's homes", there had been a reduction in the number of libraries. She considered the figures for the cost of education to be "most alarming" ("Pravda", April 12th 1929). An official appeal, written in a rude military jargon that is almost untranslatable, contained the following statement: "On the library front [*sic*], our situation is entirely unsatisfactory. We are suffering grievously from the delay on the 'front of book-circulation' " ("Pravda", August 4th 1929). The most serious matter of all was the quality of the books distributed officially to the few existing libraries. No one would read them, and quite rightly so; they were collections of empty-sounding formulæ and stale, watered-down compositions which had been published years ago in newspapers and reviews, only to be printed and reprinted again and again as pamphlets, collections in book-form, as "chosen extracts", or "complete works". They were the work of politicians of no great moral worth or intellectual ability who, moreover, were always tearing each other's entirely valueless opinions to pieces in the course of their continual bickering. Everyone in Russia knows the worth of such literature, but no newspaper can voice the general opinion, for the Press is strictly controlled by the Secretariat of the Bolshevist Party, which has at its command the most rigorous censorship and the most active police system of any country in the world.

In the political programme drawn up after the October Revolution it was proposed to establish a system of general education; it was to be compulsory, free, embracing all subjects, and open to all classes of people. In the twelfth year after the inauguration of the new régime, it is none of these things. The pupils, children of workmen, labouring peasants, and employees, were to receive, free of charge, all the necessary school requisites, books, and one hot meal a day. Now, it is no longer worth even dreaming about such wonderful possibilities. The Soviet legend may well make a great deal of a few schools, children's gardens, and model clubs which have been constructed and kept open as show-places, but that will not exonerate the Party which monopolises all responsibility and power from having swelled the number of illiterates or of having lowered the intellectual standard of a great people. The recent sacrifice, as a scapegoat, of a man like Lunacharsky, who was suddenly dismissed from his post as People's Commissary for Education by a decree to which the Press gave as little prominence as possible, as if he were guilty of some shameful act—even his immolation does not get to the bottom of the matter. And after reading some of the articles that have recently appeared in the Soviet newspapers with headlines similar to the following: "A country organised on a Socialistic system must be a country all of whose inhabitants can read and write. In two years' time there must not be a single illiterate workman in the R.S.F.S.R." (Russia proper together with Siberia, but without the Ukraine, the Caucasus, and other federated republics) ("Pravda", August 31st 1929). One is in a position to realise how slow the authorities have been to gauge the true situation and how impossible it is to rely on the fulfilment of their promises, even more so because one knows only too well the kinds of methods employed in the U.S.S.R. since Lenin's death in the application of the best of resolutions, and the vast difference that in Russia exists between putting decisions on paper and finding ways and means to carry them into practice.

Therefore the level of ignorance found in the sixth part of the globe's surface is higher than the everlasting "pre-war standard". Statistics do not show how this affects the everyday life of the masses. The Western reader will be better able to understand the full significance of the Russian expression, "the powers of darkness", if he examines a few facts and incidents which are not fortuitous in character, but, on the contrary, reveal the true mentality of a very large majority of Russian peoples.

An inhabitant of a village in Podolia addressed a complaint to the President of the local Soviet that his wife had left him and had been "illegally" united to another husband. The President caused the woman and her new companion to appear before the village General Assembly, where she explained that she had resolved not to live any longer with her first husband who beat her, but intended to enter her second marriage in the official register. Thereupon the President, having had the unfortunate woman and her companion completely stripped of their clothes, caused them to be scourged with nettles by the Soviet members in full view of all the villagers. This incident was reported in "Pravda" by the editor, who treated it as a commonplace affair without being in the smallest degree shocked or indignant at the outrage. He also confined himself to making the most matter-of-fact statement concerning a similar occurrence at Saltykov-Chedrin.

In a country district, near Yaroslavl, a peasant woman was reputed to be a witch, though without rhyme or reason. One day another peasant had an attack of epilepsy at Mass, and no one knew how to look after her. But it so happened that this unfortunate creature, chancing to meet the "witch" on the way to church, had touched her neckerchief. From that the relation between cause and effect was quickly established. A crowd assembled and dragged the sick woman to the pseudo-witch and demanded that she should be cured forthwith. That poor innocent creature declared herself unable to effect a cure and pleaded to be left in peace. Her entreaties were unavailing. A curious procession was formed; on a "teliega" (a primitive cart), driven by two moujiks, reposed the sick woman, while the "witch", her neck in a slip-knot, was dragged behind, followed by the yelling inhabitants of three villages. The "witch" was first given a severe flogging with a "knout" and then with an iron chain until she fainted; she was next thrown into the river, only to be fished out again and, finally, thrown into a wood. Her torture lasted for six hours. "Not a single sane person was forthcoming to defend her" ("Pravda", May 24th 1925).

The following is a picture of the conditions prevailing in a felt boot-factory in the province of Nizhni-Novogorod: six hundred workmen were employed there, but only between September and July; for the rest of the year they worked in the fields. They formed an extremely religious community, and twice or three times a month, on the local feast-days of the Church, as well as the ordinary holidays, only one-third of them did any work. There was practically no system of cultural development. For five years a club had been in the process of construction, but it was not yet finished; 10 per cent. of the workmen subscribed for newspapers which, however, arrived very irregularly. Coarseness, obscenity, and drunkenness went everywhere unrestrained. The behaviour of *young people in no way differed from that of older folk;* on Sunday walks, youths used to fight each other . . . ("Pravda", June 7th 1925). This factory was certainly in a remote provincial district, but more than one case of this kind could be quoted.

This gives some idea of the human foundations of the U.S.S.R. But several rungs up the social ladder inherited from Tsarism, the intellectual standard is hardly superior. Sosnovsky narrated the following characteristic story: The rural tribunal of a canton or district ("volost"), which was called upon in 1922 to settle a dispute between two citizens arising out of the division of certain personal properties, gave judgment *in default* and promulgated its decision in which it first invoked the principles of Socialist justice and then enumerated the articles to be apportioned (chairs, a watch, ikons, etc.). It was decreed that the party found guilty of opposing the judgment would be *sentenced to death.* On June 10th 1925 the Agricultural Commission (!) of the Tver province confirmed this outrage against justice. Sosnovsky emphasised that this took place in 1925 and at Tver, an important town situated between the two capitals. The peasant who was thus threatened with death went to the offices of the "Tverskaya Pravda", where his anxieties were allayed ("Pravda", July 9th 1925). Though the account of this incident is given in narrative form it exposes in a singular manner the depth of the "darkness" overspreading the land.

In three villages of the Uralsk, near the town of Lyevsk, three hundred peasants were beaten in June 1928, though by whom and on what pretext the newspaper account did not reveal. It was reported that the "kulaki" had beaten certain of the "bedniaki" because they had kept the hedges in bad repair, allowing the cattle to brouse on each other's pasture—an explanation which was extremely suspicious in view of the fact that the "kulaki" are now, no matter what untoward event occurs, held to be responsible for it. But the fact remains that three hundred "votiak" peasants, among whom were some children of fourteen or fifteen years of age, were whipped. There were thirty-six Communist members of the Party in the canton, and of these twenty-three were in office, but not one of them showed any sign of moving in the matter ("Pravda", September 26th 1928). In the German-speaking province on the Volga, the "kulaki" (?) whipped eighty-five poor peasants, with the result that several died from their injuries ("Pravda", August 13th 1929).

The leaders of the Russian Communist Party or, in other words, the Soviet Government, decided to stage an international manifestation, called a "Red day", on August 1st 1929. But throughout the Armavir region the rumour spread that the night of July 31st to August 1st was to be a "Red night" of the St. Bartholomew order, and that the Communists were going to cut the throats of the whole population, showing no mercy to anyone. To make matters worse, some Chinese were encamped not far distant with the most blood-curdling inscriptions painted on their tents. The spreading of this rumour was, of course, another of the "kulaki's" misdeeds. Cossack cultivators in the district thought their last hour had come, and on certain farms men got ready to leave *en masse* and, putting on clean shirts, tearfully bade farewell. Children were hidden in barns, corn-bins, and under hay; windows were hermetically sealed and houses barricaded. The first few hours of the night passed quietly, in deathly silence. But a youth, bolder and more curious than the others, ventured out of doors to see if the cut-throats were coming; in the darkness he bumped into another youth also bent on satisfying his curiosity, and both of them started to yell savagely. Thereupon, from every "isba", barn and corn-bin rose piercing screams and mournful cries, the clamour of a terrified people which even drowned the dismal barking of the dogs. This continued till dawn. No one was killed, but for another three nights a considerable number in this "stanitza" (Cossack community) could not sleep. Some time afterwards, having been informed of the general panic, the more advanced elements in the "stanitza" took steps to explain "the real meaning of the day of demonstration held on August 1st" (*sic*), but only at the second attempt were they able to get anyone to hear their explanation as no one had dared to attend the first meeting, for the sole reason that the "Red night" was to be the topic under discussion ("Pravda", August 30th 1929).

The most interesting fact is that "Pravda" found nothing unusual in this reign of terror, and put all the responsibility on to the local Communists, who left the coast clear for the "kulaki". In Russia, people are accustomed to eye-opening incidents such as these. In the same way no further notice is taken of the traditional fisticuff battles between the peasants of different villages and, in the towns, between the workmen of different districts and wards. Brief telegrams in the newspapers announce that these combats have begun here or there, sometimes reporting a fatality or the number of those injured. The militia do not intervene; the Party as well as other organisations wash their hands of the matter. Proletarians are free to break each other's jaws and crack open their heads or generally disable one another. Here is only one example: at Astrakhan there were struggles between the inhabitants of different wards and divisions. Hostilities were opened by men from two working districts; there were injuries of every description, but the militia made no move ("Pravda of Youth", April 4th 1928). No longer is any importance attached to news of this kind. The poor proletarian beasts in question, uneducated and unreasoning, are supposed to vote unanimously in their meetings for the multiple transcendental resolutions and complicated proposals which the officials appointed for the purpose do not even bother to read to them.

The spread of religious superstitions and the development of mystic sects is aided by the real and enforced obscurantism of the present régime. In recent years it has been impossible to avoid remarking the rapid increase of societies and brotherhoods of various kinds and the considerable progress of their propaganda. The conditions prevailing in country districts and the sentiments expressed in official anti-religious publications only favour and reinforce the tendency towards reactionary mysticism by their irrational methods of gross brutality and unnatural violence. From all sides come reports of the success attending the efforts of Baptists, Evangelists, Brethren of the Peasant Union, Adventists, Molocans, Belocrins, Trezvenniks, Brethren of Avvakoum, followers of Tolstoy, etc., in addition to the progress made by various sects of the official Churches. Their activity has greatly increased during the last year, and their influence is already being felt in factories, in the home, even in the meetings summoned by atheists, where believers are allowed to voice their hostile opinions. In a factory at Tver, sixty workmen belonged to a sect; at Moscow some young Communists became Evangelists ("Trud", March 7th 1928). "The Baptists imitate Communist methods, and among their images of saints, their texts, and illustrated bills they hang portraits of Karl Marx and of Lenin (The "Rabochaya Gazette", June 24th 1928). The churches resemble workmen's clubs with their "watchwords" and coloured posters, but they are better kept and are always full, whereas the clubs are empty ("Pravda", August 23rd 1928). Communists are being won over to religion; near Kolomna, a secretary of the Communist nucleus contributed to the Church funds, and a woman Communist from the Lenin factory in the Vladimir province joined the Baptists; the Evangelists were particularly successful in securing converts at a Moscow factory, the Red Rose, etc. ("Izvestia", August 25th 1928). According to "Pravda", the sectarians and the "kulaki' in the Novogorod district held separate meetings before the village General Assembly was convened in order to check the Soviet power ("Pravda", September 15th 1928). Religious people and sectarians imitated the Party more closely every day; at Nizhni and at Sormovo they posted up "wall news", formed agricultural clubs, established "Red corners", frequented the "isba" libraries, and posed as Leninists; at Syzrañ a deacon at the close of his sermon recommended his flock to follow the teaching of Lenin. In the Uralsk the members of a religious circle declared themselves "religious Leninists" ("Izvestia", December 25th 1928). "Sectarians of every persuasion divide the work of conversion up among themselves and become specialists in their own particular line; the Evangelists send their supporters into the factories to convert the employees. The Union of Peasants' Brotherhood have suspicious relations with Japan (?)." On every hand there were signs of religious activity ("Trud", May 26th 1929). In the Donetz, all the great industrial centres were hotbeds of religious renaissance; at Makeyevka alone there were 13,600 people who belonged to sects and 4,600 of these were young people. Their propaganda among the unemployed met with great success, their theme being: "The Communists do not give you bread, then God will give it to you"; this was accompanied by the distribution of helpful gifts. They won over a certain number of young people and taught them doctrine during musical evenings; the girls acted as "fishers of men" ("Pravda of Youth", August 15th 1929). The Baptists ceased to be a sect to become a great political, religious party. At Poltava they occupied the former Lutheran Church, which was close to the building in which the meetings of the executive committee of local Soviets were held. They built chapels in which music was supplied by choirs and stringed instruments, and in this way managed to attract the youth of the district ("Pravda of Youth", September 22nd 1929). According to the review "Zhizn Iskousstva", thousands of Evangelist and Adventist circles, Baptist communities, and Molocans, formed art groups and sang the Internationale with a slight variation of the words, though keeping its general swing and leaving the rhymes unaltered; they conducted propaganda campaigns which were exactly similar to the Party methods; they issued five reviews. "Pravda" reported that in the Ukraine alone four million books of a religious nature were printed yearly (April 10th 1928). It is worth noticing also that these publications were circulated by persuasive measures and *were read*, whereas the Communist literature which was forced upon the people was not read at all.

But it is to the ravages of alcohol, which is the most evident of all evils and has many far-reaching consequences, that the general decadence of the Russian peoples is due. The Tsarist Government had, at the beginning of the war, suppressed the distillation and sale of vodka (grain brandy). The Soviets, however, have re-established it to their own profit, thereby legalising alcoholism soon after the death of Lenin and in spite of the clear-sighted opposition of Trotsky, Rakovsky, and Krupskaya. In the course of only a few years its effects have been truly calamitous; the Russian peoples are once again weltering in the most bestial forms of drunkenness.

The suppression of State vodka had not put an end to alcoholism because the peasants themselves learnt to distill in home-made stills and produced an alcohol of very bad quality, the "samagonka", which was retailed and consumed in secret. But this filthy liquor poisoned at least only the peasants themselves, and the evil was kept within bounds by supervision and repression; its consumption could also be further reduced by appropriate measures, above all by the enlightenment of the population. With Soviet vodka on sale, town workers have been legally supplied with poison, and the "samagonka" has been continually poisoning the country districts, its secret distillation being all the more easy to conceal since the appearance of the other form of alcohol. These two evils are both active, contrary to Rykov's statement at the Teachers' Congress that the purer form of alcohol would eliminate the impure ("Pravda", January 16th 1925). Semashko and all other public speakers were of this opinion ("Pravda", September 3rd 1928). And yet Soviet vodka swells the State budget with money taken from workmen's pockets!

"Nearly all the workmen in our factories have taken to drink," wrote one of Tomsky's comrades; "that is the situation in the provinces, but it is no better at Moscow. People drink the most on pay-day; women and children wait for husbands and fathers to come out of the factory so as to extract part of their earnings from them. The workmen, knowing this, generally hurry off from the pay-desk to the pot-houses. They sometimes do not return home till the next day in the evening, with empty pockets; that means hunger, misery, quarrels in the home." Some workmen became intoxicated even at the factory, and feast-days served as opportunities for bestial carousals. Workers from the peat-bogs, after they received their pay for three months' exhausting labour, spent all their money on drink without buying any necessities for their families. "Not only non-party men but Communists take to drink, and the Communist nucleus makes no attempt to stop this habit", etc. ("Pravda", August 20th 1925). Near Ivanovo-Vosnesensk, "the conditions in the workers' barracks at our factory offer a very sombre picture; they are an uneducated, drunken crowd. The situation is the same as it was before the Revolution, and it has remained unaltered in many out-of-the-way places. Nor are these conditions found only in remote districts, but also in big factories, as at T., where there are 8,000 workmen. On holidays, whole groups of them become intoxicated; they sing obscene songs and play about with knives in the presence of children, who imitate their example" ("Pravda", March 17th 1925). At the factory N. (Moscow), 80 per cent. of the workmen were drunkards; in the Party nuclei and among the Communist youth there was much drunkenness ("Pravda", June 24th 1925). Reports from Tver revealed that the railway unloaders, of whom there were more than 1,000, "spent all their leisure in pot-houses and all their wages on alcohol" ("Pravda", November 11th 1925). In June, 27,674 vedros (74,720 gallons) of alcohol were sold, and in August as much as 41,854 vedros (113,005 gallons), exclusive of wines, liqueurs, and "samagon" (one vedro is equal to 2·7 gallons). "The increase in the consumption of brandy has led to a spread of hooliganism" (The "Rabochaya Gazette", October 2nd 1926). "The Tula workman spends as much as 15 roubles (12s. 6d.) a month, on an average, in drink." The situation in the working districts provided a heart-breaking spectacle: the roadway was strewn with the bodies of proletarians rendered insensible by drink; on every side people cried, quarrelled, stole, and fought with knives. "The working population of Tula is swallowed up in 'the darkness': very rarely are there any clubs in the working districts, and the few that do exist do not answer the purpose for which they were intended" (The "Rabochaya Gazette", October 10th 1926). And then there were the 15 roubles to be subtracted from the average salary—not only at Tula, but throughout the Union.

In one year the population of Leningrad consumed 1,819,980 vedros of vodka (4,913,946 gallons), not to mention seven million vedros (nearly 19 million gallons) of other alcoholic liquors: this resulted in a marked recrudescence of hooliganism (The "Krasnaya Gazette", May 28th 1927). At the textile factory B., near Moscow, everyone indulged in drink; fathers of families beat their wives and children; even little urchins eight years old became intoxicated and others aged five drank vodka. Diseases of all kinds spread rapidly ("Trud", May 22nd 1927). Drunkenness was one of the evils of the country districts; in a certain village in the Tver province, unadulterated alcohol was distilled in fifty out of the sixty houses (The "Krasnaya Gazette", September 2nd 1927). This newspaper published numerous letters from workmen who had returned to their villages after being absent for some time; all of them wrote in the same strain. "At the present time the workman spends twice as much on drink as he does on his lodging." The number of cases of sickness and of mental complaints and deaths due to alcoholic excess was rapidly increasing. At Leningrad 95,000 intoxicated people had been arrested *in the street*, while in 1923 the number was 2,088. At Moscow the situation was the same, and in that city only those who were rowdy or quite incapable from drink were arrested; 80 per cent. of these drunkards were workmen; at Baku, 20 per cent. were Communists. As a result of these conditions the rate of production fell. The State-Planning Commission calculated that there would be an "advance" from 36 million vedros (97 million gallons) in 1926–27 to 84 million vedros (226 million gallons) of vodka in 1930–31, a fact of which the writer of the article spoke in indignant terms. But in addition to this it must be remembered that, according to a rough calculation, 15 million vedros (40 million gallons) of "samagonka" were also consumed. The same newspaper published letters from Sormovo, Orekhovo-Zuevo, and Bryansk, showing the ghastly ravages of alcohol among the working class. There was always the same pitiful spectacle: women watching and waiting at the workshop door, husbands beating their wives and children, etc. ("Trud", December 24th 1927). The co-operatives were the chief dispensers of the poison.

In 1927 Trotsky, Rakovsky, Zinoviev, Kamenev, and others who have previously been mentioned, referred in their review of the situation to the figures given by the State-Planning Commission for the estimated growth of production and the increase in alcoholic consumption during the next five years. There would be an increase of 227 per cent. in the consumption of alcohol and only 41 per cent. rise in the output of textile fabrics. "*The production of alcohol is therefore established, according to the Five-Year Plan, as the predominating interest in industry.*" "Then it is possible to foresee how the campaign against drunkenness, which has been announced in the [official] programme, is to become a reality by *momentarily trebling the present norm of alcoholic consumption.*" In April 1928, however, an anti-alcoholic society was formed under the ægis of the Government, and in "Pravda" of April 10th 1928 appeared the following: "*Alcoholism and Socialism are incompatible.*" (Signed) Lenin. What a happy circumstance, indeed, that Lenin thought of uttering this truism!

Alcoholism was the primary cause in 25 per cent. of the nerve cases treated in the Moscow hospitals, in 40 per cent. of venereal cases, in 50 per cent. of suicides, in 66 per cent. of criminal acts, and in 74 per cent. of cases of hooliganism. "The amount which a workman spends on drink is increasing to alarming proportions." A quarter of the products sold in 1926–27 by the co-operatives was composed of alcoholic liquors, whereas meat only represented 10 per cent. and sugar 8 per cent. Bukharin, one of those responsible for the evil, said that alcoholism was becoming a menace to the whole edifice of Socialism. In 1926 more than one thousand million roubles (£41,600,000) had been expended on alcohol. In certain industrial concerns, 14, sometimes 17 per cent., of wages went in drink, while unjustified absence from work, the low standard and the bad quality of production were, to a great extent, due to vodka; women and children were also taking to the drink habit ("Pravda", April 24th 1928). But while the ravages of alcohol were being denounced in this philosophical strain, both the production and the consumption of brandy were steadily increasing. Thanks to the sale of State-controlled alcohol, it was possible to count on 825 million roubles (£34,375,000) towards the annual revenue. The Gosplan laid plans for the "future development of Socialism", at the same time computing the probable increase in the sale of alcohol, while the fifteenth Party Congress decided gradually to reduce its production. "Pravda's" report of this situation was couched in very indignant terms (October 1928). About the same time, the "Rabochaya Gazette" reported that according to information supplied by the Gosplan, the consumption of brandy had increased from 387,450,000 litres (86 million gallons) in 1926–27 to 467,400,000 litres (104 million gallons) in 1927–28; it would then rise to 580,000,000 (129 million gallons) in 1928–29 to 713,400,000 (158 million gallons) in 1929–30, and to 826,400,000 litres (192 million gallons) in 1930–31, which would then represent an average consumption per head of 5·8 litres (nearly 1⅓ gallons), children being included. But these figures only refer to the "official alcohol", the "rykovka" as it is commonly called in Russia —a term which certainly stigmatizes Bolshevism—and take no account of "samagon" of which the production is estimated by one of the directors of the Supreme Economic Council as being approximately 40 million vedros a year or about 110 million gallons—and this in addition to the output of official alcohol. For 1931, therefore, the average consumption per head of the population should be estimated at 8 litres (nearly two gallons).

The newspapers were never tired of denouncing the evil, but never attacked its principal source. (The opposition party grouped round Trotsky were alone in fearlessly expressing an adverse opinion). Certain correspondence published in the "Trud", referring to the situation in a district of the Smolensk province, gave a clear summary of the salient features found in more or less all information on this subject: drunken workmen tortured their wives and children; in the workers' barracks there were fights, shots were fired, chests and doors were smashed, men plundered and stole. On pay-days, drunkards would lose all their earnings at cards, even gambling away their shoes and clothing; games always ended in a fight. In 1927, seven workmen hanged themselves in this district alone; crowds of women took to drink and there was a great increase in crime ("Trud", March 20th 1928). Workmen often arrived at the factories in a state of intoxication (The "Rabochaya Gazette," May 17th 1928). The clubs were transformed into low-down taverns (The Kharkov "Proletarian", March 17th 1928). Lenin said that from among six million proletarians there were 400,000 inveterate drunkards, who were each arrested on an average three times a year for being found intoxicated in public places ("Pravda", June 29th 1928). "We are being deluged with alcohol", was the expression used in a letter to the Leningrad "Pravda", which described the drink problem in the country districts and gave many heart-breaking details (August 2nd 1928). In Siberia even well-paid workmen were wretched because they spent the greater part of their salary in drink; clubs were turned into drunkards' dens ("Izvestia", October 20th 1928). At Serpukhov, near Moscow, Communists were just as inebriate as non-party men ("Pravda", October 25th 1928). At the Dzervinsky factory, accidents increased three or four times in number after wages had been paid and as many as forty occurred in one day; absence from work was, in 73 per cent. of cases, due to drunkenness ("Trud", November 14th 1928). At Moscow, as well as at Kursk and Leningrad, new alcohol factories were constructed, although the existing ones would have been adequate to supply all needs ("Pravda", November 28th 1928). Before the Central Executive Soviet Committee, Larin pointed out that in one year, the militia had arrested two million inveterate drunkards who had been found incapable in the street; that 500,000 tons of grain were swallowed up in the production of alcohol, and that the Anti-Alcoholic Society was not protected by the Government, but was continually coming into collision with those authorities whose commercial operations were thwarted by it. At the same assembly, Larin estimated that one thousand million roubles (£41,600,000) had been lost to industry owing to the spread of alcoholism among the working class; the two great cultural centres, Moscow and Leningrad, drank more than the other towns ("Pravda", December 5th 1928 and following days). At Saratov, in the course of their demonstration against drink, the children proclaimed: "We are against having drunkards for fathers; we demand that it shall be possible for us to do our homework; instead of vodka we must be supplied with books" ("Izvestia", December 25th 1928).

All these workmen, Communists or pro-Communists, who have been dragged down to the state of degradation so often described in the Soviet Press, vote "unanimously" for the high-sounding proposals concerning "Socialism as the world's religion", the irremediable decline of Capitalism in Europe and America, the Five-Year Plan for production in the U.S.S.R., and all sorts of difficult and complicated problems which would cause even cultivated, conscious revolutionaries to hesitate. Still "unanimous" as ever, they ruthlessly condemn all those Communists who have been bold enough to risk even the mildest criticism of official policy and governmental methods. When the intoxicated proletarian has ruined his machine, abused his foreman, beaten his wife, and murdered his child, stolen from his neighbour, outraged his neighbour's wife, fouled his lodging of "coffin dimensions" and gambled away his only pair of trousers, he then proceeds to "demand" [*sic*] that the absurdly tolerant political bureau of the Party shall take pitiless measures against Trotsky and other "sceptics" who have been too long tolerated among the living.

In the meanwhile, in every direction this calamitous condition was gaining ground. An inquiry held in 1928 revealed that increasing numbers of the younger generation were taking to drink: as a means of investigating the matter, two schools comprising 2,420 children from eight to sixteen years old were examined. It was found that 15 per cent. of the boys and 14 per cent. of the girls were drunkards and that, in addition, 14 per cent. of the pupils used frequently to drink intoxicating liquor, and in very liberal quantities ("Izvestia", June 3rd 1928). In 1929 it was admitted that it would be impossible to reduce the sale of vodka for fear of upsetting the equilibrium of the budget; and yet drunkenness was becoming more and more a public menace ("Izvestia", January 16th 1924). A consumption of 46 million vedros (124 million gallons) was forecast for 1929 and this estimate did not include "samagon" sold in secret. The yearly expenditure on alcohol was put at one and a half thousand million roubles (£62,400,000) ("Pravda of Youth", April 2nd 1929). Last year the global consumption of brandy in towns was 75 per cent., and in country districts 150 per cent., above the pre-war figure. At the present moment, therefore, the level of consumption in Tsarist times has been very largely exceeded, taking the country as a whole. Experience has shown that the State vodka has not eliminated the "samagonka", of which there is an increased distillation ("Pravda of Youth", June 5th 1929). *In a single night* at Leningrad, the militia found 859 intoxicated people in the streets—a record number (The "Krasnaya Gazette", September 1st 1929). The "alcohol department" put up for sale more than sixty million litres (13 million gallons) in excess of the authorised amount—540 instead of 480 million litres (120 and 106 million gallons). The Anti-Alcoholic Society protested ("Trud", September 11th 1929).

This little detail was passed unperceived by the sham "friends of the U.S.S.R.", or, at any rate, there is no mention of it in their Utopian tracts.

In the foregoing pages something has been said, either incidentally or in special cases, about the condition of women. It is a sure sign of the level of civilisation in any country and it is well worth a moment's study. The "Izvestia" noted many cases in which husbands beat their wives because they took part in the "elections". In the Uralsk, a secretary of the Communist nucleus thrashed his wife, who was a candidate for the Soviet; in the province of Tula, a member of a department in the Soviet killed his wife, the President of this Soviet, with an iron bar. In the province of Gomel, all the women in one village were beaten by their husbands for having held a meeting, etc. (May 19th 1926). These are not isolated incidents but characteristic events. (In the following chapter matters relating to elections will be more fully explained.) "Pravda" in its turn denounced the harsh treatment meted out by workmen to their wives and gave numerous examples. Communists were very prominent in these cases. It recalled the many tragedies in which women workers were beaten to death by their degenerate husbands without any attempt on the part of the organisations to intervene, although they were fully informed of what was occurring. At Ivanovo-Vosnesensk, the principal textile centre and the Manchester of Russia, "women are now almost universally beaten"; the "Weavers' Voice" started a campaign against this habit of workmen striking their womenfolk, and announced that they had received numerous letters confirming these brutalities ("Pravda", April 1st 1928). In the country, morals and customs remained as barbarous as ever; the "Byednota" quoted numerous cases of human brutes who imprisoned their wives, beat them unmercifully and spat in their faces (June 22nd 1928). Among the Turcomen the Revolution has not abolished trade in women; a wife costs at least 60 roubles (40s.), but the "kulaki" have put up the prices, and though the poor peasants have endeavoured to establish a "fixed rate", they have not been able to prevent their women from being attracted by the big sums paid for wives by rich speculators ("Pravda", August 26th 1929).

The "heritage of the past" is here undoubtedly responsible for much, but the perpetuation of this cursed heritage is no less responsible for this state of things—except in the eyes of the blind, obliging tourist. There is, however, another hideous evil in Soviet Society which has made its appearance since the death of Lenin, and this is anti-Semitism. Though rooted in the distant past, yet it is due in some measure to modern conditions, and, according to the newspapers, is spreading daily. In the Russia of olden time, anti-Jewish feeling certainly existed, but it was confined to very restricted classes. To give only one example, the working class had never harboured any ill-feeling towards the Jews, nor was there the slightest trace of anti-Semitism in the Revolutionary, Socialist, and Communist Parties. But since its renaissance in the year 1925, it developed rapidly in the period that followed, and it is the proletariat which has been defiled by this form of savagery. And experience shows that, except where the Government is in sympathy with the movement, anti-Semitism cannot exist. Certainly it has been officially denounced, and in violent cases the aggressors have been severely punished, but as so often happens in cases of this kind in the Soviet Union, it is the effects of evil that are denounced while the cause is left untouched; or, to use the common expression employed in Russia which is also applicable to alcoholism and the suppression of illiteracy, "colds are treated by keeping cold draughts blowing". The chapter on the "Dictatorship of the Proletariat" will shed fresh light on this formula.

In a Leningrad factory the workmen were summoned before *two members of the Bolshevist Party*, one of whom boasted publicly that, with his own hand, he had killed 900 Jews on the Polish frontier and regretted that he had not exterminated them all (Leningrad "Pravda", June 29th 1927 or 1928—the date being indistinctly printed on the author's copy). "Never before in the course of the Revolution have we seen the Party and the Communist Youth so strongly infected with anti-Semitic feeling as at the present time", wrote Sosnovsky in "Pravda" (September 1927), and he quoted an extremely characteristic letter from one Communist to another justifying "for 50 per cent." [*sic*] the old battle-cry of the Black Hundred, "Death to the Jews, long live Russia". "Pravda" of the Young Communists (December 23rd 1927) gave a whole page to the disgraceful attitude of the Communists and working men towards the Jews; it quoted cases in which workers, without the smallest pretext, treated comrades as if they had been Jews, refused them admittance to the Trades Unions, and, in consequence, deprived them of their right to work. "Pravda" also emphasised that entire groups of the Communist Youth and "pioneers" were affected by this anti-Semitic spirit and that they had taken to assaulting Jewish children and adolescents. The same paper (May 17th 1928) pointed to the strengthening of anti-Jewish feeling within the Communist Party; at Kiev, a Communist of high rank refused to provide Jews with work, and elsewhere it was of common occurrence to find Communists ill-treating Jews. Written on a wall at the National Economic Institute, a Communist inscription read as follows: "Death to the Jews, long live the Soviets". The "Krasnaya Gazette" (June 29th 1928) revealed that a Communist director in the co-operatives arranged that purchasers should wait in two distinct queues, one being for the Jews, the other for orthodox people; he beat an old man of seventy who protested at such treatment. The paper declared that the conduct of this brute and his accomplice, the chief of militia, was calculated to provoke a pogrom (a wholesale massacre of the Jews). In the club at the October Revolution factory, a young Jew, whose arm had been paralysed as a result of an accident, was thrown to the ground and half strangled, and this with the full approval of the president of the factory committee ("Pravda", July 28th 1928). At Rostov, Dniepropetrovsk, and Kazan, etc., young Communists insulted and soundly thrashed their Jewish "comrades" ("Pravda of Youth", July 29th 1928). One of Gorev's books gave much useful information on this point, proving that "in the course of the last few years" the anti-Jewish spirit had penetrated everywhere (The "Evening Krasnaya Gazette", September 9th 1928). In the Donetz mines, Jewish workmen were insulted and ill-treated by their companions, who were often Communists and secretaries of the Communist nuclei. Communists openly regretted that they could not themselves raise a pogrom; Jewish workmen found that they were refused work, lodging, and membership of the Trades Unions, all because they were Jews. Regional Communist committees encouraged the evil by their silence ("Pravda of Youth", November 18th 1928). At the October glass-works near Minsk, the foremen insulted, persecuted, and beat a Jewish woman worker; they undressed her, whipped her, and splashed cold water over her *in the presence of all the workmen and Communists in the factory*, who, by maintaining silence, became accomplices in this outrage. Three of the blackguards who were directly concerned in the persecution of this woman were members of the Bolshevist Party ("Pravda", January 15th 1929). In the same issue of this paper, several other instances were reported in which Jewish workers in various factories were subjected to pleasantries of this order. Feeling against the Jews was running higher every day, and the "Trud" (May 29th 1929) finally admitted that it was not only a monstrous relic of the past but a phenomenon of present-day politics.

The importance of the situation is proved by the reports appearing in the Press, as, for instance, the detailed account of the scandal at the Kharkov Geodetical Institution given in "Pravda of Youth", of April 10th 1928. There, a young "rabfakovetz" (a Jewish student of the working class) had been tormented and persecuted for months on end by Communists under the very eyes of his comrades, who made no effort to help him. He was woken at night with blows from a ruler on the head, drenched with cold water, and had the soles of his feet pricked with the point of a pair of compasses; this poor tormented creature was driven nearly mad. At another hostel at the other end of the town, the same bullying methods were employed; a Jew was beaten unmercifully and left half-dead by his brutal aggressors, two of whom were secretaries of the Communist group. "Similarly striking manifestations of anti-Semitism frequently occurred in the "Vouz" (higher education establishments). At the same Geodetical Institute, some students were brutal enough to tread purposely on the stomach of a pregnant Jewess, also a student. At Belotserkov, there was an organised group of violently anti-Jewish blackguards. At Dniepropetrovsk, at the Institute of Mines, at Kharkov, at the Institute of Technology, at students' conferences, in various towns in the Ukraine, anti-Semitism found expression in acts of extreme coarseness and violence. The general assembly of the Communist nucleus at the Geodetical Institute screened those responsible for the outrages and mocked at their victims' sufferings.

It is Communists of this kind who vote unanimously [*sic*] for every resolution sent them by the district Party committee and handed down in turn through the town and provincial committees and the Central Committee of the Party from the Political Department of the Party Secretariat itself.

If this fact is borne in mind, the statement made by Maxim Gorki in "Pravda" (September 26th 1929) is bound to cause some astonishment. "Is it possible to believe the malevolent declarations appearing in the refugees' Press which accuse Communists of being infected with this anti-Jewish spirit?" Then it would appear that Gorki pays no heed to the Soviet Press. He is evidently employing an artifice of style, for he ends his article with the following sentences: "There cannot be any question whether to combat those who are hostile to the Jews. Two questions must be answered; are they being sufficiently and diligently opposed? and what measures should be taken to combat them?" These questions have still to be answered and will remain so while they remain within the scope of the present political system. For the question cannot be settled without touching upon all the problems of the system, which, since the death of Lenin, has been built up upon the "powers of darkness".

CHAPTER VI

THE "DICTATORSHIP OF THE PROLETARIAT"

The Soviet Constitution—Citizens and subjects—Communists and non-party men—The Comsomols—Constitutional rules and practical realities—Communist, Sovietist, Trade-Unionist, economic, co-operative, police and housing "machinery"—The bureaucratic pyramid—Lenin's intentions—The State and the Party—Press and censorship—The quality of the élite—Rights and liberty of the proletariat—Governmental methods—The chronicle of scandals—The truth about the Trades Unions—Co-operatives—Bureaucratic monstrosities—Justice.

The Soviet Constitution, the legal outcome of the dictatorship of the proletariat, is a destructive document in the U.S.S.R. of to-day. Several thousands of Communists and other revolutionaries are at the present time imprisoned, interned, or deported because they claimed its principles or wished to make use of the rights of citizenship which, in theory, it gave to them. This is not the first time in history that a Constitution has failed to be respected by those entrusted with its manipulation. But it is certainly *an unique case* of a Constitution which *has nothing in common* with the Governmental system of which it is supposed to define the organisation.

This singular state of affairs was not established in a twinkling; it has gradually taken shape since the death of Lenin and has become comparatively crystallised in successive stages after the death of the founder of the "Federated Socialist Republic of the Soviets". This condition of affairs will not endure for all time, but since it is one of the realities of the hour, those who do not want to be taken unawares by any future turn of events would do well to study it.

In principle, all the inhabitants of the U.S.S.R. who live by their labour without exploiting their fellow-workers are citizens, electors, or eligible for election; they have the right to express their opinions and to attend meetings. As an actual fact, out of the 150 million and more Russians and kindred peoples, *one individual alone* enjoys all the rights, and *the rest* are responsible for all the duties. This exclusive, privileged citizen is the Secretary-General of the Communist Party.

The population of the U.S.S.R. is divided into two great categories, those who are members of the Party and those who belong to no party. The Communists alone have, to a varying extent, a few undefined rights which depend in quantity and quality according to their position in the ruling class. A Communist has less rights than his comrade who, by virtue of his office, is placed immediately above him on the ministerial ladder, but yet he has more rights than the man just below him in the official scale. Nevertheless, he has more rights than an individual who belongs to no party at all, for this unfortunate is completely barred from playing any part in vital urban or national affairs.

The only right possessed by non-party people is to approve the proposals advanced by the sole existing party in the U.S.S.R. Disapproval of all kinds, whether it be distinctly stated or only implied, any criticism, whether of the most timid order or made with every possible justification, even complete silence (for this may be interpreted as being of a hostile nature), all these render the non-party man liable to a charge of being an enemy to the Revolution and brings the most dire consequences in its train, from the loss of his work, and, consequently, his daily bread, to deportation to Siberia and lifelong imprisonment.

In the non-party class, there are two sorts of people: "sympathisers" and the rest. In order to be a "sympathiser" there is no need to be in sympathy with Communism: it is enough to declare one's support, to feign allegiance and then take precautions not to be caught red-handed in a hostile act. In consideration for his apparently sympathetic attitude, the sham supporter is granted small favours in everyday life—assistance to find work and lodging—and these are appreciable advantages if the living and working conditions which have been objectively described in the foregoing chapters are once more called to mind. Besides, the real or sham sympathiser, if he shows exemplary docility, may be chosen *by the Communists* to figure on the waiting-list of non-party people destined to be "unanimously elected" at forthcoming elections; in this event, he becomes a member of one or several Soviets, and this may, *in some cases,* procure him certain amenities. Electors' assemblies are held in the factories and an individual may only attend the one of which he or she is a registered member. The local committee of the Party alone has the power, either directly or through the medium of a Communist nucleus or the factory committee which is under its orders, to summon a meeting. In this way, anyone attending these meetings is known to, or easily identified by, the factory management or the Communist officials. No one may open his mouth or move so much as an eyelid without immediately attracting attention, and any expression of opinion which does not conform most strictly to the official view, renders him liable to any corrective measures that the officials of the Party may think fit to employ. The assembly committee, whether Communist or chosen by the Communists, is therefore elected unanimously, and the orders of the day, the resolutions or the lists of candidates drawn up by the Party are necessarily "voted" with similar approval. This sham method of voting is carried out by a show of hands after the president has stated the motion and followed it with the sacramental question, "Who is against it?" If the matter is an important one, it is impossible for a member to dissent without running the risk of losing his occupation—and eventually his daily bread—as well as his lodging, for workmen's houses are under the control of the factory authorities. In view of the widespread unemployment and the gravity of the housing question, everyone keeps off dangerous ground by abstaining from raising a dissentient voice. When the prospect of loss of work, etc., is not sufficient to stem the tide of heresy, there are other more direct and energetic measures which may be adopted. These will be examined later in this chapter. Unanimity of the hundred per cent. order is, therefore, assured. In the country districts, the situation is not quite the same. There, owing to the interposition of several additional grades of voters which do not exist in the towns, as we shall see later, the electoral base is more remote from the elected "summit", added to which the peasants' interest is more keenly centred on local affairs. This results in less official pressure and supervision in country districts, though, in any case, this is bound to be so, because there is an insufficient number of rural Communists. The immense proportion of illiterates and drunkards in the population still further limits the desire for progress. The greater the importance of the sphere of authority belonging to an assembly or congress, the more strictly is the Communist control enforced so that nothing may be left to chance.

It has been shown in a previous chapter how none of the non-Communists is, in general, anxious to belong to a Soviet, for the sole mission of that body is to raise taxes and to find recruits—two of quite the most unpleasant tasks imaginable. It is more often the well-to-do peasants who find it to their advantage to worm their way into the Soviet in order to benefit from the privileges which such an office confers upon them, and to be in a position to force their poorer comrades to do their will. One might almost say that in the big villages and the small and medium towns, the Soviet, once elected, never meets again; it is the committee that does its work, and a Soviet member's title is hardly, therefore, of great value. Instances have been frequently cited where, owing to the loss of the list of Soviet members, these singular deputies were nowhere to be found as the majority of them were even in total ignorance that so great an honour had been conferred upon them. In some cases, when the name Ivanov appeared on the list drawn up by a committee of the Party with no indication as to the Christian name or patronymic, it was impossible to find out to which Ivanov it referred from among the dozens of Ivanovs who are invariably found in any community in Russia. In the great towns the Soviet very seldom meets at all and then only for propaganda purposes and in order that its executive and sub-committee, which are both appointed by a Party committee, may be obligatorily but "unanimously" approved. The Soviet member is far from being worn out by his public duties, but is fortunate enough to have a ready-made excuse to leave his work and smoke a few cigarettes in the corridors of the Soviet assembly hall; he also receives gratuitously all official "literature", a free pass on the trams, and other privileges of a like nature.

Non-party persons, who are not classified as "sympathisers" by the Party committees with which they are connected by reason of their place of work or domicile, are entitled to live in the manner described in previous chapters—if they are lucky enough to have a lodging of "coffin dimensions" and not to be numbered among the unemployed. But this is on condition that they abstain strictly from all interference in politics except to applaud wholeheartedly the decisions of the powers that be.

The members of the Party are in their turn divided up into several categories. There is a kind of Communist proletariat, humble and obscure members who devote themselves to thankless tasks; a medium class shares the modest but less laborious posts and is better paid; a bourgeoisie fills the relatively important economic and administrative appointments; an aristocracy which monopolises political and all responsible offices; finally, an oligarchy from which are recruited the *de facto* rulers, who are not always rulers in name. They encircle the "summit" of the Communist hierarchy as represented by the Secretariat of the Party.

Each category of Communists owes a passive obedience to the categories placed above it; on the other hand, it may demand a similar obedience from the "lower layers"; the nethermost class retaliates upon non-party persons. This is what is officially miscalled the "Dictatorship of the Proletariat". No one has the authority to doubt his superior but is, on the contrary, expected to criticise his own actions and those of his equals and inferiors. This is called self-criticism. In this way, the Secretariat of the Party is out of reach of all attacks.

Since the death of Lenin, it is not necessary to be a Communist in order to be a member of the Communist Party. *It is even preferable not to be one.* A genuine Communist has the choice between silence, prison, or Siberia. A sham Communist lives more or less comfortably in office if he leaves unmolested the Secretariat of the Party.

Doubtless there are thousands, if not tens of thousands, of Communists who earnestly apply themselves to their tasks, fully conscious of their responsibilities: but of these, the great majority is not found within the Party. Besides those who have been deported to Siberia, Turkestan, even to the shores of the Arctic Ocean, or interned in concentration camps and prisons, or sentenced to solitary confinement (and it is difficult to estimate their exact number owing to the secrecy with which revolutionary ideas are suppressed), there are some discreet, prudent men who, in factories and Soviet institutions, are awaiting the hour when they may safely express their opinions. As has already been pointed out, there are some Communists of this kind within the Party, but they are likewise silent and circumspect and, unwilling to sacrifice themselves without sufficient cause, abstain for the present from making known their inmost convictions.

On October 1st 1928, the Party included 1,360,469 members or "candidates" (probationers who had not yet been definitely admitted into membership); this number was, according to statistics, made up of 169,264 peasants, 479,579 officials and employees, together with 141,095 "various", or, in other words, intellectuals, technicians, artisans, etc. (*Statistical Year-Book*, Moscow, 1929). All these workmen are members of one or more committees in the factory and in their homes, as well as belonging to one or more Soviets in the district in which they live, and to councils, Trades Unions, or co-operative commissions, or to one of those "voluntary" organisations which have previously been mentioned in the chapter on wages. All these peasants are members of their cantonal, regional, or provincial Soviets. All those in the "various" category are members of the administrative, economic, or political "machinery" of State. Therefore, all these 1,360,469 recognised Communists are the wheels in the Soviet governmental machine. They constitute the principal, privileged, social category of the system.

In a political sense, they form a patriciate which monopolises authority. But from the economic point of view, their position is rather different. Communists have the advantage of being, with few exceptions, safe against unemployment and better paid, better housed than the masses, though they cannot, however, openly accumulate private funds. The Party has fixed the maximum monthly wage of its members at 225 roubles (£7 10s. 3d.), whereas the workers' so-called average salary is three times smaller on paper (75 roubles, or £2 10s.) and at least five times less (45 roubles, or 30s.) in reality, as has been shown in an earlier chapter. But in addition to this theoretic payment of 225 roubles, Communists benefit from special privileges—good houses, maintenance allowances, accommodation in habitable rest-homes, allowances when on special missions and travels abroad at official expense. Then, as already noted, writers or occasional contributors to newspapers and reviews may earn as much as 600 roubles (£19 9s.) and more a month. The half million workers included in the membership figure are specially privileged in the factory, workshop, and in the home. That is the only reason why they exist at all. The Party membership card represents a kind of social insurance and it is much sought after, for it provides the necessities of life and a relatively certain guarantee of security. Anyone who can produce this card of membership is far more easily able to keep his place in the factory and far more difficult to expel from his lodging. He has, moreover, the additional advantage of being in a position to obtain some appearance of civic rights.

At the present time the Party's numerical strength is no clue to the influence of Communist thought upon the country as a whole. The Party's difficulty is not to find recruits but, on the contrary, to refuse them. During a given period, approximately up to the death of Lenin, the title "Communist" implied sacrifices and devotion to duty, but for the past five years it has been, above all, an advantageous and profitable designation. The number of members in the Party (1,360,569) could easily be multiplied by ten or divided by twenty without increasing or diminishing the actual number of genuine Communists.

Apart from this entirely fictitious figure of Communist numerical strength, there is an organisation called "Communist and Leninist Youth", comprising approximately two million members, of whom several thousands are genuine, earnest Communists and a few hundred others are fully conscious of their creed. But most of them are members because they have been deprived of their right to refuse their support and are entirely ignorant of the principles of Communism. These children and young people are practically forced to enter the only legal political organisation that exists besides the Party itself, of which it is an antechamber, a channel leading towards the privileges of citizenship. As Comsomols, they may be elected to the Soviets, and to Trades Union, factory, co-operative, and housing committees, an honour which gives them small privileges both in the factory and in the home. They run almost no risk of unemployment in a country where everyone lives in constant dread of losing his work and daily bread; they benefit from various illegitimate favours and reductions in price when they go on excursions and on visits to museums; when they arrange sports meetings, processions, and reunions. In short, like their elders in the great Party, they have practically the right to ride roughshod over the 150 million non-party people.

In all the scandals which have besmirched the history of the past five years, the Comsomols and recognised Communists have taken a very prominent part. They have been guilty of acts of tyranny, abuse of power, embezzlement of public funds, sexual offences against women, brutal treatment of children, aggressive anti-Semitism, bribery, and debauch. From time to time, the Secretariat of the Party has ordered a "campaign of purification" in order to get rid of hot-heads, critics, and discontented members, for at every election some of these manage to obtain membership and no effective methods of ensuring their permanent exclusion has been discovered. At the same time, a certain number of thieves and assassins of various kinds are eliminated. But for every one of these caught, scores or even hundreds remain at liberty—and the reason for this will be easily understood when a fuller knowledge is gained of the working of the system.

The Constitution provides that the "Soviets" or delegate councils of workmen, employees, peasants, soldiers, and labourers of all categories, shall be elected in each locality by all wage-earning citizens, who, without distinction of age, sex, or original nationality, live by their work without exploiting their fellows. The local Soviets elect their delegates for the Congresses of cantonal Soviets, which elect delegates for the Congresses of district Soviets; these, in their turn, elect delegates for the Congresses of provincial Soviets, which do the same for the Congresses of the Federated Republic Soviets, which elect delegates for the Congresses of the Soviets of the Union. This last body elects—still according to the constitutional theory—the Central Executive Committee of the Union. This theoretical Parliament is, therefore, in principle, *the result of a sevenfold election.* The Constitution of the U.S.S.R. is more or less bourgeois-democratic, and yet in no other country in the world is suffrage so indirectly operated as on the Soviet system. The Central Executive Committee appoints a Council of the People's Commissaries, a Council of the Union, and a Council of Nationalities. Then, besides this, the Congress of Soviets of each Federated Republic elects a Central Executive Committee for that republic, which in its turn appoints a Council of the People's Commissaries. Finally, each village Soviet has a Presidium or Standing Committee, each Soviet congress elects an Executive Committee in every canton ("volost"), in every district ("uyezd"), and in each province ("guberniya"). The town Soviets send their representatives direct to the provincial Soviet Congress without passing through either the cantonal or district committees. Only by continual reference to a plan of the system would it be possible to understand anything about this pyramid of Soviets, Congresses, Committees, and Councils. But no such plan will be given here for the reasons given below.

In actual fact, elections are not conducted and electoral bodies are not constituted in the manner laid down by the Constitution. Any attempt to apply constitutional principles would be severely punished. The following is a description of the manner in which the Government is in reality carried on.

It is not within the scope of this book to follow up the historical events which led to the formation of the Party Secretariat, and it must, therefore, be taken as an established fact. But with regard to its functions: it elects the delegates for the Party Congress and causes them to elect from among the Congress members a specially selected Commission, which draws up the list of members (who will be unanimously elected) for the Central Committee and for the Central Commission of Control. *These delegates are certain of unanimous election* for, being all selected by the Secretariat or by officials already chosen by the Secretariat, they nominate a Commission conforming to the purpose of the Secretariat, and this Commission draws up the lists for the Central Committee and the Central Committee of Control in accordance with the wishes of the Secretariat. Once the Central Committee has been thus constituted, in its turn it appoints its Political and Organisation Bureaux (Politburo and Orgburo) which are entrusted with carrying on its duties because it very rarely ever reassembles. As regards the Central Commission of Control, it appoints an executive to which it delegates its authority, owing to the fact that it assembles still less frequently than the Central Committee. These three permanent Executives are constituted according to the orders of the Secretariat. The Political Bureau controls the two others: *this is the real Government of* the U.S.S.R. Practically speaking it is part of the Secretariat. Before Lenin's death, the Political Bureau had the Secretariat under its control, but since his departure the order of things has been reversed. The Secretariat is, strictly speaking, the legal representative of the Political Bureau, but while the former body carries on the Government from day to day, the latter only meets to promulgate its decisions once a week. The Secretariat, acting in the name of the Political Bureau and employing its Organisation Bureau and various other services of which the Utchraspred (Party members' Distribution Bureau) is one, either directly or indirectly nominates the principal and secondary committees of the Party in the Federated Republics, in departments and provinces, in urban centres and their divisions, in country districts, cantons, and villages. As a general rule, the Secretariat is able to depend on each of the Party Committees to use their own judgment in the formation of the committees under their control, but it exercises direct intervention whenever circumstances seem to require it, and distributes its political agents among the principal posts, rectifies unsuitable appointments, and dismisses or nominates the committee Secretaries in every connecting link of the governmental machine. In order to carry out its task, the Secretariat employs a staff of 1,200 officials and special clerks in its offices in the Staraya Ploshchad at Moscow. The Central Commission of Control, or, more correctly, its Bureau, is placed as the apex of a pyramid of local, cantonal, district, and republican control committees; it surveys the whole organisation through its inferior committees and suppresses any dissentient tendency. Finally, every Party committee saddles the basic organisations, the Communist nuclei and "zones", with secretaries and officials who, to use the Russian expression, are "in the line", or, in other words, blindly and tamely accept the decisions of the higher authorities.

The whole constitutes a pyramid of secretaries, officials, committees, and commissions with the Secretariat at its "apex". The Soviet pyramid which has been previously described is a parallel case. For every organisation in the Soviet system there is a corresponding one in the Party system. But the function of the Party is to give orders and of the Soviets to carry them out. The reason for this is quite simply that each Soviet body is nominated by the Communist organisation which corresponds to it in the district. In every assembly charged with the election of a Soviet representative body, the Communists constitute a disciplined party which is forced to vote unanimously for the election of candidates appearing on the list drawn up by the Party committee proper; any breach of this obligation would entail the exclusion of the guilty member from the Party, the loss of his work and livelihood, and often his lodging. The non-party members of the assembly necessarily vote also for those on the list, for besides the fact that they are already delegates under the authority of the Party, the slightest opposition on their part renders them liable to be deprived of their work and lodging. In this way, any move within the Party automatically operates the appropriate wheel in the Soviet machine. The Secretariat, in the name of the Central Committee of the Party and of its two principal Executives, appoints the Council of the People's Commissaries (which is constantly under its orders), together with the Central Executive Committee of the Soviets of the Union; it also nominates the President and his Presidium (Standing Committee) by drawing up the lists and "proposing" [*sic*] candidates for the electoral assemblies through the medium of its groups and committees. The Central Committees of the Party follow the same methods in each republic, making use of their Executives and secretaries. The Committees of the Party at Moscow, Leningrad, Kharkov, "elect" their Soviets in the same way. The functions of every Party Committee are likewise carried out, and the Soviet staffs are consequently subjected to the strictest control by the Communist personnel; there is the closest co-operation between the two in important offices, and Party members monopolise the most important posts of all in each system, and with the aid of a collateral network of commissions of control, keep a close watch over the whole organisation.

This monumental masterpiece of bureaucratic structure is only a mere fragment of the general Soviet system. In addition to the Party and Soviet "machinery", with their complementary organisation of the Communist Youth, there is the apparatus of Trades Unions (in Russia, professional Unions), of Soviet economic, industrial, and commercial systems, and of the co-operative establishments; there are the police and military "machines" together with a network of housing committees and co-operative societies. These innumerable appliances of government, all interpenetrating, all intertwined, constitute the most formidable, the most labyrinthine system of government that has ever encompassed, bound, gagged, and paralysed a people or individuals. Neither past nor present has seen the like of it and, as far as one can see, nothing will ever surpass it in the future.

The "machinery" of the Trades Unions is closely modelled on the Soviet system, and consists of a pyramid of committees with the local assemblies as its base and the Central Council as its apex. But there is an additional complication in this case, for each branch of industry has its own organisation and this overlaps the territorial system. All wage-earners are registered as members of the Unions whether they like it or not, and now the stage has even been reached when the number of Union members is given as being higher than the total number available for membership! This has been already noted, but there are two points worth considering in connection with so brilliant a result. No clause in the Constitution laid it down that the membership of these Unions is obligatory, but the Constitution, as we have been previously forced to remark, is a seditious document. In actual fact, the wage-earner is made a Trades Union member by the decision of the factory assembly, which, if he attends at all, he does so as a silent onlooker. This decision is really dictated by the Party Committee, which gives its orders to the Communist group in the factory. The Union member must choose between submission on the one hand or the loss of his work and livelihood on the other—very often his "coffin-dimensioned" lodging as well. Based upon the hunger-forced resignation of the workers rises the pyramid of bureaucratic Trades Unionism; it is dovetailed into the two other pyramidic systems, and united to them by the confused distribution of functions and of responsibility in positions of administration and control.

In the Soviet economic, industrial, and commercial systems, the production and exchange of goods has been to a considerable extent nationalised—a change affecting all industries of the heavy branch, the great and medium manufacturing industries, transport in its entirety, soil, and subsoil, waterways and forests, a small part of agriculture, banks, and loans, nearly all wholesale and all foreign trade. The Soviet State has had, therefore, to build up a vast technical and administrative organisation in order to administer these industrial fields on a collectivist basis. Its management is entrusted to two principal Councils: the Supreme Economic Council, the Work and Defence Council, assisted by the Planning-Commission, the Conjunctural Institute, the Principal Concessions Committee, the Central Board of Statistics, and the People's Commissariats: Finance, Commerce, Agriculture, Workmen's and Peasants' Inspectorates. The Supreme Economic Council has its ramifications in district and local councils. Industries are grouped in trusts; commercial establishments are organised in shareholding societies of which the bonds are held by economic organisations. An enormous staff of experts, politicians, and employees is at the service of these various departments. The Party Secretariat directly nominates all the chiefs and leading officials and through the medium of its trusted agents, committees, "fractional groupings", and nuclei, indirectly appoints the subordinates. The proportion of the Communists is considerably less in this apparatus than in the others, but it is strictly controlled by the Party, and its management is in the hands of specialised Communists.

Town dwellers, and a part of the rural population, are enrolled as members of the co-operative stores, which absorb most of the retail trade. People have no choice but to submit to the system which is forced upon them. The Constitution did not provide for enforced membership of this kind; it did not command the abandonment of true forms of co-operation for a system of State trade, labelled co-operative. But the Government, or rather the Party, left the proletarian consumer no choice in the matter; private commerce on a small scale was abolished by fiscal methods, and the consumer was practically forced to give his support to a co-operative movement in the management of which he had no say nor any controlling hand. His interests were not considered either in the goods offered for sale or in the prices demanded for them. In juxtaposition to other organisations, the co-operative system employs a huge staff of officials and employees furnished, administered, and supervised by the Party Committees.

Apart from the militia entrusted with the maintenance of public order, the Soviet State keeps up a political and criminal police (the Ogpu), and a permanent army. The Ogpu has the right of life and death over all citizens; it has the power to prosecute, arrest, and imprison any individual of whom the Secretariat of the Party wishes to be rid; it may judge him without witnesses, condemn him without proof, sentence him to lifelong exile, and banish him for ever from the face of the earth. There is no other example in bourgeois society of a police system with such extensive and complete authority; it might be termed the most "perfect" inquisitorial organisation in the world's history. At its command there is a close network of public and secret agents, paid officials, and willing informers, together with certain military forces which are directly under its orders and tactfully termed "special duty" or "vone" detachments. Its actual budget is unknown as it is maintained to a great extent with grants from secret funds, but in 1926 these were admitted to amount to 27,122,778 roubles (£904,000), besides 36,825,000 roubles (£1,227,500), which was the cost of the special military detachments (The "Finansovaya Gazette", May 9th 1926). The Ogpu may, in the majority of cases, utilise as auxiliary agents all Communists and Comsomols, Soviet officials, the militia, and non-Communist members, as well as thousands and tens of thousands of factory, Trades Union, co-operative, and housing committees: they are all subdued by its all-powerful hand. In the towns, half the population spies on and informs against the other half. The Ogpu gives no account of its actions to anyone. In principle, it is only responsible to the Council of People's Commissaries, one of whom holds the office of Commissary of Justice. But as this Council, together with the executive body of the Ogpu, is nominated by the Secretariat, the latter serves as a cover for all the operations of the police by automatically giving them its approval through the Political Bureau. In other words, the Ogpu is not responsible to any authority but its own. By its orders, prisons, detention camps, and deportation centres are filled to overflowing with workmen, Communists, Socialists, Trades Union members, free-thinkers, Zionists, and even Tolstoyans—thousands of them all sentenced without any semblance of a trial. The militia (the street police) are both part of the Soviet apparatus and of the Ogpu; their misdeeds are continually reported in the Press. An official inquiry revealed that they were guilty of coarse, insolent, and violent behaviour towards citizens, and were venal, drunken creatures ("Pravda" and "Pravda of Youth", May 8th 1928). The standing army, with its nucleus of professional soldiers, is under the orders of a "Revolutionary Council of War" which, like the People's War Commissaries, is also nominated by the Secretariat of the Party. Tens of thousands of officers and non-commissioned officers of the regular army are thus under the control of the Party, and are subjected to the same blind discipline which is encouraged by the Party itself.

But it was Lenin who said at the first Congress of Soviets: "A republic which will create—not in words but by deeds—a strong central authority *without police or a standing army*—this is the transformation worthy of an institution like the Soviet system (*Complete Works*, vol. xx., p. 551). At the first Peasants' Congress he had advocated "the government of the State by Soviets, *not through the agency of police, agents, or of a standing army*, but with the aid *of a people's militia formed of armed workmen and peasants*" (*ibid.*, p. 464). Some time before, he had proposed in "Pravda" "that with firm tread we should move smoothly forward gradually, step by step (as was only fitting), towards the establishment *of a militia chosen from among the whole people*, and towards the substitution of the nation-in-arms in place of *the police and of the standing army*" (*ibid.*, p. 439). He also wrote: "Russia must be a *democratic republic*. We want a republic where there are no police to mock us; we desire that all officials, whether of high or low degree, shall be nominated *exclusively by election*, and that they shall be dismissed at any moment if that be the people's wish; that their salaries shall not be higher than the wages of a good workman; that the army leaders *shall be elected*, and that the standing army, which is now distinct from the people and is commanded by men of social classes entirely foreign to them, shall be replaced by the nation-in-arms and by a militia drawn from the people as a whole" (*ibid.*, p. 410). Then again: "The establishment of a *body of nominated* officials cannot be tolerated. None but the administrative body set up by the people in each district may be recognised. The idea that it is necessary to put all administration in the hands of officials nominated by higher authorities is an entirely misleading experiment as well as being anti-democratic, Cæsarean, and Blanquist" (*ibid.*, p. 365). And yet again: "The Party is struggling to create a proletarian and peasant republic which will be more democratic than at present; from which police and permanent army will be completely banished, to be replaced by a general arming of the people, or, in other words, by a militia to which all citizens will belong; in which, office will not only be elective but revocable at any moment at the wish of the electors; and in which the salaries of all officials, without exception, will not exceed the average wage of a good workman," etc. (*ibid.*, p. 343). And again: ". . . These are the claims of a proletarian and peasant democratic republic (or a state without *police*, *permanent army*, or a privileged body of officials)", etc. (*ibid.*, p. 319). And yet again: "We are in favour of a republic which, throughout, will be *without police or standing army*; in our opinion, the whole people in arms must take their place; there must be no body of officials who enjoy privileged bourgeois treatment and permanency of office" (*ibid.*, p. 223). "The real task before us is to abolish the *standing army, the corps of officials*, and the police, and to put in their stead a vital force, *the whole people in arms*" (*ibid.*, p. 263). "The State must not be governed *by the police*, or by *officials who are not answerable to*, but are placed over, the people, nor yet by the permanent army; it is the people in arms united by the Soviets who must govern" (*ibid.*, p. 162). It would be possible to give an endless number of similar quotations. In the Communist programme of 1917, it was proposed to suppress the police, the standing army, and the official classes, and provision was made for the general arming of the people (militia), and the power to elect and transfer official personnel; it was also laid down that the functionary's salary should be equal to the workman's wage. *Twelve years have passed by*, and it is now impossible to imagine methods more contrary to the principles of the programme: the police, the army, and a parasitic officialdom play their part in an even stricter maintenance of order; wages are grossly unequal, the people are totally disarmed, and the powers of the police are monstrously augmented. If the workmen and labouring peasants had been organised into militia bands, and had been therefore armed, the political system of the U.S.S.R. would not, doubtless, have become what it is to-day. The proletariat is forbidden to carry arms: the Communists alone are armed.

Finally, there is the machinery of housing and co-operative committees: it rounds off the work of all the other machines of government by controlling the life of the ordinary mortal in his home by meddling with his private affairs, by throwing him, with his wife and children, out on to the street at a signal from docile Communists acting under the orders of their committees and secretaries. These committees and co-operatives are not paid for their services, but they avail themselves of many advantages in kind; they decide the living-space available in each dwelling, distribute the inhabitants among the houses, crowding them in as they think fit. They have the right to go into any house whenever they choose: in short, they are able to make life unbearable for the people as a whole. In this way the worker may, if the Party deems it necessary, be rounded up in his last refuge—his lodging.

No official figures are available to show the vast number of permanent officials and of auxiliary committees employed in the working of the gigantic bureaucratic machine. At the Fifteenth Party Congress, Ordzhonikidze, the committee reporter of the Commission of Control and the Workers' and Peasants' Inspectorate, declared: "There are 3,722,000 officials employed by the Government, including the staff of the Education Department. The administrative organisation finds work for approximately 2,000,000 officials who cost the country in the neighbourhood of two thousand million roubles (£83,000,000)." (Press of December 1927.) To the number of State officials (3,722,000) must be added those serving in the Party, the Communist Youth, Trades Unions, and co-operatives. In the co-operative service alone there were 400,000 in 1925. Dzerjinsky said that their salaries amounted to 90 million roubles (£3,700,000) in 1925, and that their number had increased considerably ("Pravda", April 20th 1928). Their total must now be about five millions. Then, again, in addition to these, there were, so to speak, the part-time officials who performed their public duties in addition to their ordinary work. Such is the extraordinary bureaucratic machine which has been gradually built up during the last ten years and which for approximately two years now has made invulnerable a system intimately known in Russia as "the Dictatorship of the Proletariat".

The Soviet machine, which turns the wheels of all the governmental mechanism briefly described in these pages, is of relatively solid structure; it depends for its strength on the fact that the trusted servants of the Party hold as pluralists all the principal offices and act as the driving-belts in the machine, mechanically transmitting the thrust of the Secretariat. Let us attempt to give a concrete example of this. Before he was banished from the Party, Kamenev, one of the three real chiefs of the Union at that time, was simultaneously a member of the Central Committee and of the Political Bureau of the Party, President of the Work and Defence Council, President of the Moscow Soviet, Vice-President of the Council of People's Commissaries, member of the Board of the Supreme Economic Council, a member of the Central Executive of the Union and of the Executive Committee of the Soviets of the Russian Republic; a director of the Lenin Institute, co-director of the "Bolshevik", the Party's official organ, and doubtless member of various committees and assemblies of minor importance. Then to compare this striking example with the case of a Communist taken from the thousands reported in "Pravda": a young man and therefore member of the Communist Youth, he complained of being overburdened and threatened with an excess of social duties; he enumerated sixteen offices and appointments held by him in the Soviet organisation, in the Party and Communist Youth, in the Trades Unions, and in various other bodies; some were permanent offices and others, though they were temporary, were continually cropping up again ("Pravda", March 21st 1925). These two examples show the limits of the scale of responsibilities. First Zinoviev, and later Bukharin, filled almost as many responsible posts as Kamenev. In Lenin's time, Trotsky, who did not seek after appointments, found that his personal intervention was required on all occasions where the difficulties of a situation, the gravity of a crisis, or the serious consequences of a governmental break-down necessitated the presence of a man of exceptional ability. At the present time, the commanding positions in each department are still in the hands of the same pluralist office-holders and in every grade of parallel bureaucracies this pluralism is repeated: a member of the Central Committee of the Party is also a member of the Revolutionary Council of War, of the Ogpu Collegium, and of Soviet executive committees. Another takes part in the various supreme economic councils of committees, in the assemblies of economic commissariats and in the Soviet executives. This method ensures so close a connection between the various offices that it is often impossible to ascertain which of the regular authorities is responsible for the decisions taken. Complete chaos results from this fusion of governmental functions. There was a time when certain forms and ceremonies were respected, but after the death of Lenin these were discarded as being entirely superfluous. In consequence, there has been the spectacle of a Trotsky "openly" dismissed from the Commissariat of War, a Soviet appointment, by the leading groups in the Party—an event duly noted in high Soviet circles. Since that time, there has been a series of startling dismissals in the Soviet organisation as a result of Party decisions dictated by the Secretariat and carried out with no regard for normal, or, rather, constitutional procedure. On August 16th 1926, the Chief Secretary of the Party, the President of the Council of Commissaries, and the President of the Supreme Economic Council, all signed a manifesto, just as if the Secretariat of the Party was technically the supreme authority in the State. The nominal Government is answerable for its actions, not to the Soviet Congresses, but to the Party assemblies which publicly issue instructions to this falsely appointed authority. There is no trace in the Constitution of prerogatives assigned to the Party. But the Party, by its skilful manipulation of all other organisations, has caused the complete disappearance of the Constitution itself.

In every State institution, whether great or small, there is uncertainty and confusion concerning the assignment of prerogatives and of responsibilities. Governmental duties are not shared out on any definite system but just as dictated by chance circumstances and curious considerations. Decisions are taken sometimes by one department, sometimes by another, and often, quite unexpectedly, by the one least qualified to act. The principal authorities mutually encroach on each other's territory, and strive to nullify their respective efforts. In his attempts to gain a clear understanding of the situation in Soviet Russia, the author continually consulted persons of the highest authority, but he was never successful in obtaining an explanation as to why, for instance, a question should be settled by the Commissaries' Council instead of by the Bureau of the Executive Committee or by the Council of Work and Defence—or *vice versa.* His would-be informants all admitted that they had no explanation to offer. If a compositor were to make an error with regard to the title, sub-head, or signature of an important resolution or decree when setting it up in type for publication in the "Izvestia", the public would not be in any way astonished at his mistake. Only a few officials directly concerned in the matter would notice that anything was amiss. The same resolution or decree could be attributed on an average to half a dozen different official bodies. To take an example from the thousands or hundreds of thousands available: a certain decree was to be passed in connection with the cotton-growing industry in Turkestan, but the question was—by whom? One would be tempted to suppose that the responsible authority would be the economic body to which the textile trust was attached, or the Commissariat of Agriculture or the Supreme Economic Council; perhaps, more strictly speaking, the Council of Work and Defence or one of the Executive Soviet Committees. But the resolution, which filled four columns in the newspaper, was headed as follows: "*The decision of the Central Committee of the Party upon the report submitted by the Principal Cotton Committee and the Workers' and Peasants' Inspectorate*" ("Pravda", July 28th 1929). This anomaly is quoted at random and with no intention of emphasising any particularly striking case of confusion in administration. The same conditions prevail on a smaller scale in local organisations. In a town in the south of Russia, where the author lived for some time, the Secretary of the Party nucleus, which used the power-station as its headquarters, for reasons doubtless best known to himself ventured to cut off the electric supply from certain inhabitants. Any complaint addressed to the proper authorities was invariably met with the formula, "Go and see the Secretary of the Communist group about it." A secretary who plunges houses into darkness is by no means a rarity in Russia, but quite the reverse. In the eyes of anyone who has lived the life of an average Russian, he has a symbolic character. The fact that such an occurrence is possible shows the true character of the whole situation.

The only legal party in the U.S.S.R. is the Communist Party; the only legal opinion is that expressed by the Secretariat. No Communist political programme ever prescribed the suppression of rival workers' and peasants' parties, nor did it forbid divergencies of opinion in the Party. On the contrary, seven weeks before the October Revolution, Lenin made the following statement, which is here quoted word for word: "Alone, the power of the Soviets could ensure a widespread, constant development of revolutionary influence, *a peaceful rivalry of parties within the Soviets*" (September 14th 1917: *One of the fundamental questions of the Revolution*). A little later, he repeated this: "The parties' struggle for power *may be peacefully carried on in the heart of the Soviets*, provided that the latter desist from distorting democratic principles" (September 16th 1927: *The bugbear of civil war*). The ideas of Lenin, the theorist of Bolshevism and the founder of the Soviet Republic, are limpid clear. Moreover, when the country was in the grip of war and the Soviet régime was passing through a most critical period, political parties like the Mensheviks, Socialist Revolutionaries of the Left, Ukrainian Borotbists, the Bund, and various anarchist groups, which did not oppose the system with force of arms, all enjoyed a legal existence. Their disappearance was the logical result of the war and of civil strife, which culminated in a paroxysm of fury and a reign of terror; but their suppression should have been but of a temporary nature, like terror and warfare themselves. The danger of war once over, the Revolution moved forward along the paths of peace and Lenin's programme once more became an actuality and should have recovered strength and meaning: *peaceful rivalry of parties within the Soviets.* But Tomsky, a member of the Political Bureau and President of the Party Secretariat and of the Central Council of Trades Unions, made the following pronouncement on the matter: "The main difference between the Party systems in Western Europe and in Russia, is that, with us, *only one thing is possible: one party is in power and all the rest are in prison*" ("Trud", November 13th 1927). Such was the progress made between 1917 and 1927. Lenin had spoken of a *peaceful rivalry of parties within the Soviets*, but Tomsky declared that *one party was in power and all the rest were in prison.* The inevitable perpetuation of this method of government had led to the imprisonment and deportation of all those who actively opposed the Secretariat of the Party; amongst them were Lenin's most faithful comrades in arms, headed by Trotsky.

The sole existing party has its exclusive Press. All newspapers in the U.S.S.R. are under the direct control of the Party Secretariat or of the bodies to which it has delegated its authority. Only the opinions of the Secretariat may be legally expressed. The Board of Censors, which is impudently and ironically termed the Glavlit (lithographic centre) allows nothing to pass which may overshadow the Secretariat or which appears in any way to be of a suspicious character. The Press, literature, theatres, arts—everything is censured. The writings of Trotsky have been forbidden as well as the stage representation of the *Brothers Karmazov.* Even Lenin's sayings are suppressed if the Secretariat finds them embarrassing. The censors go as far as to force authors to accept interpolations having no reference to the text and threaten to withhold the imprimatur if objection is raised. One writer was obliged to include in his book on a European subject a whole passage about the Chinese Revolution—a "suggestion" from the Party Secretariat. (This is a mere nothing in a country where the farandole from *L'Arlésienne* is introduced into the second act of *Carmen* and where the tricolour in Delacroix's picture "Liberty on the barricades" is changed into a red flag, quite regardless of historical accuracy and of the painter's real intentions.) A special service examines correspondence and foreign mails in particular; thousands of officials waste their time in this way and the proletariat has to pay them for it. It is an incontestable fact the Soviet Press publishes the hard truths concerning the real situation in Russia; innumerable complaints, criticisms, protests, and correspondence contradicting the official optimism are fully quoted, filling whole pages at a time. Even this book, in which the number of references and examples have been voluntarily limited, bears witness to this fact. But only as long as they remain fragmentary and refer to special circumstances and not to the general situation, are these disclosures made. Nothing is ever published which may assign responsibility to the proper quarters or cause the invulnerability of the dictatorship of the Secretariat to be less respected. These revelations are the safety-valves by which the stifled anger of the masses, weighed down by misery and bureaucratic rule, finds an outlet. They belong to the policy of self-criticism; they do not harm the chief culprits, nor do they refer to the source of the evil. On the contrary, the masters for the time being use them as indictments and so keep their enterprising agents more closely under their control and divert public attention from fundamental questions. One cannot quote Lenin's opinion on this point without some feeling of bitterness. "If some big Soviet newspapers were published, having the sole right to make announcements, *a much greater number of citizens* would be enabled to express their opinions; for example, any group which could obtain a certain number of signatures, would be entitled to publish its views. Thanks to this transformation, the liberty of the Press would become much more democratic and infinitely more complete" (*The Liberty of the Press*, September 15th 1917). This was what Lenin said in 1917. Ten years later, Trotsky was deported to Siberia for having attempted to disseminate his ideas in a limited circle of readers with the aid of a gelatine duplicator. Such was the evolutionary curve of Bolshevism.

The "Pacific rivalry of parties in the Soviets" (to quote Lenin's phrase) is not only impossible to-day in the U.S.S.R., because there are no longer any parties or Soviets in the initial meaning of the term, but because the sole existing party is not a party in the generally accepted sense. The bureaucratic institution, which is still labelled "Communist Party", no longer resembles a party, nor hardly can it be called a Communist "Party" (which it certainly is not), for its "members" are forced by economic necessity to give it their support and are in no way influenced by Socialist or political considerations. Nor is it Communist, for slavery and Communism are incompatible in the eyes of anyone versed in Communist doctrine. In the minds of a few thousands, the true conception of the Party still lives on, but in the present circumstances it has not been embodied in any political movement or in any group of individuals. This reincarnation will inevitably come about as soon as the pressure from this bureaucratic dictatorship is relaxed and at the moment, neither Party nor Soviets exist in the "Soviet first signs of proletarian awakening. For the present Union"; Trades Unions and co-operatives are likewise non-existent in spite of the imposing organisations bearing these names and the impressive columns of their statistical data. They are not, because they are not free to be, or not to be. History has already known republics without republicans; the world now sees a Communist Party without Communists, Soviets without electors or elected, Trades Unions without members, co-operatives without customers. On the other hand, there are five million officials employed in the offices of this "Party", these "Soviets", "Trades Unions", and of "co-operatives". Supposing, then, 50 million out of these 150 million inhabitants are employed by the State, that gives one official for every ten citizens. Now to see these millions of officials at their work.

The Party is reputed to represent the élite of the proletariat and the flower of civilised humanity. The organisations and institutions under its control are staffed by its officials, who are—in theory—the best, the most conscientious, and the only really disinterested politicians. They have deliberately sacrificed—again in theory—personal for collectivist interests. They have exerted all their intelligence in studying social development and its bearing on history; and by reason of their principles, their political programmes, and their activity, deserve to be appointed as leaders of the irresolute masses, to lead them towards progress, unfettered labour, and to a life free at last. But to what extent have these abstract definitions been carried into practice? One may well ask also what manner of men are these superior persons. It will be interesting to discover their level of intelligence, the nature of their public acts, and of their relations with the proletariat (which owes its freedom to them), and the daily happenings in their meetings, offices, and at their daily work. To what extent are they worthy of the public trust reposed in them and how do they exercise the absolute, undivided power which the workers "unanimously" grant them? It should have been possible to gain some idea of the characteristics of the average Communist from the study of the foregoing pages; a more complete, accurate picture will now be painted.

In 1924, when a Party "purge" was in progress, Yaroslavsky, the principal controller, wrote: "It has been discovered that many members *do not know their Party and take no interest in it*, and after being several years in its ranks, know nothing about Communism, and yet are counted as Communists. This applies particularly to pupils from the *higher grade schools*". He was speaking of White Russia, where on one occasion, when a "revision" was threatening, the bookshops were suddenly cleared of books by Communists anxious to acquire the elementary facts of Communism. In the other republics of Russia, no one would have troubled to do this, as will be seen later ("Pravda", September 25th 1924). Turning to a few issues of the official journal of the Party for 1925, we find that a workman wrote in one of them: "The idea of a Party is a good one but unfortunately *the immense majority of its members attend first to their own interests* and only as a second thought to those of the Party. At the present time, a great number of responsible, militant officials have become so bureaucratic that *they are worse than the functionaries of Tsarist times*" ("Pravda", March 24th 1925). This workman openly stated the views of all his comrades; moreover, Lenin himself declared that there was nothing to choose between the Sovietist bureaucracy and the Tsarist régime. The secretary of a cantonal committee *ordered a military agent* to go and take the Party card away from a man who had been deprived of his membership; he told the Soviet executive committee of this district: "I command, therefore, obey!" He monopolised the powers of all the representatives of the district.

In one case, a Communist nucleus was in need of money; the secretary made a list of the small traders in the locality and forced them all to pay a contribution ("Pravda", March 26th). Incidents of this kind in various shapes and forms are to be found nearly everywhere. One Communist nucleus was entirely composed of poor peasants who had joined the Party in 1920. They were all nearly illiterate except the secretary. None of them read the papers or did any intellectual work. They were entirely ignorant of the most important political questions, and not one of them had heard of Trotsky. According to "Pravda": "The authority of the rural Soviet is in reality centred in the president; he notes the decisions of the higher authorities and carries them out" (April 1st). Such nuclei and Soviets are not the exception but the rule; the exceptions are the genuine Communist nuclei and Soviets. "At Tver *the militia, commanded by the chief officer*, arrived with measured tread to attend a meeting; the motion was read and the vote mechanically taken" ("Pravda", April 4th). A report of a co-operative meeting to elect the managing board had the following as a heading: "There must be a change of methods", and as a sub-title: "It's pressure, not management." The secretary of the Communist nucleus presided, and purposely prolonged the meeting in order to tire the members. At midnight the vote was taken and the Communist nucleus proposed a list of officers. The assembly suggested that the old president of the board, a Communist held in the highest esteem, should be added to it. It was then announced that the president of the assembly would not permit the list of candidates to be examined, and the passing of the list was sanctioned: that was all. Many members went away saying, "What was there for us to do there? We need not have bothered to come." "Comrades who were not loved by the labouring masses were elected in this manner and none dared to speak against them *because of their fear of the secretary of the Communist nucleus*" ("Pravda", April 5th). This is a very common occurrence at all meetings; the Communist secretary commands and everyone submits; and if the motion is one of local interest, that is why someone ventures to express his wishes, only to be quickly suppressed. If it had been a great problem of vital importance, no one would have dared to have outlined a proposal. "Whether we are there or not, it's of little importance" was the heading of one report of a meeting. Workmen say: "Why do they make us come, for it's always the same whether we are there or not" ("Pravda", April 23rd). Near Rostov, "certain Comsomols" considered themselves to be the supreme authority and recognised no law. Two of them recently carried out a search in a peasant woman's house at night—an entirely illegal procedure ("Pravda", May 14th). In a village in the Stavropol district, the peasants hated the Communists in "responsible" positions and called them "a set of drunkards"; one of them was the ex-president of the Soviet, the other the ex-secretary of the Communist nucleus, and the third was the ex-president of the executive committee; even when banished from office, these undesirables still continued to dictate orders ("Pravda", *ibid.*). "Our rural militants are backward, and ignorant of political matters: they often know nothing of, and do not understand, Party politics. Many do not read a newspaper" ("Pravda", *ibid.*). Spurred on by appeals, resolutions, circulars from the centre, and finally roused to activity, some Communist nuclei were anxious to recruit more active members, but when they received papers from the district committee about their election, they wondered what they meant and whether a new party was to be formed ("Pravda", May 24th). Two members and a candidate composed the staff of a

Communist nucleus in the Uralsk. They took to drink and indulged in hooliganism when they were intoxicated. In another, in the province of Moscow, the Communists and Comsomols were fond of knife play ("Pravda", *ibid.*). In another Communist nucleus in the Don district, only two members had had anything resembling a political education and the rest knew nothing nor wanted to learn anything; many of them were drunkards ("Pravda", *ibid.*). One must have lived in Russia to be able to guess what a "resemblance to a political education" really means; it probably signifies that they knew the name of the President of the Republic. Two of the members of a Communist nucleus in the Vladimir Province had been presidents of the cantonal Soviet committee; they were generally in a more or less intoxicated condition ("Pravda", *ibid.*). The secretary of a Party district committee declared that Communists and Comsomols had not the right to criticise office-holders, for that would weaken the authority of the Party and assail Communist ethics [*sic*]. "We would punish them, even to the extent of expelling them from the Party" ("Pravda", June 2nd 1925). "In our district of Southern Ossetia, a number of Communist groups in out-of-the-way districts are unable to transact any business" ("Pravda", June 7th). A demobilised soldier joined with three other persons to subscribe to a newspaper. Some peasants came to hear it read, but two Communists found fault with the originator of the plan, for "it was forbidden to assemble in such numbers to hear the newspaper read: not more than three were allowed. The subscribers wondered how many could safely meet to read a newspaper" ("Pravda", May 12th). At a halt on the Ekaterinoslav railway, two Communists, who were the lords of the district, "so terrified the workmen that they were frightened of speaking at the meetings". A secretary asked why they were silent and a workman answered: "They do well to keep silent; no one wants to lose his occupation" ("Pravda", May 12th). In a "stanitsa" where the Communist nucleus had ten members, the secretary, B., decided to increase the number to one hundred and admitted some undesirables on his own initiative. The same secretary, speaking of himself, said: "When B. speaks, Communists must keep silent. If B. makes a statement, then it has the force of law, as he who does not believe in B. does not believe in the Party" ("Pravda", May 12th). In short, this local satrap was expressing the ideas of the Secretariat of the Party. At the election of factory committees, "many Communists reasoned thus: What was the good of going to workmen's meetings when everything has been decided in advance at the Party meeting?" On one of these occasions, a Communist declared: "The list has been adopted by the Communist nucleus, so let us vote for it without discussion." At other meetings, the Communists would say: "Your intervention is futile, for we can always get our candidates elected" ("Pravda", June 11th). A comrade wrote to this newspaper: "Can there be many members of the Party who are not drunkards? If there are, then they are very few and far between." "Religious prejudices, drunkenness, indiscipline, and the gross behaviour towards non-party people, all the maladies which are attacking our organisations, and certain of their members must be mastered at all costs" ("Pravda", June 14th). "Up to the present time, the system of arbitrary control by secretaries of the Communist nuclei and by Party committees has been adopted in our district; illegal pressure has been brought to bear on the elections and there has been a complete absence of comradeship, etc." ("Pravda", June 16th). In the Communist nucleus at Kharkov "criticism was not permitted. If some bold person ventured to criticise, he paid for his daring. He was immediately denounced and banished from the Party." "The bureau expelled three "rabcors" (worker newspaper correspondents) from the Party because they had written critical articles in the Press without the permission of the Communist group" ("Pravda", July 8th). "Workmen do not and will not vouchsafe any information at the meetings, for they do not want to be dismissed." "A workman dare not speak to a Communist for fear that evil may result therefrom" ("Pravda", July 8th). At a meeting in the Donetz, a workman declared that "he felt that his presence was not required and, being unwilling to vote as he was ordered, left the hall" ("Pravda", *ibid.*). The secretary of a Communist nucleus at Moscow submitted his own list of candidates and, in spite of the fact that it was unanimously opposed, entered it as having been elected. He alone had the right to speak in the Party group ("Pravda", *ibid.*). "Anyone belonging to a "cell" in the province of Kostroma who ventured to criticise was treated as a counter-revolutionary; consequently, no one dared to open his mouth. At a meeting in a factory in the province of Ivanovo-Vosnesensk, the door of the assembly hall was shut to prevent workmen leaving after their day's work and to force them to be present" ("Pravda", July 12th). Only 25 out of the 300 members in a big Communist nucleus at Moscow took any active part in affairs ("Pravda", July 17th). Any member who criticised the secretary of a Moscow Communist nucleus was to be treated as an enemy to the Party and must expect to be expelled from it ("Pravda", July 21st). This would mean the loss of his livelihood as well. "For a long time past our workmen have simply registered their votes and kept silent, but now in secret they are whispering together, complaining and recriminating." "The working masses passively accept the proposals and decisions of the

Party because they may neither be modified nor criticised" ("Pravda", July 21st). "After an important Party conference it was stated that many of the local militants did not even know what had been the decisions of that Conference. In one Communist nucleus, for example, 33 out of the 45 members had read nothing concerning it" ("Pravda", July 26th).

The real character of the Party is accurately reflected in these statements, which are drawn from only *half a dozen* issues of "Pravda". It would be an easy matter to take other striking facts and testimonies from the *same* pages and to accumulate a host of them by referring to all the issues of that paper for a given period and by verifying their accuracy in Communist organs: it is simply a question of time and paper. The few facts quoted have been chosen because they are most likely to be understood by Western peoples and can be easily summarised; yet they are not the most damaging to the Communist character. No one will seriously deny that these are signs of a definite, established condition. The last few years have witnessed no weakening in these fundamental and organic characteristics: on the contrary, they have been accentuated in all vital problems affecting the régime and have been sometimes stripped of all considerations of secondary importance and of purely local interest. Outstanding, world-famous events have taken place without exciting any interest or feeling on the part of the people: there was Leon Trotsky who, though enormously popular and warmly applauded in every assembly, was "unanimously" condemned by men forced to vote contrary to their conscience. Next came Zinoviev, "unanimously" approved by the Leningrad organisation and yet disgraced—again "unanimously"—within twenty-four hours. Then Tomsky, the President of the Trades Unions, also elected "unanimously", has recently been dismissed with the same "unanimity". Finally, Bukharin, the theorist of the régime, also "unanimously" acclaimed, has suffered the same fate as his predecessors. This is a slave-like unanimity.

The Sovietist versifier, Demyan Byedny, gave the general assembly of the Party an account of a conversation he had had with Karl Radek. The latter had read a passage concerning the Eskimos in a scientific work, *A Sketch of the Development of Social Forms*. "The Eskimos brought with them from the South a rich and supple language, the tongue spoken by the first generation of immigrants in days gone by. Their songs and legends bear witness to their distant past. But their history seems to have suffered a break. Amidst primitive surroundings and influences, their language has itself become primitive. Conditions no longer render natural the use of their old, rich language. The old chants and stories still exist, but they are unintelligible to the Eskimos of the present day. If the singers are asked what they understand of the meaning of their songs, their answers are vague." "Therefore", said Byedny, beside himself with wrath, "we are political Eskimos; we are always referring to Lenin and using Leninist phrases, but, like the Eskimos, we do not understand the meaning of the words we use" ("Pravda", November 1st 1927). We would add that the parrot-like prattle of the Eskimos is inoffensive and that they do not pretend to impose on the Universe. A few further examples will show whether Radek was exaggerating. A report of a political examination held in a Communist nucleus in the Saratov Province recorded the questions asked and the answers given to them.

"In whom rests the supreme power in the U.S.S.R.?"

"In Rykov."

"No, Rykov is not the supreme authority."

"Well, surely the Comintern is the supreme body," corrected a member of the Soviet.

"Is Capitalism firmly established?" was the question asked of a Comsomol in charge of the educational course in politics.

"Evidently—and permanently established," was the answer ("Pravda", September 5th 1925).

A more recent report reveals the answers given in an examination by some Comsomols from the *higher grade* schools.

"The League of Nations is a Trades Union to which the U.S.S.R. belong."

"Karl Liebnicht is still alive."

"Lenin was the Commissary of Work."

"Stalin is Commissary of Finance."

"Bourgeoisie no longer exists with us, but if the bourgeois are not entirely extinct, then they must be the Trotskyists in the towns" ("Pravda of Youth", August 1929).

Such reports are very common and have been quoted at random, but even the average story one hears on Russia to-day shows the incredibly low level of intelligence. Besides, Yaroslavsky admits that the "political level is extremely low" among the majority of rural Communists ("Pravda", August 25th 1929). In the examinations intended to verify Communist culture, the examiners' knowledge is often quite as weak as the candidates! "The members of the Commission asked questions and were themselves hopelessly confused as to the correct answers. Some of the questions, like the following, had nothing to do with politics. "Why did you marry for the second time?" "How many drinks do you take at a time, and do you drink from small glasses or cups?" ("Trud", August 3rd 1929). The following shows the manner in which lessons in political economy are conducted: The lecturer reads a paragraph from his book and then makes his hearers repeat each sentence in chorus, as, for example, "The Trades Unions are the schools of Com—*munism!*" "Industrialism is the road to So—*cialism!*" etc. ("Pravda", June 27th 1928). This is how the élite are trained! This élite lived so well up to its reputation that in 1921 174,900 members had to be expelled from the Party, and 264,140 in the following years ("Pravda", April 30th 1929). But in what respect did those who were not banished differ from the others? A Comsomol sent his newspaper some verses dedicated to Lenin's memory; they were composed in imitation of Lermontov's cradle-song:

Sleep, little babe, sleep my pretty one,
Sleep, pretty baby of mine.
The moon looks sweetly down on thee;
Sleep, my little babe, sleep.
The moon shines softly down
Into thy mausoleum.

("Pravda of Youth", January 1929).

This was an entirely typical young Communist, but a number of his congeners did not even attain his standard of purity of motive, as will be seen later. A committee secretary telephoned to the district committee, asking: "Is there any class warfare at the moment in your district?" A deputy-president of the cantonal committee [*sic*] solemnly entered in his report that "from January 5th to the 10th, there had been no class warfare in the canton" ("Pravda", February 1929). And this is the élite! When sixteen out of forty-six little girls between the ages of eight and fourteen, belonging to a school in the Samarkand district, had been violated by their teachers, the local administration, on being informed, not only kept silent but attempted to hush up the affair ("Trud", April 13th 1929). This was the élite again. The most active chiefs of officialdom in White Russia were, politically, entirely illiterate; some of them did not even know why the Party was called Communist ("Pravda", July 30th 1929)—the élite again—and these were *men in official positions and leaders* to boot! Therefore it is difficult to imagine what can be the intellectual and moral condition of the masses whom they are supposed to lead. Everyone voted "unanimously" for Trotsky's deportation to Siberia (and if the author persists in alluding to Trotsky's fate, it is not because his person seems to him to be sacred, but because that episode shows how an ignorant, obscure proletariat may be treated).

The Soviet methods of government are in keeping with the people's wretched living-conditions, which have been described in an earlier chapter, and are of the same quality as the Communists who operate the system. The following facts serve as illustrations of this. On January 21st 1924 the militia went the round of all the porters (dvorniks) in Moscow and ordered them to hang out flags veiled in crape under penalty of fine. This was done, though the reason was not known. Passers-by saw these signs of mourning for what was obviously an important person, but did not know for whom. The next day people learnt through the newspapers that Lenin was dead. In July 1924 the author was present at a great demonstration in the streets of Moscow; he questioned some of those taking part, but none of them knew *the object of the demonstration.* The committee responsible for the arrangements had summoned the workers to attend at a certain hour after the factories closed and that was all they knew. A great many Communists were questioned in an attempt to throw light upon the matter. Some tried to explain it by suggesting that the demonstration was to commemorate the July insurrections (which were suppressed in July 1917 at Petrograd), but it was an untenable hypothesis. The newspapers provided no information, and, finally, the author learnt the next day that the parade was held to celebrate the opening of the International Communist Trades Union Congress (the Profintern). No one knew this except a few discreet officials. One day in August of the same year the author entered a barber's shop in Yalta but found the proprietor with his arms crossed, steadfastly refusing to attend to the wants of his would-be customers. He said that the militia had come in and ordered that no work was to be done. The barber himself was entirely ignorant of the reason, and no one had a plausible suggestion to offer. Several Communists were questioned but in vain. It appeared that the shops had been ordered to close, but it was impossible to find out why. Some people *supposed* that it was in honour of the Medicsantrud (a day on which the medical and sanitary services made their inspections). Finally it was announced that the celebrations were for the Feast of the Assumption (Uspenie). No one could possibly know this, for the Church kept the feast according to the old calendar and on another day. Yet this was the excuse offered for the stoppage of work which had been forced by the militia on a people who did not even dare to inquire the reason. Some time after, seeing Moscow decked with crape-veiled flags, we were determined to satisfy our extreme curiosity and discover the reason. Though we inquired right and left, no one could tell us for whom the nation was in mourning, but, happening to dine that evening with some Communists, we learnt that a comrade of the Moscow Committee, Likachov by name, had died—hence the crape and flags. No one had heard his name even when he was alive, and now they were kept in ignorance of his death! When employed in a Soviet institution, the author witnessed the following practice: A quarter of an hour before work stopped in the evening, a small boy or girl used to come into the offices and cry out that the whole staff must assemble at the door of the building for "demonstration purposes". Of course *no one knew* the reason, but the departmental chiefs and their underlings kept so strict a watch on the employees that they were unable to escape without running the risk of being severely punished, or unless they had a very good excuse to offer. We actually saw with our own eyes the details of the inner workings of the demonstration—outwardly so magnificent—with which the English Trades Union leaders were deceived. It is strictly true to say that in no country in the world does the government treat the people in this way, scorning to offer them, even as a matter of form, the smallest explanation for its conduct. And how could the intellectual and political level of this people be raised under such a system?

Meetings and elections, whether of Party, Trades Unions, Soviets, or others, are all alike inspired with the same spirit. Communists stamp them with their own mark. Often factory meetings cannot be held unless the doors are shut to prevent the workmen escaping. At the Red Proletarian factory at Grodno the workmen fled away, hid themselves, and jumped over walls in their attempts to escape, and the president and secretary of the committee, who chased them, only managed to collect 180 out of the 400 members ("Trud", June 17th 1926). The workers' feelings of repugnance for these meetings, their systematic absenteeism, and their indifference to debates and resolutions are due to their fear of being dismissed by the officials. Outside these assemblies, they hold animated discussions ("Trud", July 2nd 1926). At Pskov, the workers found the door of the meeting-place open and made good their escape; the committee reporter stated that the officials took the names of those persons taking part in the debates and in consequence hardly anyone came to the meetings ("Trud", October 16th 1926). Zorich summarised present methods as follows: "Is there any opposition? No. Complete unanimity with one exception. I invite the comrade who abstained from voting to come and see me after the meeting." This journalist quoted a series of facts proving that the Communists trample upon the workers' rights and opinions ("Pravda", January 9th 1927). The Central Committee of the Party passed a resolution at its conference in February 1927 prohibiting the system by which orders were issued to electors and by which candidates were forced to stand for Soviet elections, thereby admitting the prevalence of this practice. Nevertheless, electoral commissions rob hundreds of thousands from among the worker, peasant, and even Communist, electorate of their right to vote ("Pravda", February 6th 1927). "Attempts were made to entice workers to attend the meetings at which they were so unwilling to be present by offering them cinema shows, etc.; the doors of the assembly halls were kept shut and the workers threatened" ("Trud", June 2nd 1927). At the election of a workers' committee in the Uralsk, the district secretary forced his candidate to be nominated though the majority of the workers voted against his election ("Trud", June 2nd 1927). "Workers are no longer interested in the meetings; the same stories are always drummed into them; they are made to listen to lectures on China and, tired beyond their endurance, ask for peace" ("Trud" March 23rd 1928). The management of the Bukharin factory *sent for the militia to expel* workers who criticised the group-contract plan ("Trud", June 15th 1928). A sketch which appeared in the "Crocodile" (a comic paper) showed an assembly chamber quite empty with the members crowded together on the platform. The comment ran as follows: "Everyone present has been made a *member* of the bureau so that none can escape" (No. 40, 1928). "Meetings have wearied everybody;

hardly anyone ever attends or takes any interest in them, and decrees and resolutions are treated as mere scraps of paper." To take one example: at a factory in the Ukraine, 1,353 meetings or conferences were held in five months, and 6,797 resolutions were passed during that period ("Trud", November 14th 1928). At a conference of agricultural labourers, delegates from Kharkov declared that they were afraid; and others from Sverdlovsk said that their bachelor friends were welcome to criticise, but that they, as married men, did not want to join the unemployed. (The "Evening Krasnaya Gazette", December 6th 1928). Some workers at Samara found the doors closed when it was time to leave off work and were forced to continue for an extra hour to make up for the time lost in listening to the Soviet report ("Trud", March 23rd 1929). Metallurgical workers in the Uralsk were *afraid* to make even verbal statements at a Trades Union inquiry. Workers were dismissed from several factories for daring to speak at meetings ("Trud", March 30th 1929). Two workers were discharged because they offered criticism; "rabcors" were frightened to write for the newspapers because the factory committee and management would quickly settle their account" (Supplement to the "Trud", September 6th 1929). And this is the "Dictatorship of the Proletariat"!

Soviet newspapers publish a great number of reports recording the proceedings of these meetings and elections, which show in the clearest possible manner the apathy, ignorance, and fears of the masses, and the tyrannical insolence and brutal rudeness of the pseudo-Communists towards them. But all such reports cannot be summarised in a few words. Let us again observe these features of the infinitely varied physiognomy of the Bolshevist Party. "The standard of learning among our officials and in our bureaucracy is lamentable: it requires to be twenty thousand times higher. If that is to be effected, a minimum of education is necessary. The 'Dictatorship of the Proletariat' should in no way consist of insulting behaviour towards all non-Communists." Bukharin gave this as his opinion at the Congress of Comsomols, and he also said: "Lenin's wish was that a guilty Communist should be punished ten times more severely than an ordinary mortal, but in actual fact, very often the very opposite occurs ("Pravda", March 21st 1928). Yaroslavsky admitted that alcoholism was very prevalent among the Communists, and described it as a "general phenomenon"; and not only the ordinary members had taken to drink but the leaders as well (The "Krasnaya Gazette", March 16th 1926). In another report on rural Communist nuclei, Yaroslavsky acknowledged that complete ignorance of politics (in 30 per cent. of these nuclei) and the low level of culture among the majority were also "general phenomena". Hardly anyone read the papers and the secretaries monopolised all authority. The abuse of power, drunkenness, and the embezzlement of public funds were very frequent. The Commission of Inquiry expelled from the Party 25 per cent. of the group secretaries appearing before it. Turcoman Communists bought themselves wives; one of them sold his daughter for 500 roubles (£20), and others trafficked in minors ("Pravda", June 2nd 1927).

All the irregularities cited here and thousands of others are vigorously denounced from time to time in the Soviet Press and with the soundest reasoning: but it is precisely this method which is termed in Russia "nursing a cold by keeping the draughts blowing". It is forbidden to point out the fundamental causes of the evil (these are hidden deep beneath the faults of the régime), and superficial, half-hearted observations only stimulate the evil and deceive its victims. The apparent sincerity of this policy of self-criticism in reality belongs to the system of Soviet autocracy: it may strike at unimportant provincial secretaries, who will be followed by men of the same stamp or worse, but it leaves intact the monstrous power of the Party Secretariat and will never curtail the imperfections begotten by its administration.

In a letter to Trotsky, Sosnovsky quoted a very characteristic case, which shows the atmosphere existing in the Party and in the factories, and indicates the feeling which governs the relations between Communist and proletarian (Opposition report. No. 3–4, p. 24). At the Clara Zetkin tobacco factory in Leningrad, a woman worker who spoke of rationalisation at a meeting was treated as an enemy of the proletariat. The under-manager made some insinuations which terrified her, and in the night of May 1st she *died of fear.* The workers declared that they would never again attend meetings nor utter a word in public ("Trud", July 3rd 1928). At Leningrad, the "cradle of the Revolution", as Russians love to call it, the directors of the Sevzaptorg (the commercial department for the North-West) were arrested for extortion, debauchery, and tyrannical conduct, etc. Such incidents are of daily occurrence and no one pays the slightest attention to them, but the following is of general importance: "Honest comrades in the Party who tried to raise their voices against these abominable practices were persecuted. Three of them could no longer stand such treatment; the first threw himself out of the window, the second cut a vein, and the third blew out his brains. The Party and the Trades Unions turned a blind eye to these tragedies" ("Trud", September 4th 1929). It has already been remarked that in reality the Party and Trades Unions do not exist at all, but, in their place, only an administration and its officials, both hostile to the interests of the working class. This is proved by the facts given below.

In one of the most prominent institutions of Soviet life, the Commissariat of Finance at Moscow (and not in a village in far-away Kamchatka), the Communist nucleus was quite recently "disintegrated" or broken up by the iniquitous behaviour of its members. They were guilty of embezzlement, drunkenness, abuse of authority, non-payment of pensions, hooliganism, and unlawful demands made upon their woman comrades in office. They had been obsequious, bureaucratic, quarrelsome, caring for nothing but their own interests; they had put obstacles in the way of new members and were found to have deviated from the paths of righteousness [*sic*] in their official capacity, etc. This obsequiousness (which in Russian is "podkhalimstvo" and means servile vapidness and ignoble compliance) had reached such a pitch that, for example, a Party member, fearful and cringing, looked silently on while a drunken Communist outraged his wife ("Pravda", August 7th 1929). This creature of a husband, who through cowardice and ambition became the accomplice of his wife's seducer, is a truly symbolic character. He is the incarnation of the Party "discipline" which makes all members accomplices in the violation of the principles of Communism and in the destruction of the ideals of the Revolution, which is working out its course day by day under their very eyes. Moreover, such facts and others similar to them have become commonplace in their profusion, but they are very rarely made public. But this end will not be achieved except as a result of a political conflict which will cause the leaders to cast aside all scruples of discretion and will rouse them to combat their adversaries by all the means at their disposal. These Communists, together with their brothers and their cousins, all of the same kidney, vote enthusiastically for proposals such as "Socialism to make the world one", while at the same time approving the imprisonment or deportation of the last remaining Communists who are struggling towards their ideals.

But the most marked effect of the "degenerate" and "disintegrated" state of the Communist Party (the Bolshevist Press itself uses these expressions) and of the Soviet apparatus is seen in the scandalous *affaires* which during the last few years have thrown a strong light upon the realities of the Russian situation and have revealed the profound corruption of the Revolutionary personnel. In view of the widespread character of these scandals, their continual recurrence throughout the country and in all important industrial centres, the number of Communist officials or "sympathisers" implicated in them, and the multitude of less serious cases which are, nevertheless, equally valuable indications, it was clearly a waste of time to point to the failures of individuals, monotonous though they were, as the source of every evil. The leaders of the Party have laid bare these evils, at the same time affirming the sound condition of the organisation for which they are responsible. The reader will judge for himself whether any body so covered in sores could possibly be said to be healthy.

The gangrenous state of the Communist and Soviet administration in Nakhichevan, Kherson, and in other places has been pointed out in an earlier chapter, but the report made of the conditions at that time now seems to be an entirely unimportant addition to history. In July 1925 it was found necessary to arrest all the upper ranks of the Kiev militia, who were found guilty of various heinous offences—embezzlement, theft, and abuse of authority. Among them were "an old recidivist robber" who was "an ex-chief of militia from the central district", former police-officers, spies, and gendarmes of the counterrevolution ("Pravda", end of July and August 1st 1925). Men of this long-lived breed were constantly being discovered by the "purging" commissions. They had been versatile enough to adapt themselves in all outward appearance to the new régime, but were yet free to carry on the methods of the old. In the province of Poltava, a village nucleus organised the assassination of a peasant family; the three ringleaders, the secretary of the nucleus, the president of the Soviet, the president of the poor people's committee, were arrested. While still in prison, the secretary threatened that the throats of all the members of twenty families would be cut by the Communist nucleus if one of his accomplices was not set at liberty ("Pravda", May 26th 1925). At Zakarievka, in the province of Odessa, the heads of Communist organisations and Soviet institutions were arrested. Among them were the secretary of the Party, the president of the executive committee, the director of the co-operative, the judge and the principal controller. They had been guilty of robbing the public funds, of indulging in drunken orgies, and of forcing female teachers into immoral relations with them ("Pravda", October 20th 1926). In the Kirghiz Republic, two district secretaries of the Party, a member of the Central Executive Committee of Soviets, and other Communist officials were arrested. This band had been infamously ill-treating peasants, shooting them without trial, confiscating their horses, etc., and ransoming them by making them pay huge taxes. The robbers divided the proceeds among themselves ("Pravda", October 20th 1926). At Leningrad, on August 22nd 1926, forty workmen seized a young girl and outraged her in turn; several of them were Communists ("Pravda", September 11th 1926). This affair led to the discovery of a whole series of others, less important, in which Communists and Comsomols had been particularly prominent. At Artemovsk (formerly Bakhmut) in the Donetz, the proletarian capital of the great coal basin, the chief police officials and the staff of the militia, who had been relying upon the co-operation of the Soviet officials and the influence of the Party committees, were suddenly arrested, tried, and condemned for rape, drunkenness, and tyrannical methods, etc. The local newspaper, "Kochegarka", on being informed of this, maintained a discreet silence, and high Communist officials, beside themselves with fear, did not dare to say anything. Several committed suicide ("Pravda", and other newspapers, February 1928). Three members of the Proletarian Authors Association were arrested for having carried off a young Communist girl, whom they first made drunk and then violated. Their victim committed suicide. (The "Rabochaya Gazette", March 31st 1928). Faced with such evidence, the Press decided to recognise such infamies as having been absorbed into the manners and customs of the people. At Sotchi, in the Caucasus, all the local Communist leaders were arrested on a charge of squandering the public funds and of drunkenness, for having assaulted women on numberless occasions, indulged in debauchery, and for having ruled as tyrants ("Pravda", April 8th 1928). In the Crimea, the President of the Central Executive Committee of Soviets, Ibraimov, and all his confidants were common robbers in the eyes of the law. They were convicted of innumerable and abominable crimes—assassinations, torture, extortion, theft, embezzlement—of every shameful act imaginable. The report ran into five volumes—3,800 pages in all (The "Evening Krasnaya Gazette", April 30th 1928, and all newspapers). In the Uralsk it was discovered that the Communist leaders in one district were guilty of bribery; that they had become debauched and had cultivated acquaintance with the riff-raff of the place ("Pravda", May 22nd 1928). An old militant of the Party was amongst the Soviet officials arrested in Turkestan for having embezzled enormous sums from the public funds. At Ryazhsk it was stated that almost the entire administration was in intimate relations with some robbers of the district ("Pravda", May 6th 1928). At Stavropol, the secretaries of the regional Committees of the Party and the other Communist officials were all arrested; they had raped some women teachers, indulged in drunken orgies, and were guilty of other abuses ("Pravda", May 12th 1928). But the most malignant abscess of all, as doctors would say, was undoubtedly the situation at Smolensk.

In the town and in the surrounding country, in the cantons and districts, the whole Bolshevik-Sovietist administration was rotten through and through. Party committees, Soviet, and Trades Unions, all competed with each other in oppressing the workers, violating the women, plundering the public funds, and behaving in a drunken, dissolute manner. In one factory, where quite half the employees were Communists, the president of a Trades Union division exacted a "consideration" in money from the workmen, and "in kind" from the women. This had been going on for several years. Seven workmen who were worn out by the régime committed suicide, all within a short space of time. A "commune", which was composed of prominent Party officials and military agents, was closely connected with some bandits; several cantonal secretaries were convicted of extortion and dishonesty. A peasant woman tried to hang herself after her last ewe had been confiscated. In order to protest against the criminal conduct of the local authorities, a group of Comsomols secretly printed a pamphlet setting out the facts of the case. The Party organs co-operated in hiding the truth by maintaining an unbroken silence. A start was made by arresting sixty officials, the majority being Communists ("Pravda", May 12th 1928, Zaitsev's article, as well as all other newspapers; "Pravda", May 18th, resolution of the Commission of Control). Yakovlev, officially appointed to investigate the affair, emphasised its general significance ("Pravda", May 16th; "Izvestia", May 22nd). The entire Press sounded the alarm and roused public opinion to react against the moral decadence of a considerable number of State employees and of officials in Government service (the Party, Trades Unions, and co-operatives). For several months a "purging" campaign was carried on; the organisations in the Smolensk district and elsewhere were thoroughly cleansed. In one canton alone, thirty-three officials were brought to justice; among them were the chief military agents, who had stolen horses from peasants, and the judge, who had fined one murderer 100 roubles (£4) and had acquitted others. Thirty "revisers" had inspected the district in the previous year without noticing anything amiss ("Izvestia", June 9th). At Vladimir, the directors of the textile Syndicate abused their position of authority; a female employee was outraged ("Pravda", June 19th 1928). The Party chiefs at Tuapsi took to drink, and one of them screened a brothel; the co-operative managers were impeached in court and the magistrates convicted of arbitrary conduct ("Pravda", June 19th). The directors of the tramway service in Odessa forced unemployed women into immoral relations with them before they would give them work; the secretary of the Communist nucleus and the municipal employees were all inveterate drunkards ("Trud", June 19th). The Soviet and Communist organisations at Irkutsk were corrupted by officials formerly belonging to the Tsarist régime ("Pravda", August 4th). An inspector who had been sent into the Maryisk district reported the demoralised state of the principal officials, the Communist militants, and the committee secretaries, etc.; they were drunkards, peculators, and robbers of women ("Pravda", August 8th). At Yakutsk, the Communist organisation was responsible for disturbances, robbery, and numerous crimes. The Crimean administration, which was already unpleasantly notorious, shielded Whites, Nationalists, and undisguised *saboteurs* ("Pravda", August 11th). In the province of Riazan, 1,139 out of 5,100 officials in the Finance department were dismissed for embezzlement, bribery, drunkenness, and forgery ("Pravda", November 11th).

In 1929 fresh "abscesses" were always being discovered on the "healthy body" of the Soviet bureaucracy. The "Pravda" (January 3rd) admitted that the Communist nuclei were overrun with ex-gendarmes, pogromists, monarchists, or "kulaki", according to the district. At the beginning of January, the remarkable "kabuki" affair occurred at Moscow. The whole staff of the building syndicate, guilty of waste, debauchery, and abuse of authority, were denounced as a result of an erotic outburst in the public street ("Pravda" and others, January 6th and other days). Then there were syndicate directors who did not distinguish too finely between the syndicate money and their own. One of the principal committees of the Communist Youth at Leningrad was "purged" on account of bribery and corruption. The Communist organisations of Sir-Daria were simply swarming with thieves, robbers, and all kinds of scoundrels ("Pravda", January 9th). At Tver, the tribunal had been for several years in league with all the officials, who were guilty of dishonesty, turpitude, and various abuses ("Pravda", January 19th). At Bryansk, the provincial committee of the Party shielded the Communist leaders of the N. district who had been found guilty a month before of public debauchery and abuse of power, etc., and whom they had first of all decided to expel from the Party. At Astrakhan, 200 Soviet officials, who had been robbing the State in various ways with the complicity of the Communists, were arrested; fifty-seven members of the Party and later some others were expelled. A gigantic trial was set in motion which lasted several weeks. ("Pravda", "Izvestia", July, August, September). In Uzbeskistan, the Municipal Workers' Union (or, in other words, their leaders) were accused of various crimes, which likened it to the "kabuki" affair at Moscow ("Trud", August 3rd and 4th). At Rybinsk, the same hotbed of infection was discovered as at Astrakhan. At Syzrañ, Grozny, Kharkov, and Stalingrad conditions were the same ("Trud", August 3rd, 4th, 22nd, and 27th). At Baku, the People's Commissary of Finance and a number of high officials in his department were brought to justice ("Trud", September 3rd). At Leningrad, the commercial administration was rotten to the core and the regional Party commission of control was guilty of complicity in many shameful acts; in four years one hundred persons had been the subject of denunciatory letters sent to the Press without effect; the editorial staff of the Leningrad "Pravda", among others, were guilty of refusing to publish them ("Trud", September 3rd). At Nizhni-Novogorod, the Communist organisation broke down and the officials behaved in a highly suspicious manner ("Pravda", September 6th and following days). From Tula came the usual story of embezzlement and debauch, this time in the Finance department, the commercial section, the co-operatives, and the tribunal. Thousands of corrupt officials had been expelled by the "purging" commissions from the Vniechtorg (foreign trade service) and yet they continued to increase. Hardly a day passed in July, August, and September 1929 that the "Trud" did not denounce some fresh signs of "degeneracy", "deviation", or moral "disease" among the heads of the Trades Union organisation or in the basic committees. The attention of the public was drawn to conditions in the textile organisation at Tver (July 10th), in the Crimean syndicates, and in the Number One factory at Moscow (August 21st). The "Trud" revealed that in a canton in the province of Tver the secretaries conducted themselves in a manner worthy of the Middle Ages. A woman teacher whom they persecuted committed suicide (August 23rd). At the big factory at Bryansk, the Red Profintern, the lightermen's central committee, went bankrupt (August 25th). But only the main features of the most important cases are given here, and the reader is spared the tedious task of studying the more complicated Press extracts packed with statistics and confused explanations. But enough evidence has been produced to show how impossible it is to make any allowance for these political persecutions and moral "purgings": the zeal of the Trades Union chiefs for these "cleansing" campaigns is clearly inspired by the Party Secretariat's struggle against Tomsky and his supporters, who so recently were masters of the professional organisation.

Amid the general disorder, it is impossible to define the boundaries of the Party, the Soviets, and the Trades Unions: as has been already explained, they are bound together, cast, and welded into one. The same officials, generally in the closest co-operation, monopolise all offices in the three systems. That is the reason why they are arrested in batches of ten, fifty, or a hundred and more. The sub-title above the report on conditions in Number One factory at Moscow declared in heavy type that "there had been revolting incidents in connection with the disintegration of the Party into groups." These "disintegrated" militants were found in the Trades Unions, the co-operatives, in the district Soviets, and in the housing committee, etc.—in fact everywhere. As a general rule, all information concerning the Party is available to the Trades Unions and vice versa; the same applies to the Soviets and the co-operatives, etc., and to the various organisations and institutions which are carried on by the same Communist personnel.

For some years past, the Soviet Press has been obliged to record a "wave" of embezzlement and an "epidemic" of dishonesty—to use "Pravda's" expression—in the Trades Unions ("Pravda", April 15th 1925). "Tomsky declares that if this wave does not subside, it will be necessary to inflict a capital sentence on these peculators" ("Pravda", May 28th 1925). A circular letter from Kursky, the Commissary of Justice, warned all magistrates and legal officers and requested them to deal severely with cases of embezzlement (June 21st 1925). Every day cases of dishonesty were reported in the Press, and in the province of Moscow alone there were 285 in nine months. In the postal service and at Kharkov the same trouble existed; 83 per cent. of the thieves were Communists ("Trud", March 2nd 1926). In Siberia, the State, co-operative, and Trades Union funds were robbed in 1,500 cases (The "Krasnaya Gazette", March 19th). At Leningrad, 2,274,000 roubles (£94,750) were stolen in seven months; one-quarter of the 2,702 cases occurred in the Trades Unions ("Trud", September 8th 1926). In the Moscow Province, the Trades Union funds alone were robbed on 342 occasions in 1925, 281 in 1926, and 245 in 1927. Tomsky more or less admitted at the eighth Trades Union Congress that everyone stole, the Communists, Comsomols, and non-party people alike. (A report in the "Trud", December 15th 1928 and following days.) In 1928 the appropriation of public monies increased by 53 per cent. over the previous year in the

Moscow Trades Unions; half of those responsible were Communists ("Trud", March 29th 1929).

Nowhere else in the world is there anything like this or approaching it. There are cases of bribery and corruption in every country as well as officials unworthy to be in positions of trust and responsibility, but nothing can be compared with the conditions prevailing in the Russian Trades Unions. And the explanation is simple: these bodies are Trades Unions only in name. Wage-earners and proletarians in the U.S.S.R. have no Unions in the proper sense; they are nothing more than committees which are controlled by bureaucrats hostile to the interests of the people. So-called members have never consented to join the Unions. They were not consulted, and all that was wanted of them was part of their meagre wages and still more work. In the course of a very critical speech at Leningrad, Tomsky made the following pronouncement: "If I had made this speech in certain local assemblies as an ordinary Trades Union member, I should have been considered *a waster and a disgrace to the organisation; in other words, I should have been expelled*" ("Trud", May 20th 1925). Nothing could have been clearer. And banishment from the Union means dismissal from the factory and death by starvation, as has been already explained. It is the same in the Party as in all other organisations. Tomsky personally experienced similar treatment in that year; having opposed the Secretariat of the Party, he was simultaneously expelled from the Trades Unions and from his office as chairman. And the Secretariat, if it had wished, could have caused him to disappear, unjudged, for ever—by a simple order to the Ogpu. Trades Unions do not exist.

Dogadov, another Trades Union leader, reported the following significant figures to the Central Council of these sham Trades Unions: in 1925, the budget of the

Central Workers' Union was approximately 70 million roubles (£2,958,000), of which nearly a half (47 per cent.) had been squandered by the officials ("Pravda", December 9th 1926). But one cannot be sure that a part of the other half did not go indirectly into the officials' pockets. In the Moscow Metallurgical Workers' Union, there were 700 officials and only 130,000 members ("Trud", June 12th 1928). The parasitic bureaucracy which constitutes the sham Trades Union needs no comment. Now to turn to the life of these so-called Trades Union members. What do they receive in return for this dearly bought privilege of membership? The "Vyestnik Truda" (No. 10, 1926) remarked upon the poor attendance at meetings, the lack of interest among the workers, and the bad effect of coercive and authoritative methods—the closing of the factory doors, for example. The "Trud" (March 29th 1927) admitted that all decisions were taken by the "executive" bodies outside the Trades Unions. It stated that workers took no interest in the resolutions which kept pouring in upon them; it was a waste of time to attend these meetings (November 14th 1928). This was confirmed by "Pravda" when it published letters from "rabcors": people no longer troubled to go to these meetings because no attention was paid to workers' opinions. In his speech before the Eighth Congress, Tomsky could not avoid speaking of the *strikes* which had occurred unknown to the Trades Unions. Workers who were driven out on strike by the Soviet Government took good care to appeal for help to their professional Unions. He was obliged to admit that there was a traffic in membership cards quoted in secret like stock-exchange shares because they represented privileges. At Kiev, an inspection proved that the Unions completely disregarded the members' interests ("Trud", March 20th 1929). The Union bureaucracy indulged in "higher politics" and neglected to regulate working conditions ("Trud", August 26th 1929). This newspaper called "higher politics" the back-kitchen of the Party, for their object was to replace the ordinary officials by men specially chosen by the ruling gang. Since Tomsky's downfall, permission has been granted, or, rather, orders have been given to state openly that for years all has not been well with the Trades Unions, whereas before he was disgraced, it was taken for granted that they would be recognised as being in excellent running condition. At the present time, the Trades Unions tend to become corporate, bourgeois institutions, entirely foreign to the spirit of the age, added to which they are cut off from the masses and operate most unsatisfactorily ("Pravda", September 6th 1929). But the actual truth is simpler than that: Trades Unions do not exist.

The co-operatives are in every way similar. "We continue to trade according to Oriental or gipsy methods", as Lenin said. The customer is forced to buy what he does not want, and anything he does want is not sold to him ("Pravda", March 26th 1925). In the co-operative stores of the Amo factory at Moscow, provisions were of bad quality, sometimes even rotten, and were dearer than elsewhere ("Pravda", July 7th 1925). In another store in the province of Moscow "there was poor choice of provisions of an inferior quality" ("Pravda", September 11th 1925). "Why do workers show no interest in the co-operatives?" was the headline in a paper; and the article explained that disaffection had been caused by the intrusion of Communists, who had put in their own men as employees—often entirely worthless creatures ("Pravda", September 30th 1925). It was stated at a co-operative conference that the prices charged were so high that they lowered the *real* wage by sometimes as much as 8 per cent. ("Trud", April 3rd 1926). It was repeatedly declared that the co-operative officials speculated with Capitalists; the "Ekonomicheskaya Zhizn" gave an example of this in its issue of March 27th 1926. In one year as much as 5,323,000 roubles (£222,000) were squandered in the co-operatives ("Torgovo-Promyshlenaya Gazette", May 23rd 1926). The staff stole and plundered in the co-operatives in the Leningrad and Yaroslavl districts (The "Rabochaya Gazette", June 13th 1926). Theft and plunder was the general rule. Profiting by its monopoly of retail trade granted by the State and guaranteed by force, the co-operative management engaged in unrestrained mercantilism and exploited the consumer, or, rather, the poorest classes, with the result that it made a clear profit of 200 per cent. by employing the most disgraceful Capitalist methods ("Pravda", February 1st 1927). "Workers who come to make their purchases at the co-operative are received like dogs; the employees are arrogant and insulting, the goods are of bad quality and very dear, added to which customers have long, tiring waits in queues" ("Trud", August 18th 1927, from workers' letters). The capital of more than half the co-operatives was squandered by the personnel, and this was continually increasing (The "Evening Krasnaya Gazette", November 13th 1928). Bukharin said: "One cannot tell the difference, even with a telescope, between an ordinary shop and a co-operative" ("Pravda", December 2nd 1928). There is one difference, however, but it is not to the credit of the co-operative store. "These stores ask much too high prices and their general charges are very considerable" ("Ekonomicheskaya Zhizn, January 4th 1927). At Saratov, Stalingrad, and Rostov, in fact everywhere, the employees stole and plundered ("Pravda", January 13th 1929). No improvement had been observed in the quality of co-operative goods since the time when Dzerjinsky severely denounced its fallacious prosperity ("Pravda", January 13th 1929), and the monstrous parasitical administration, with its 400,000 officials, receiving 90 million roubles (£3,750,000) in salaries a year—figures which have very much increased since. The whole Russian Communist Press for August, September, and October accused the co-operatives of negligence, wilful destruction, and wholesale frauds, the disastrous effects of which were borne by the labouring masses.

To be able to give an adequate study of the Soviet bureaucracy in general would require a book in itself. We must confine ourselves to giving a succint enumeration of several facts which show the characteristics of this hypertrophied monster, the Soviet administration. It is useful as waste-paper, harmful, costly, a sterile system with a sterilising influence, a thing corrupted and yet a thing corrupting. It is insolent towards the humble, cringing before the powerful, remaining always an enemy of the Revolution. Whether as the instrument of the Party, of the Soviet, or of the economic Services, it does not belie its reputation. The scandalous affairs discussed earlier in this chapter pointed to the moral. Now to turn to the system in actual operation.

"Every member in our group is expected to answer in writing eighty-four questions a month" ("Pravda", April 23rd 1925). That makes a thousand a year per person; no one reads them and millions of tons of fatuous inquiry papers are stacked up on the dusty office floors; and yet there is a serious scarcity of paper. Children are without exercise-books and money is lacking for education and industry.

"The number of instructional circulars received by Communist groups varies in certain places between thirty and one hundred a month" ("Pravda", June 7th 1925). Still more paper uselessly piled up in offices—and it is the proletariat that pays! The character of the Soviet local administrative apparatus is red-tapist in the extreme. The provincial committee usually sends out two or three circulars a day on every conceivable subject: having done that, it considers that it has fulfilled its duty ("Pravda", June 7th 1925). This entails more millions of wasted sheets, not to mention the ink! "We are inundated with circulars and instructions," many group secretaries complained, "and they are hardly of any use." After a meeting in a Communist nucleus of some out-of-the-way village, the secretary exhibited a "small sheet measuring exactly 6 feet 6 inches long by 1 foot 7 inches broad". This was an inquiry form which needed filling in. "If all the members of the group were placed one on top of each other and the circulars and inquiry forms, etc., were piled up beside them, this heap of human beings and paper would be higher than the group building itself" ("Pravda", June 12th 1925). This was an example given *by the Party*; it was contagious, as we shall see. "The decision concerning the local reserves of seed was published by the Central Executive Committee in 1922 and it has still not been applied ("Pravda", September 25th 1925). But, after all, that was only three years after the decision had been taken; besides, in 1929 it has certainly been forgotten altogether and millions of others with it. "Factories are forced to give the most varied information, reports, and statistical data, which forms a torrent of paper necessitating the employment of an excessively large staff and swamping creative work. A sea of papers is the result and hundreds of people are engulfed in it." "Accounts and statistics are in a calamitous condition; industrial establishments are weighed down with the burden of having to furnish information in hundreds of different shapes and forms; reckoning is now made in pouds." This was Dzerjinsky writing in "Pravda" (June 23rd 1926).

A forest department sent a circular to district officials demanding information concerning the number of partridges, quails, grouse (*Bonasia ketulina*), hares, bears, and wolves, etc., found alive in the various districts—the data to be forwarded within a week (The "Krasnaya Gazette", May 14th 1926). The annual report of the Yugostal would weigh 12 pouds (418 lb.) if it was produced according to rule ("Ekonomicheskaya Zhizn", June 17th 1926). The Commissariat of Transport had already sent out approximately 10,000 orders which were never read and which had been published after a delay of one to three years (The "Krasnaya Gazette", June 6th 1926). "A flood of reports": in the space of only two months, 643 books of factory reports were published in Moscow; there were approximately 1,200 pages in each and "hardly anyone read them". During the preceding four months 1,866 had appeared; a considerable amount of money was thus wasted ("Pravda", July 29th 1926). At Chereopovetz, the communal authorities laid down a plan of administration for the next 200 years (The "Krasnaya Gazette", August 23rd 1926). To obtain information from the Commissariat of Commerce, the inquiry had to pass through thirty-seven different services (The "Evening Krasnaya Gazette", August 28th 1926). It was not uncommon to find that certain goods had to pass through ten to fifteen services before reaching the consumer, and the general expenses exceeded the initial value of the article ("Izvestia", September 19th 1926). The inquiry form for a children's dispensary produced 127 questions; a trust in the Uralsk printed a report of 9,459 pages; the railways spent 9 million roubles on reports comprising 18,000 pages, in which the required information could never be found. The Commissariat of Finance in Adjaristan cost more to maintain than the country received in revenues

(The "Evening Krasnaya Gazette", December 22nd 1928).

The management of the railways received reports representing 30 million pages with portraits of the local Party chiefs [*sic*], but lacking information concerning the trains. The Mostorg answered 477,085 questions in one year, the Moscow Co-operative Council 622,393, and a textile factory 629,000 ("Pravda", February 3rd 1927). A State education bureau sent parents of school-children a questionnaire consisting of 100 idiotic questions ("Pravda", February 19th 1927). The Commissariat of Transport alone spoilt 420,000 pouds (6,620 tons) of paper in one year, nearly one-quarter of the total production and about ten train-loads of approximately forty trucks each ("Izvestia", February 4th 1927). The children of a school in the Uralsk found that they had to answer 180 absurd questions in writing. The following one was addressed to the parents: "Were you not drunk at the time when the child was conceived?" ("Trud", April 29th 1927). The Workers' and Peasants' Inspectorate calculated that in the accountancy department of State industries alone, 500,000 clerks were employed, costing one thousand million roubles a year ("Trud", May 30th 1927). The Kharkov Department of Hygiene sent a circular of 47 pages and 127 questions to all the villages in the district. One of the questions was: "Indicate the nationalities of those using the wells. Say whether they are Ukrainian, Jewish, Russian, or Polish" ("Pravda of Youth", September 24th 1927). At the fifteenth Congress of the Party, Stalin quoted the following facts: a disabled soldier had to wait seven years for a set of false teeth; the report on the leather industry submitted to the Commissariat of Commerce contained 27,000 questions, and an agricultural report from the Ukraine had as many as 20,000 questions, etc. ("Izvestia", December 11th 1927).

A workman who had a claim to make against the management of an industrial concern had to transact his business through twenty-four different offices ("Trud", January 14th 1928). *The provincial agricultural office circularised the cantonal executive committees to the effect that they must count the earthworms found in the fields* ("Pravda", March 1st 1928). We are under the impression that the record set up by this attempted census will never be beaten. A local executive committee sent the village Soviets a questionnaire containing 348 questions, just at the height of the sowing season ("Pravda", April 18th 1928). The authorities of one factory entered 210 comments on each workman in their register and one must remember that the personnel was always changing ("Trud", August 5th 1928). According to Ordzhonikidze a watch imported into the U.S.S.R. was examined on 142 occasions by the Customs ("Izvestia", December 9th 1928). He also stated that more than half the decisions taken by the higher authorities were never carried out ("Pravda", December 21st 1928). The Institute of Agricultural Research issued an inquiry-form concerning tractors, which was 16 feet by 19 feet and covered with questions ("Byednota", April 14th 1929). An inventor who had come to Moscow to carry out experiments on his discovery, set out to find a room; after a year and a half he had not yet met with success, but he had a fine collection of papers, certificates, resolutions, declarations, protocols, and decisions—more than 400 documents in all ("Vechernyaya Moskva", June 1929). The foundations of a factory were laid . . . three months before the constructional plans had been approved. The newspaper which remarked upon this fact called it "a curious little detail". In fifteen months, the Supreme Economic Council was required by the Government to carry through 866 plans of which 446 did not receive attention.

Many other institutions were in the same plight ("Izvestia", July 31st 1929). There was an increasing number of cases in which buildings were completed while the constructional plans and estimates were still being passed from one office to another or had been already pigeonholed. In studying the Soviet economic system it would be necessary to take this fact into account as it is a valuable aid to the true understanding of the situation.

The bureaucratic régime of the U.S.S.R. weighs all the more heavily on the proletariat and the labouring peasants, because it is not possible to have recourse to legal methods in order to counterbalance the effects of the political, economic, and administrative tyranny of the dictatorship of the proletariat as instituted by the Secretariat of the Party. And in the first place, in the only republic which has taken "Socialist" as its designation, legality does not exist at all. There is an infinite number of laws and decrees which even bewilder the best-trained and most expert of Soviet jurists, and which the Secretariat of the Party, with the help of its Ogpu, is well able to disregard. Besides, no one minds stating bluntly that "the dictatorship of the proletariat, in common with all other dictatorships, is a power which is bound by no law". This phrase occurred in a letter to the "Izvestia" (September 7th 1926), in which the writer refuted the statement made by Krylenko, the Procurator, who expressed as his opinion that this dictatorship *should be made* part of the legal framework of the modern State. Therefore up to the present time the dictatorship has not been sanctioned by law. Moreover, the Soviet Press has repeatedly denounced its abuse of power, its arbitrary and unjust actions, and its violation of laws; it has continually declared its disapproval of its decrees, ordinances, regulations, statutes, instructions, and official circulars, which prescribe exactly how the Soviet individual shall conduct himself, and which inculcate respect for the "legality" of the Revolution. Bugoslavsky, Soltz, Krylenko, and others have filled many newspaper columns and accumulated innumerable reports and papers in connection with this subject. But their method has been once again "to nurse a cold by keeping cold draughts blowing". Since the dictatorship is not bound by any law, what is the good of wasting time in discoursing on its legality? It is enough that the local, provincial, regional or general secretary of the Party commands, and that the people submit. As for popular tribunals, they are part of the bureaucratic machine and support a respectable number of bureaucrats. Surely this is in keeping with the system as a whole?

The Workers' and Peasants' (or, more correctly), the Bureaucratic Inspectorate, set up an inquiry into the administration of justice in the U.S.S.R. It revealed that in 1926 more than a million individuals were torn from their work to imprisonment in the R.S.F.S.R. (the All-Russian Republic), not to mention witnesses and experts, etc. In the Ukr.S.S.R. (the Ukrainian Republic), 15 per cent. of the population appeared in the courts of law during the same year. This caused serious congestion on the cause-list, which nothing short of a general amnesty could relieve ("Izvestia", October 11th 1927). At the fifteenth Congress of the Party, Stalin employed these figures to denounce the chaotic conditions in the bureaucracy, of which he was high priest ("Izvestia", December 11th 1927). "Pravda" of February 2nd 1929 condemned the illegal actions of local authorities, which gave rise to an ever-increasing number of complaints, and, yet again, enjoined respect for revolutionary legality which does not exist for the Party and cannot, therefore, be claimed by the State. The "Izvestia" (June 11th 1929) declared that all laws were invariably trampled under foot in the country districts, or, in other words, throughout the length and breadth of the Soviet Union. This meant illegal taxes, perquisitions, and illegal arrests, faked elections, and unjust fines. The local budgets were supported by these fines and it was a simple matter to issue summonses to the peasants at every turn concerning matters of which they knew nothing.

"The struggle against bureaucracy." This is one of the watchwords of the Soviet Government and there are others bearing the same meaning. It is one of the *leitmotive* of the cradle-song with which the higher bureaucracy soothes a people exploited and oppressed by bureaucratic officials of all ranks, grades, and classes. It now belongs to the collection of the ritualistic formulæ of the official doctrine and has become one of the commandments of the Leninist religion, to be recited docilely and without comprehension by young "pioneers" and Comsomols, and to be despised by men when they attain a certain degree of social and political consciousness. This watchword—"an end to bureaucracy"—will only take on its true meaning when it issues from the lips of the masses themselves.

CHAPTER VII

"SOCIALISM IN FIFTEEN YEARS"

Party prophecies—The new idealists—Socialism in fourteen years—The author's point of view—The present stage and a question of direction—The standard of production—The Five-Year Plan—The sacrifice of a generation—Capitalism without Capitalists—A transitional phase and constitutional perspectives—The Party and the proletariat—Towards Capitalism or Socialism.

What the Soviet Union will be in fifteen years. This was the title of an article which appeared in "Pravda" on August 29th 1929, from the pen of Larin, the recognised idealist of present-day Bolshevism. This theorist of Leninism—the religion which came into being after the death of the great leader—only recently came into prominence, but has, since the repudiation of Bukharin, acted as the official purveyor of ideas to the Secretariat of the Party. He is still quite unknown outside the Russian Socialist movement in which, as a patriot in the days of Nicolas II, he only played a humble part before rallying to the flag of present-day Communism. In this article he gave an account of a book which has only recently been published, *The U.S.S.R. in Fifteen Years.* Sabsovich, its author, is quite unknown. Larin subscribed to his general opinions and conclusions, and caused them to be adopted by "Pravda", the central organ of the Party. (When "Pravda" does not print the note "article for discussion" below the writer's signature, that signifies that the article expresses the opinion of the editorial body and, therefore, of the Party.) It is important to notice that for twelve years Bolshevism has produced no new striking personality in spite of its material resources and of the protection which it affords to politics. In every realm of its activity and in every strata of its society, ideas, initiative, and the deeds that count, all have come from the October generation;

it is, therefore, extremely interesting to watch a new man, this Sabsovich, taking his first steps on the stage of Soviet actualities.

Larin was emphatic in stating that Sabsovich's plan was for *the establishment of Socialism in the U.S.S.R.*, with the suppression of classes and the transformation of the mode of life, of manners, and customs, etc. "It is perfectly clear that this is the only conception possible for us. In actual practice, the experience of the first two years of the Five-Year economic Plan (one complete year and the second on the point of termination) has fully strengthened our view. The results obtained have been shown to be more satisfactory than was estimated, not only as regards the Gosplan's Five-Year Plan, but in connection with Sabsovich's own forecast. The point is, therefore, not that the scheme is objectively impossible, but that an aptitude for utilising the existing resources must be developed, apart from the unknown reserves hidden in the possibility of utilising future discoveries and inventions." Then the Secretariat of the Bolshevist Party definitely promises that at the end of fifteen years Socialism will have spread over one-sixth of the globe's surface. Socialism will be realised, therefore, in the U.S.S.R. in fourteen years' time.

Socialism means the social régime immediately preceding the final stage in human development—Communism. It signifies a society without class distinctions and the realisation of the formula "*from each according to his ability*", the inevitable transition towards the final Communist formula "*to each according to his needs*". "Our generation", wrote Larin, who is not young in years though young in Bolshevism, "can see Socialism with their own eyes. And they will not even contemplate for an instant the possibility that war, for example, may thwart the grandiose plan. On the contrary, it must be admitted, as the basis of the plan, that our country will be called upon to defend Socialism with the sword. *Preparations have been made for any eventuality*."

Our rôle in these pages is not to contrast one proposal with another, but to reveal the realities of the Soviet régime, which have been obscured by the Soviet legend after being misrepresented by the counter-revolutionary campaign. A knowledge of those realities is essential for the true understanding of any thesis that may be advanced. We have given a true picture of the moral and physical state of the labouring masses, and this is the limited object of our task in this restricted plan. We did not spend long examining the situation of the privileged social categories found under the present system, but only briefly observed proletarian housing conditions, wages, lack of employment, and civic rights. Privileged treatment certainly exists in the U.S.S.R. for certain minorities forming the pillars of the State, and this fact explains why a situation in which conditions are such that few foreigners can distinguish between partial truths and general facts, or can avoid confusing the exception with the rule, produces seemingly sincere, if not clearsighted, testimony in its favour. The violent contrasts in Russia are reflected in statements which though accurate in themselves yet are contradictory, and they do not all have a general bearing on the situation. Our description is based on observations which have a general value for a given period of the Revolution.

But it is obvious that this stage will be superseded, and the question arises of foreseeing in what manner this will come about, and whether the state of Soviet inequality tends to develop or to disappear. Are these privileges the vestiges of an earlier social order or the signs of a social system which is still to come? It is impossible to approach this problem without a knowledge of the present condition of those classes which brought about the October Revolution, and this work should be of some assistance in this connection. But it will be still necessary to ascertain the state of industry and the advance of economic development in the U.S.S.R. in their relations with the economy of the Capitalist world. But an analysis of this other element in the destinies of the Revolution would be out of place at so late a stage in a work of this kind. A study of Soviet political economy and a comparison between their various policies would equally have no place in these pages. But the author may perhaps be allowed to give in brief outline and without statistical data his impression of what the future holds in store—to prevent, at any rate, opinions which he does not hold being attributed to him.

In ten years, agricultural and industrial production in the U.S.S.R. has been restored to the pre-war level, with appreciable progress in certain branches of industry and a decline in others. The volume of business on commercial exchanges is lower than was formerly the case. The quality of production is considerably inferior and the consumption per head has decreased. This period has brought great privation and suffering to the poorer classes. The progress which has now been made in the working of the Five-Year Plan must compensate for this slow recovery, and may then allow for an improvement—on paper—in the standard of life. This plan was intended to triple at least pre-war industrial output at its highest point, while increasing agricultural output only by half, in actual figures, and taking no account of the increase in the population; this would still not increase production enough to enable the workers of so vast a territory to live in conditions equal to those enjoyed by the "sweated labour" in Capitalist countries. Besides, the State cannot continue to built up its vast industrial and agricultural undertakings, except by seizing an ever-increasing share of the national revenues by every available means: continual internal loans, camouflaged indirect taxation, confiscation of a large portion of the crops, the issue of paper money without security, etc.; in other words, reducing the buying power of the population. In a country where the scarcity of all manufactured goods is already severely felt, it will become a matter of sheer necessity to enter in competition on world markets. The scarcity of manufactured goods is becoming increasingly acute, and for the past two years there has been a growing shortage of agricultural produce. "For the twelfth anniversary of the advent of Soviet power we are without almost all agricultural produce", was Ordzhonikidze's admission in "Pravda" of September 29th 1929. To admit the existence of a problem will not solve it. And other problems are arising of which the Soviet autocracy will not be able to dispose by issuing decrees or by employing violent measures.

Industrial development and Socialist progress are two distinct issues, but there is a definite connection between them; they may coalesce or diverge according to whether productive property is private or collectivised, or whether the social nature of the State is bourgeois or proletarian. These conditions are never of a clear-cut or determined character, but in the case of Soviet Russia, where neither the bourgeoisie nor the proletariat is in a position to dominate the State, their nature is particularly complex. Lenin aimed at Socialism through the N.E.P.—an economic policy which acknowledged a transitory co-existence of the economic forces and organisations controlled by the State, master of the key-positions in the economic system. At the present time, the Soviet Government intends to establish Socialism by virtually abolishing this N.E.P. and by eliminating Capitalist elements with the aid of police methods and administrative measures. Its Five-Year Plan is the expression of a new economic policy which the Communist "opposition", grouped round Trotsky, lays claim to have inspired in general principles, if not to have been entirely responsible for its application.

Whatever the value of the data, calculations, and forecasts for this Plan, the destiny of Soviet Russia will henceforth depend to a great extent on its application. And the actual immediate consequences may well be inconsistent with recent theoretical conclusions. In the immediate future, the present Soviet Government will show that modern industry can dispense with Capitalists, but that has already been shown in bourgeois States where the great public services are industrial in character; it will demonstrate that the extent and rhythm of an industrial system supported by State revenues checks individual initiative and competition, though the ultimate fate of such a system governed by many other factors cannot be foretold. But if the Soviets build up an industrial system in the same way that the Pharaohs built up the pyramids they will be digging their own graves, and the experiment could not be fully tested for, actively or passively, the oppressed classes would resist its realisation. As far as it is possible to judge from the available documentary evidence, the Plan is only partially realisable by the imposition of forced loans, by low wages, high prices, and fiduciary inflation, all of which indirectly rob the workers; and even then it will only be possible with the co-operation of foreign Capitalists. It demands that a downtrodden generation shall be sacrificed to the betterment of conditions for future generations and to the theoretical provisions of social progress. As a result, industry will be much developed, and agriculture better equipped. But in what does this economic system differ from Capitalism?

There is this difference: the most evolved form of Capitalists—bankers and industrial leaders—has disappeared, and the Capitalist type only continues its precarious existence in the persons of a few well-to-do peasants, country moneylenders, small oppressed traders, and some impecunious manufacturers burdened with taxes. The proletariat produces merchandise and receives wages as in Capitalist countries, but instead of the bourgeois as an individual taking a share in the profits, the State as a collectivised unit appropriates them all—a method of confiscation which is the outcome of the wasteful methods of a parasitic bureaucracy. That is what Lenin called State Capitalism, an expression which is disputed by the Communists.

But a point which is not disputed is the transitory nature of this régime, which must lead to the establishment of Socialism or to the restoration of Capitalism.

The State is only an instrument of economic and social transformation in so far as it identifies itself with the interests of the classes concerned in the Revolution, and therefore of the party which becomes the conscious and active agent of that great movement. Without even discussing the complex social character of the Soviet State or the possibilities for the realisation of the Five-Year Plan (both very debatable questions), it is enough to know the relations between the Bolshevist Party of the present time and the proletarian mass to be able to perceive a marked divergence of their respective interests which may even bring about a rupture. If this rupture comes about, no Five-Year or Fifteen-Year Plan will check the advance of Capitalism; on the contrary, any industrial plan would promote its development by freeing the productive forces which the State would be powerless to control. And instead of "Socialism in fifteen years", we should have "Capitalism in five". It is impossible to forecast with any accuracy the future course of Soviet development. The Russian Revolution is far from having exhausted its resources and its ability to exist.

But its power as a social movement to outlive the stabilisation of international Capitalism is weakened every year that Communism continues to be nothing more than a theory preached by Communists who never carry it into practice. A bourgeois revolution is all that can be accomplished against the working classes. The bourgeoisie will return to power under the banner of the dictatorship of the proletariat if the masses are still forced to live in misery, ignorance, political unconsciousness, and slavery.

The point is whether this economic system is made for the workers or if the workers exist for the Plan. It is for them to say, if they can. According to whether they will submit to the Plan or will adapt the Plan to their own interests, so will they advance either towards Capitalism or towards Socialism. The question that history asks them is not whether they want Socialism in fifteen years, but whether they want liberty—now and at once.

We have resisted the temptation of giving more than one extract from the Soviet Press to illustrate each problem. By this method it has been possible to show the inaccuracy of official statements on all matters.

In the opening chapter of this book we showed, by a reference to the "Humanité", the statements made by impostors in the service of the Soviet bureaucracy concerning "the truth about Russia". A short extract from the same paper will reveal the inaccuracy of its information concerning the Five-Year Plan.

In the issue of October 18th 1929 the following telegram appeared: "Soviet Motor Industry—Moscow, 17th October ('Humanité'). The motor-car factories of Nizhni-Novogorod have, as the result of last year's work, made an increase of 20 per cent. over the estimates for the economic year 1929–30. Their output will be 70,000 lorries, 20,000 motor vans, and 30,000 touring cars, making a total of 120,000 vehicles." But *there are no* motor-car factories at Nizhni. They do not exist, but no documentary evidence is available to prove this for no one previously thought of writing and printing statements for the express purpose of revealing the non-existence of an industrial concern! But nothing is easier than to prove that these factories do not exist at Nizhni. And even if a photograph had been published, purporting to be of this non-existent factory, that would not alter the fact that up to the present time Nizhni has not produced a single car. The U.S.S.R. manufactures approximately 500 cars a year at the Amo factory, which was established by the Fiat company, near Moscow (Ossinsky: *Statistics of the Motor Industry*, Moscow, 1927), and at Yaroslavl, where the Baltic factory was transferred from Riga during the war. This output is quite sufficient to make good the wear-and-tear in the total number of vehicles, which is approximately 11,000. Of these, 5,000, and later 3,000 more, lorries were bought from foreign countries. Ossinsky gave other figures; according to him, the total number of cars was 18,300 in 1925 and 21,000 in 1927. Soviet statistics were at fault again and Ordzhonikidze recently admitted that they "were very lame all along the line", adding: "The council of experts in our statistical service are hopelessly muddled with the figures" ("Pravda", September 29th 1929). How can a country possessing 15,000 to 20,000 cars and turning out about 500 a year increase its production in one year to 120,000 with the assistance of a non-existent factory?

With a series of telegrams all bearing the same glad tidings the Five-Year Plan could—on paper—be realised in five minutes!

This example is worth noticing, for this is the kind of information concerning Russia that the "Humanité" has been in the habit of publishing since its honest and reliable editors were dismissed in 1924. In the end, no one will believe its statements, even when it announces that Ford, the well-known Leninist, has completed the construction of his motor-car factory at Nizhni—at present nothing more than a plan in the making.

An article recently published in the same paper revealed the kind of arguments employed and reasons given to show the progress of Socialism in Russia. Under the title: "Irrefutable evidence concerning the establishment of Socialism", the following passage occurred quoting the words of "a learned gynæcologist" [*sic*]: "The telephone system works as admirably in Moscow as it works badly in Paris." We are able ourselves to confirm this "irrefutable evidence", but would not add anything about the "establishment of Socialism". The telephone system in question is quite first class; it was installed in Moscow by a Russo-Dano-Swedish Capitalist concession, and at Leningrad by the Swedish Capitalist firm of Eriksson —both in Tsarist times. There, the happily combined efforts of the Russian autocracy, Scandinavian Capitalism, and French gynæcology have resulted in the instalment of a Socialist telephone system!

Then there was the same "irrefutable evidence" concerning the Moscow emergency surgical hospitals: "I have seen similar institutions at Rio de Janeiro and in Santiago, but I have never seen anything so well organised as the Moscow service." This was most unexpected and welcome—a comparison with the Socialist system of surgical aid as found in Rio and Santiago. Fortunately we are able to reveal how fallacious was the parallel drawn: in Russia, as in every other country, there are some model establishments of this kind, but they do not affect the conditions of 150 million Russians nor the state of Socialism in Russia. The learned gynæcologist also said: "I saw one maternity home in which thirty or forty children were born every day and which *appeared* to me to be perfectly organised." Exactly: forty children are born in that home, but 10,000 are born every day in Russia. Under what conditions do the 9,960 (to count only those who survive their birth) come into the world? There is no place for them in this maternity home. Here is the question. If there were ten of these institutions, that would still leave the problem unsolved from the gynæcological and obstetrical point of view—and all the more so in Socialist eyes.

We have emphasised the word "*appeared*" as used by the prudent gynæcologist, who was not responsible for the grotesque interpretation of his straightforward report, but who evidently knew full well that there is a great difference between the *appearance* of a medical service as shown to a visitor and its working in practice. In spite of the information already given on this subject, it would perhaps interest the reader to hear the most recent, the most remarkable, and the most general evidence concerning health resorts and sanatoria. They are institutions which more than any other appear convincing to hurried tourists and obliging witnesses. The "Trud" of October 19th 1929 described as follows the conditions prevailing in these establishments during the summer season of that year: "It was not infrequently that the patients were three to five days without drinking-water. The feeding got worse and worse, and dirt and filth increased in a most incredible fashion. [Most health resorts have no sewerage system.] Contagious diseases have not decreased in number, but have rather shown a tendency to increase." In short, the Board of Management of the health resorts stated that "with regard to hygiene and organisation, the situation was extremely unsatisfactory and *was, in fact, abominable*". These five lines utterly destroy the thousands written concerning "the irrefutable evidence as to the establishment of Socialism", and all official statements contain equally damnatory remarks on questions which are the subjects of misleading information.

One last example, referring to the dominating question in Russia at the present time. "Pravda" of October 9th reported "a *revolting* case of forced self-criticism". In a Communist nucleus an unemployed man had in perfect justice pointed out a series of illegal actions on the part of some committee. He was arrested the next day by the Ogpu and kept in prison for a fortnight. The rumour was then spread about that he was "an enemy of Sovietism and almost a terrorist". But this "revolting" case of injustice on the part of subordinate officials is a legitimate and praiseworthy practice, because, throughout the vast scale of administration and on the responsibility of the Party officials, acts of this kind occur daily. Not for fourteen days but for fourteen months thousands of workmen and revolutionaries have been imprisoned and deported by the Ogpu for having "in perfect justice" pointed out "a series of illegal actions" of an all-powerful committee, and one is still waiting for the liberation of the victims and for the punishment of the guilty.

If the reader felt the slightest misgiving concerning the genuineness of this book in spite of the mass of documentary evidence at his disposal, these few extracts taken from the Communist Press in 1929, after this book was finished, should be enough to dispel all doubts.

INDEX